The Art of Reading Italian Americana

The Art of Reading Italian Americana

Italian American Culture in Review

Fred Gardaphe

Bordighera Press

Library of Congress Control Number: 2010912897

Cover art: Joanne Mattera, *Joss 59,* 2008, gouache on paper, 22 x 22 inches. Courtesy of dm contemporary, New York City

© 2011 by Fred Gardaphe

All rights reserved. Parts of this book may be reprinted only by written permission from the authors, and may not be reproduced for publication in book, magazine, or electronic media of any kind, except in quotations for purposes of literary reviews by critics.

Printed in the United States.

Published by
BORDIGHERA PRESS
John D. Calandra Italian American Institute
25 W. 43rd Street, 17th Floor
New York, NY 10036

SAGGISTICA 4
ISBN 978–1–59954–019–1

The Art of Reading Italian Americana

Introduction
    The Art of Reading Italian Americana 11

Authors
    Joe Amato 13
    Tony Ardizzone 15
    Tommaso Astarita 18
    June Avignone 19
    Michael Bacarella 20
    Helen Barolini 22
    Joseph Bathanti 27
    Adria Bernardi 28
    Lucia Chiavola Birnbaum 30
    Mary Jo Bona 32
    Peter Bondanella 35
    Dorothy Calbetti Bryant 36
    Anne Calcagno 39
    Philip Cannistraro 39
    Mary Cappello 42
    Peter Carravetta 43
    Michael P. Carroll 45
    Mark Ciabattari 47
    Edward Cifelli 48
    Rita Ciresi 49
    David Citino 54
    Joseph Colicchio 55
    Stephen Cooper 56
    Pietro Corsi 57
    Paola Corso 58
    David Cowan and John Kuenster 61
    Antonio D'Alfonso 62
    Rachel Guido DeVries 66
    Stephen DeFelice 67
    Emilio DeGrazia 69
    Luisa Del Giudice 71
    Don DeLillo 73
    Tina De Rosa 74
    Louise DeSalvo 77

Diane di Prima	80
Lawrence DiStasi	82
Louisa Ermelino	83
Marie Hall Ets	86
David Evanier	87
John Fante	89
Joe Fiorito	93
Anthony Fragola	94
Remo Franceschini	95
Richard Gambino	97
Anthony Giardina	98
Maria Gillan and Edvige Giunta	99
Maria Mazziotti Gillan	101
Daniela Gioseffi	106
Edvige Giunta	108
Jennifer Guglielmo and Salvatore Salerno	109
Thomas Guglielmo	110
Josephine Gattuso Hendin	112
Carmine Biagio Ianacce	113
Luciano Iorizzo	114
Salvatore La Gumina	115
Marisa Labozzetta	119
Victoria Lancelotta	122
Maria Laurino	122
Frank Lentricchia	124
Billy Lombardo	127
Martino Marazzi	128
Leo Luke Marcello	129
Elizabeth Messina	131
Ben Morreale	133
Gloria Nardini	136
Michael Palma	137
Vincent Panella	138
Paul Paolicelli	140
Joseph Papaleo	143
David Prete	144
Stanislao Pugliese	145
Mario Puzo	147
David A.J. Richards	148
Giose Rimanelli	150
E.R. Romaine	153
Mark Rotella	154
Jane and Peter Schneider	156

Felix Stefanile	159
Ross Talarico	160
Thom Tammaro	162
Gioia Timpanelli	163
Bill Tonelli	165
Adriana Trigiani	165
Bea Tusiani	167
Joseph Tusiani	168
Anthony Valerio	170
Steven Varni	173
Richard Vetere	175
Robert Viscusi	176
Justin Vitiello	177
Chuck Wachtel	178
Janet Zandy	180

Review Essays

"Could This Be the End of... Gangsters in Fact and Fiction"	183
"The Italian American Audience: Cave People Culture"	188
"Italian Americans Over the Edge"	190
"Radically Italian American"	192
"Working Class Culture"	195
"Writing as a Reader: The Deserted Village of Jay Parini"	197

Index

Books Reviewed	207

INTRODUCTION: The Art of Reading Italian Americana

This book is the latest milestone in my life-long search for the book I wanted to write. I used to think that someday, some way, I'd find the book that would tell my story, and then I wouldn't have to write it, but over time I realized that this could never be done. If you don't write your book, no one else will. It's as simple as that. Along the way I've come across a lot of great writing that has inspired, taught, and challenged me in many ways.

The search has lead to the reading of every book I could find that was written by or about Italian Americans. There once was a time, not too long ago, that I used to boast of having read every book that had been published on the Italian American experience. I had standing orders with every publisher to send me works as soon as they were ready for review. Sometimes, in order to meet my editor's deadline, I'd have to root out writers who had published their own books in order to fill my monthly column in the *Fra Noi*. These days, I can't even keep up with just knowing about the hundreds of books that come out each year, let alone find the time to read and review them all. Today I have the same problem that my late buddy Studs Terkel used to have — books come in from all over and pile up waiting for me to get to them. Unlike the mountains in Studs' office, mine are stacked neatly on shelves waiting their turn.

I have been reviewing books, primarily for the *Fra Noi*, for over twenty-five years. That work resulted in my first compilation *Dagoes Read: Tradition and the Italian American Writer*. The title came from my sincere and perhaps somewhat naïve attempt to take on the prejudices of the past. While I still believe in the artistic reasons behind giving the book that title, I wonder sometimes if the title had been a bit less ironic would the book have had a better reception. Too late now for that first book, and so this next one will not get named "Dagoes Read Too."

With this collection I want to celebrate what I have come to see as the Art of Reading, for I have learned that reading can become an art when the reader talks back to the writer. This is done in two stages: first I find myself talking back to the author while I am doing the actual reading of the book, then I talk back to the author through the writing of my reviews. I don't want to suggest that every reader by virtue of tossing eyes over text becomes an artist, but I do want to acknowledge the artistry involved in crafting a considered and careful response to the artist.

Art without response is only self-realized, and for many artists, this is enough. However, when an other gets to experience the art, and the self gets feedback from that other, the art becomes totalized and has a possibility to shape the way others view the world. This dialogue, between artist and audience, writer and reader completes a work of art in important ways, and those who strive to respond to those artists in careful and dedicated replies, I would argue, should be seen as artists of a different ilk.

This book covers the ten-year period since *Dagoes Read,* 1995–2005, and I've included most of the reviews published in the *Fra Noi* during that period. I've also included a few, longer reviews and review essays published elsewhere because they help to provide a more in-depth look at the production of Italian American writers. The dates that follow most of the reviews indicate the issue of the *Fra Noi* in which they appeared.

My own thinking and writing have been shaped by the books I've read and this book is a tribute to all of them. Over the years since I first began reviewing books in 1985, Italian American culture has grown to produce best-storytelling writers such as Tony Ardizzone, Rita Ciresi, Louisa Ermelino, best-thinking writers such as Robert Viscusi, Mary Jo Bona, Anthony Tamburri as well as best-seller writings such as David Baldacci, Lisa Scottoline, and Adriana Trigiani. This book then, is a final answer to the question Gay Talese raised so many years ago in the *New York Times*: "Where are the Italian American Writers?" They were always there Gay, all you had to do was take the time to read them, and had you written about them, you too might have enjoyed the art of reading Italian Americana.

And finally, this book is dedicated to my newest grandson, Anthony Nicholas Lomuto, part of the new generation of Italian Americans. May he grow to read and appreciate the work that was done to make way for him.

Authors

Joe Amato

That's right, there are WX pages in this so-called book. So what does that mean? You've got to figure it out for yourself. And that's the least of the challenges thrown your way in Joe Amato's latest work. Taking his cue from a John Dewey quote about how new techniques are the result of "the need for new modes of experience," Amato's book-to-end-all-books is really one made of many. Amato is hunting for the difference between reality and representation in these days when virtual experiences have taken over our pursuit of the actual. You will read this book not to make sense of the world, but to see what can happen when someone attempts to redesign the very act of reading. Amato accommodates a variety of thoughts that are normally shuffled into different books such as literary criticism, poetry, biography, autobiography, television viewing guides, cook books, and more.

You might want to skip the "Introduction," since it just tells you how you might try reading the book. Entitled "The World's Body as Information Network," this section examines the changing personality of literature as the literary agent shifts from the typewriter to the writer type. The most traditional of all this books pieces, it contains the central point of his experiment: "The development of electronic media, as I see and feel it, prompts me to conclude that it will simply no longer do to consider the articulation of such feelings as disconnected either from the contents of the forms of technology." As I typed that sentence into my new Word 97 program it was underlined, programmed as an aberration. This is the key to understanding Amato's work; we change the world and it changes us back. We don't know what will happen to us when we adapt to new technology. And if we keep doing the same old things we've done forever, we won't control our own destiny.

The remaining five chapters, all different anatomies, make up the bulk of the book and from what I can only call an amusement park of the literary mind. Amato fashions a bridge out of theory that brings us through poetry, prose and traditional forms of information gathering, and in doing so asks us reengage our senses with our selves. Much of the book must be read (said) aloud in order to appreciate the new sounds he has composed. Amato uses language like two mirrors facing each other; what's trapped in between is endlessly repeated, giving the illusion that one is many.

In "Anatomy of a Mind: Writing the life and death of the mind," Amato tells us that a wasteland is a terrible thing to mind. In synapses of sentences and through juxtaposition of quotes, he wreaks havoc with the normal way we make sense of other's words. Smack in the middle of this chapter is the work's bibliography with sources listed as ingredients on a label. Read it and imagine how the writing will taste, but it is the cooking that makes the taste, and the container is the writer we get when we open a book.

This section gives way to "Anatomy of a Soul: For and Against Virtual Space: The Anxieties of Writing in Real Times," an argument about how

> the world does not exist to be put into a book. the book does not exist to be put into virtual reality. the world does not exist to be put into virtual reality. the book and virtual reality are aspects of the world's body. we are aspects of the world's body. the world incorporates the book and virtual reality into the reality of the body....

Be sure to turn off your AutoCorrect feature if you're going to quote from this section.

In "Anatomy of a Heart: 1001 Onlines: 4 Anthems," we get some version of some one's stories. Whosoever it is, it is sprinkled with Italian signs and so might or might not be traceable (follow the money) to the very Joe Amato, who as author must be getting the royalties. "Anatomy of a Body," dwells on the fuel that feeds the physical. Here's where you find the evidence of Amato's Italianita; he gives us nothing less than the Amato family recipe for spaghetti and meatballs. But he doesn't tell you why no matter how you try, you'll never make it taste like an Amato made it. Guess.

Books are static. No matter what you do, the same words remain forever on the same pages. While superficially that is true about this book — the book will change the next time you read it; You can bet this book won't read twice the same to you and to write a review now only marks one reading. Something tells me that two people can have a conversation on this book and someone overhearing the conversation would never be able to tell that they're talking about the same book. I don't know about you, but I'm making an appointment to come back to this book in five years, to see if it's still there. Reading *Bookend* was like going out on a wild weekend and forgetting where the weekend started. Amato's writing formula is intellectual LSD; which defamiliarizes as it demystifies the complexity with which we normally weave academic tomes. Because everything is so unfamiliar, it requires an intense concentration that logically progressing, logocentric writing does not.

Bookend is the latest contribution from the SUNY Series, Postmodern Culture, edited by Joseph Natoli. Amato, a poet disguised as an Assistant Professor of English in the Lewis Department of Humanities at the Illinois Institute of Technology in Chicago, is author of *Symptoms of a Finer Age.* When you are done with the reading you have to do for work, when you are weaned off the last drop of theory, turn your attention to Amato. You might just get a sense of where all this reading and writing is taking us. After reading this book, you just might find yourself searching for new ways of writing: happy to take pause:\\wonderfully wise writing.amato@cuttingedge.com

(*Voices in Italian Americana* 1998)

Joe Amato, *Bookend: Anatomies of a Virtual Self* (Albany: SU of New York P, 1997). Pp. WX. 079143401X; 0791434028 (pbk.).

Tony Ardizzone

If you don't know Tony Ardizzone's writing by now, then do yourself a favor by picking up *Taking it Home: Stories from the Neighborhood*, his latest collection of short stories. Ardizzone, one of the best short story writers around, has been winning literary prizes for years. His *Larabi's Ox: Stories of Morocco*, "published in 1993 earned the Milkweed National Fiction Prize, the Chicago Foundation for Literature Award for Fiction," and a Pushcart Prize. His first story collection, *The Evening News*, from which come half of the stories in *Taking it Home*, won the prestigious Flannery O'Connor Award in 1986. Ardizzone's stories have been and continue to be selected for important anthologies, and this new collection could very well have been subtitled "the best of Tony Ardizzone."

Taking it Home features stories set in Chicago and filled with Italian/American and Catholic themes and characters. "Baseball Fever," the opening story, tells the tale of Danny Bacigalupo, a good Catholic boy from Chicago's north side, who hits a line drive in a game of alley baseball that changes his life. When Ardizzone juxtaposes the mystical world of the Catholic Church to the wonderful world of sports, he comes up with a humorous tale driven by tragedy.

"Nonna," a virtual workshop in narrative point-of-view, is the story of an old Italian grandmother who heads out of her home to shop in a neighborhood that's changing from Italian to Mexican. As she walks through the near west side of Chicago we are given the history of this once thriving Little Italy through the eyes of a survivor. She is confused and the changes in the neighborhood are explained through a mix of her immigrant memories. "Nonna" is one of those stories that you will want to read again and again.

"The Eyes of Children" shows how a Catholic education fashions a child's imagination so that a variety of realities are made possible. When children report a man bleeding in the church, young Gino thinks it must have been Jesus. But what he comes to realize is that when doubt pierces the cloud of his Catholic training life can become even more terrifying and complex than the simple division between good and evil and heaven and hell.

"My Mother's Stories" is a map of the shift from oral to literary tradition. It is also the story of a legacy being passed on from mother to son. The mother tells the stories that the son writes down, and he writes them down, not because she can't, but because he has to: "I stand here, not used to speaking about things that are so close to me. I am used to veiling things in my stories, to making things wear masks, to telling my stories through masks. But my mother tells her stories openly, as she has done so all of her life." Ardizzone nicely captures the difference between two generations' use of stories.

"Ritual" rivals the best of Ernest Hemingway's Nick Adams stories
Ardizzone's love of language turns this story of a fishing trip into a natural rite of passage, a moment in which a father allows his son to become the father. Ardizzone's descriptions of the movement in nature — of a heron's flight, a mother duck feeding with her brood, a fish swimming — contrasts wonderfully with the near-stillness of the father and son fishing to create.

Any one remembering the days of corporal punishment in Catholic schools will shiver with recognition when reading "The Language of the Dead" in which When Vinnie is given the third degree by Brother Stan, "the school's most viscious" disciplinarian, for his role in a high school fight. "The Man in the Movie," is a literary "Taxi Driver" about a Vietnam vet who can't tell the difference between reality and his own memories. A writer always takes a risk by entering a mind gone mad, but Ardizzone's risk pays off in a sincere and soul shaking account of insanity.

"The Daughter and the Tradesman" is a haunting story of a young girl's search for the truth behind her father's death, and how comes to understand him better through the young boy she attracts and fights off. In "World Without End," Ardizzone shows how the Church and family create frames for expected and acceptable behavior. A mother's criticism of her son's life style leads into an argument that is solved only when the son tells his mother what she wants to hear.

"Ladies Choice" brings back the early 1960s days of greasers, doopers and climbers and the nights of Catholic Church sock hops. "Idling" tells the story of how a young boy's life changes when he quits the football team and takes on a new attitude toward everything that's expected of a "guy who had a rep." And the last story, "Holy Cards," is a marvelous series of vignettes that present key teachings of the Catholic church through the eyes of a young boy. From mortal sin in milk bottles, to martyrs and saving the world's pagan babies, Ardizzone's humor is full of respect and reverence for the way it used to be.

Taking it Home recreates a bygone era of Chicago history, and at the same time shows us how good stories can transcend historical boundaries, especially when they remind us that, in Bruce Springsteen's words, "It's hard to be a saint in the city."

Tony Ardizzone, *Taking It Home: Stories from the Neighborhood* (Urbana: U of Illinois P, 1996). Pp. 155. ISBN 0252064836; $12.95 paperback.

When a gifted writer turns his skills toward the stories of his ancestors we usually end up with historical classics the likes of which were penned by a Homer or a Hawthorne. With Tony Ardizzone's latest novel, *In the Garden of Papa Santuzzu*, Italian America can claim another writer in the ranks of these world class storytellers.

Adrizzone, whose earlier work has earned such prestigious awards as The Flannery O'Connor Award for Short Fiction, the Pushcart Prize, and the Milkweed National Fiction Prize, has been dipping into his Sicilian American background here and there throughout his earlier work — one highlight being the short story "Nonna," which is widely anthologized. In this latest book, he embraces Sicilian culture and doesn't let go until he wrings out a masterpiece composed of different points-of-view.

Papa Santuzzu knows that La Merica holds a fortune for his family, but he is reluctant, if not afraid, to leave the land where he was born, so he sends child after child, until he is left alone with his visions and his memories. As Rosa Dolci tells us at the opening, "This is his [Papa Santuzzu's] story and the story of his children. It is also the story of people like me, whose destiny it was to marry into the Girgenti Family. God willing, one day you'll pick up the thread and tell these stories to children of your own."

Why might you do this? Because this is also the story of people like you, children, grandchildren, and great grandchildren of immigrants to the United States. Rosa, who opens the storytelling and serves as the guide through a couple of caesuras that threads the twelve tales, helps turn "The Garden" into a celebration of family past, present, and future.

"The rope is la famigghia, see? Each of us is a thread, wound up in it. Before you were born, a rope connected me to you. Once still does, figghiu miu." And as we know, that rope is the blood that we share and the stories that keep us aware of the importance of that blood sharing.

Throughout the other eleven stories, we learn of the trials of travelling across the ocean, of how the mafia came to be, of work in Sicily as a fisherman and in the US as a baker, and how to survive selling newspapers in "the City that Works," especially when you must "grease the right wheels." You don't have to come from Sicily to be affected by these tales, but if you're not familiar with Sicilian culture, you will find explanations of such traditions as the St. Joseph's table, Easter Bread, and the Black Madonna.

Ardizzone's clever imagination rises above reality to create a sense of a super-reality, a magical experience with words. This novel is a veritable primer of how to deal with the theme of immigration to the United States through a mix of story, history, and song. Along the way, through witty phrasing and through incredible imaginative energy, Ardizzone retells ancient origin myths and creates original myths of his own that will have you wondering where one begins and the other ends. Proverbs, poetry, and song lyrics are inserted here and there to give the work a community spirit.

The author's strength lies in his ability to create lyrical language that creates voices that you will hear over and over again in your mind, like that of Luigi Girgenti: "Hell's a lonely place. You don't have to ask me how I know. I know. I know because one bright night...."

Unlike pure folktale, these stories delve deeply into the conflicts that arise between self and family, old country and new, to offer us new understandings of the impact immigration had on everyone involved. Not since *Christ in Concrete* (1939) have we had a novel so rich in language, so strong in story, so vivid in its telling, and so filled with in history that it can be read over and over again. *In the Garden of Papa Santuzzu*, should be required reading for everyone who is or knows an American of Italian descent.

Tony Ardizzone, *In the Garden of Papa Santuzzu* (New York: Picador, a division of St. Martin's P, 1999). Pp. 339. ISBN 0312203071; $24 hardcover.

Tommaso Astarita

Tommaso Astarita, born and raised in Naples, and now a professor of history at Georgetown, has written a popular history of the region from which emigrated the majority of America's Italians. *Between Salt Water and Holy Water: A History of Southern Italy,* surveys the highlights and lowlights of the various cultures that contributed to the making of what was once called "The Kingdom of Two Sicilies" and covers the period from early Greek settlements to the establishment of Italy as a geo-political nation.

The combination and sometimes clash of cultures Norman, Byzantine, Arab, Sicilian, African, and European, makes for a rich story whose history has never been presented in such a popular form. Astarita's material and spiritual history of the area proves a more balanced view of the south than we've had in previous attempts to tell the story of the south through the separate sacred and secular histories that have come to us through the lives of saints and tales of the Inquisition.

Chapters have promising titles such as "Where the Romans Met the Greeks," "From the Terror of the World to the Wonder of the World" The Italian South in Antiquity," "Sicily Splits and Naples Rises," "The Indies Over Here," "Paradise Inhabited by Devils," "Reason Truly is Always Beautiful," "Feast, Flour and Gallows," and fulfill most of their claims.

Early on Astarita focuses on the arrival on the Italian peninsula of Greeks looking for better lands, creating Magna Graecia, or Greater Greece, as though cities such as Neapolis (Naples) were simply outposts of Greek civilization. He looks at the early Norman kings who had an influence on the development of the South. In 1016 forty Norman pilgrims after reaching their destination in Puglia decided to send for their friends and family to join them permanently. The subsequent invasions of other southern areas down to Sicily, where the likes of Roger II and Frederick became kings and Holy Roman emperors, represented the first of many formidable powers to come that would challenge the rule of the Catholic Church. The Norman invasions resulted in the creation of the Kingdom of Two Sicilies, organizing for the first time a strong state out of a diverse population out of which the cities of Palermo and Naples would arise as major centers of culture.

Because he has so much ground to cover, he must necessarily skim over periods and events out of which others have fashioned whole books. So look for an orientation and and not a deep critical discussion. Astarita accomplishes this through his emphasis on description rather than analysis. His work does help us understand both the triumphs and the pitfalls of the culture of the Italian south. He also explores and explains the origins of various stereotypes that still exist today. As a descendant from Puglia and Calabria, I was hoping to have encountered a bit more on those southern regions, but since so much more as been written and preserved about the historical cultural centers of Naples and Palermo, it makes sense that the author's focus is there.

Astarita's given us a great look at the sacred and secular stories that helped make the history of this complex and misunderstood region of the ancestral homes of most Americans of Italian descent. He steps back and lets the historical record come through. Fifty illustrations help give a sense of the art and images that came from the region and helped to visually record the stories he tells. If you want to better understand Italian Americans who hail from the south, then you've got to read this book.

Tommaso Astarita, *Between Salt Water and Holy Water: A History of Southern Italy* (New York: Norton, 2005). Pp. 352. ISBN 0393058646; $24.95.

June Avignone

On Going Home Again is June Avignone's bold artistic essay that redefines autobiographical possibilities for writers and artists alike. Each page of this booklet is a unique enough work of art that you don't need page numbers. In fact such usual conventions become meaningless when you have to turn the book upside down and around to take it all in.

"A writer wrestles with memories. A writer puts words into memories and makes stories. So how can I make grandma happy?" writes Avignone as she attempts one of the most difficult and artistically dangerous maneuver an Italian American writer: the dead grandmother story. Sooner or later we all have them, but few of us have the skill to reach beyond self-pity and mundane similarities to create new ways of experiencing the life and loss of an ancestor. Avignone has that talent. More than a writer, this woman is an artist with words and images. Using a palate of photos, poetry, prose, drawings and paintings, many by other artists, she creates a way to keep her past from leaving her alone.

Avignone reaches beyond the personal to capture the odyssey of leaving home and returning in spirit, if not substance, to the feelings of beginning, to times when ends were means of finishing stories that fashioned limitless possibilities. Histories, public and private, collide and collapse into one another in this work. Avignone's montage creates a multivocal, multilayered autobiographical flash that attempts to capture a lifetime in a blink, or is it a wink?

Avignone is the author of *Cianci Street: A Neighborhood in Transition* (Italian Girls Press), *Traveling Small Distances* (Chantry Press), and *A Place Like Paterson* (The Mill Street Forward). She is presently at work at a collection of short stories called *The Day John Reed Left Town and Other Tales From Synthetic City*.

June Avignone, *On Going Home Again* (www.SyntheticCity.org, 2002). ISBN 9965462811; $8.00 paperback.

Michael Bacarella

When most of us were taught the history of the US Civil War, we learned that it was a series of battles between the North and South over the emancipation of the slaves. What comes back in memory might be some of the battles, such as Bull Run and Gettysburgh, and perhaps the names of a few of the generals, such as Robert E. Lee, Ulysses S. Grant, Stonewall Jackson and George Sherman. But how many of us ever learned that both armies contained large numbers of experienced volunteers fresh from European conflicts such as the battle for the unification of Italy.

In *Lincoln's Foreign Legion: The 39th New York Infantry, The Garibaldi Guard*, author Michael Bacarella presents new insights into the history of the American Civil War, in a clear and interesting study. Bacarella, an amateur historian in the true sense of the word (he is not a PhD, not a professor of history, and his studies were not funded by grants) hunted through such resources as the Newberry Library, the National Archives, various state archives, libraries and historical societies. Driven by a need to learn about that which he wasn't taught, Bacarella scanned a variety of sources such as personal diaries, regimental histories, muster rolls, newspaper and magazine accounts to document the incredible support given to both the Union and Confederate armies by countries from Alsace to Wurttemberg. Much of this information is reproduced in the valuable, one-hundred page appendix, but the real purpose of his book is to retell the story of the civil war through the experience of the 39th New York Infantry, also known as the Garibaldi Guard.

As Bacarella points out, just as Italy was unifying itself, the United States was falling apart. Many of the soldiers who bravely fought for the unification of Italy — legions from Poland, Hungary and many other countries — were anxious to join in the fight to free the American slaves. Led by Giuseppe Garibaldi, whose life was saved twice by a freed slave, these soldiers were chomping at the bit to follow a Garibaldi-led army that would fight for a people's freedom. When Garibaldi, perhaps the most famous freedom fighter of his time, turned down a proposed commission in the US Army because his request, that the freeing of the slaves officially be declared the cause for the war, was not granted, men who had served under him decided to fight under his name in what they called the Garibaldi Guard.

Lincoln's Foreign Legion opens with a chapter on the relationship between the United States and Europe, told through the story of Giuseppe Garibaldi. For those who have never understood the struggle to unify Italy, Bacarella provides a crystal clear retelling of the historical events. From there he moves into the stories of those who served with Garibaldi who committed themselves to the US Civil War. "Count Luigi Cesnola became the colonel of the 4th New York Cavalry. Captain Alberto Maggi was commissioned the colonel of the 33rd Massachusetts Infantry. Garibaldini captain Carlo Lombardi would be commissioned a second lieutenant of the 39th U. S. Colored Troops." The names go one and on, and the sheer listing of these men should be enough to make us see that the Civil War was, as Bacarella reminds us, "A rich man's war, but a poor man's fight."

More than simply retell the various battles, imprisonments, charges and retreats of this illustrious foreign-made US infantry regiment, Bacarella uncovers conspiracies, scandals, and heroic deeds done by men who have never had their often life-giving contributions recognized in even the smallest of history books, let alone those from which he have traditionally learned what we know about this signal event in US history.

Bacarella devoted ten years of intense, voluntary research to the gathering and writing of this material that, while it might have been staring us all in the face, remained invisible until he began asking questions and searching throughout the country for answers. He has produced an original historical work of great significance and provided us all with information necessary to counteract the stigmas of negative stereotypes which have been attached to some of America's most hardworking and loyal minority cultures. *Lincoln's Foreign Legion* should dispel any doubt as to the multicultural make up of the forces that fought in the US Civil War and add a new perspective to the international dimension of this great intranational conflict. Bacarella has done what a good historian must, he has enabled the past speak to the present for the benefit of the future.

(August 1998)

Michael Bacarella, *Lincoln's Foreign Legion: The 39th New York Infantry, The Garibaldi Guard* (Shippensburg, PA: Whit.e Mane, 1996). Pp. 330. ISBN 1572490160 (alk. paper) $34.95 (hardcover)

HELEN BAROLINI

Traditionally tied to the home, Italian/American women often contributed to the family income by bringing work into the home. "Ritaglia di tempo," which literally translates as "time cuttings," was the Italian phrase for piecework. In a similar light, when Italian/American women add the work of writing to the demands of caring for the family and establishing a career, the result is that their autobiographies are likely to be created in bits and pieces and published as articles in journals, magazines, and newspapers.

The writings of Helen Barolini, novelist, essayist, and critic, are perfect examples of this experience. Long in shadows of the spotlight given to her husband, the late Antonio Barolini, Helen Barolini has struggled to establish her identity as a writer. In an earlier essay she encouraged women to reconsider this "work at home" tradition in terms of creating literature: "A revolutionary concept," she wrote, "could be based on the fact that Italian American women, by preference or not, have traditionally worked at home — taking in lodgers, making artificial flowers, doing piecework and embroidery, cooking for others.... Why not, then, work at home as writers?"

This suggestion, which came to us in an essay entitled "Becoming a Literary Person Out of Context," is one that Barolini followed herself. And while this essay, along with her classic introduction to the groundbreaking anthology, *The Dream Book,* do not appear in her latest book, the ideas presented in these essays are at the heart of the fifteen we find in *Chiaroscuro: Essays of Identity.*

Though Barolini has not written an autobiography, in the traditional sense of telling the story of one's life in one book, she has, over the past twenty years provided us with a sense of one through her various essays, critical writings, two novels and with *Festa: Recipes and Recollections. Chiaroscuro* represents an important step in the literary career of this American writer of Italian descent.

"If I go back through the years to try to locate what was at the root of my wanting to write, it was my wanting to explain to myself what troubled me." What troubled Barolini was "conflicting signals" she was getting at home, school and in the larger world. Each of these powerful essays deals with the experience of receiving those conflicting signals. In fact, the entire book serves as a map of the journey this writer has made from her early uncertain as an Italian/American daughter to her adulthood in which she comes to understand her position as an American woman writer.

From the beginning, her foreword that she entitles "Forward" — which in

Italian would be "Avanti!" — signals the advancement the image of Italian/American women beyond the simple madonna/whore versions presented in media stereotypes. Even the artwork on the book's cover, by Ann Gillan, accents Barolini's argument that Italian/American women are much more complex and varied than we may have publicly been led to believe.

Identity begins at home, and Barolini's "How I Learned to Speak Italian," demonstrates how a path traveled down in our youth can become the direction our future will take. The narrative bent of this essay brings out Barolini's talents as a storyteller and in the next essay, "The Finer Things in Life," she presents a the story of her mother's assimilation into American culture which is nicely contrasted by the author's assimilation into Italian culture. If ever a life was made for writing about culture clashes, it is Barolini's.

"On Discovery and Recovery," "After-thoughts on Italian American Women Writers," "The Case of the Missing Italian American Writers," "Looking for Mari Tomasi," and "Writing to a Brick Wall" are pieces of the intellectual map of the author's discovery that Italian/American literature was unknown to mainstream America.

As a professional librarian, Barolini knew the major resources for finding information on American writers, so when she began compiling a bibliography for a course on Italian/American in Literature and Life, and kept coming up empty, she knew that Italian American culture was in trouble. The same held true for the absence of recognition of Italian American writers in the *New York Times Book Review*. While falling short of presenting a conspiracy theory, Barolini does make an important argument.

> By not reviewing authors, by the non-presence of Italian American surnames on "Times" bylines, and even by neglecting our letters, the "Times" contributes to a perceived lack of Italian American status, and a negative cultural image. This, in turn, reinforces the low self-esteem that has been documented among Italian/American students as contributing to a high drop-out rate....

The answer? We need to insure that Italian/American models of success appear in all areas of American life. In her own search for literary models, Barolini compiled the first anthology of Italian American writing in *The Dream Book*. And now she presents us with models of how to make sense of our lives through language.

Chiaroscuro needs to be on the shelves of every American library and in the minds of every Italian American. It should be dipped into, and not read from cover to cover, the way you might read a novel or a book that presents a critical argument. In this way, the repetition of ideas will not seem bothersome; remember that these are concerns that were not resolved once they were raised, and only through her relentless pursuit over many years have they begun to make sense, first to her and now to us.

(November 1997)

Helen Barolini, *Chiaroscuro: Essays of Identity* (West Lafayette, IN: Bordighera, 1997) Pp. 164. ISBN 1884419119; $15.00 (paperback).

At the end of Part One of her novel, *Umbertina,* Helen Barolini has the matriarch of a family sitting by herself near a tree during a family reunion picnic. She looks around and is proud of what she and her husband created out of the little that they had brought with them to America over a half-century before. But then, there is a sadness that overcomes her to the point of tears when she comes to realize that of all the relatives here, there is no one to whom she can tell her story. Not one of her daughters or sons, granddaughters or grandsons, can, nor will they ever, know her story. "She had won, but who could she tell her story to? At times the doubt came to her whether she had really won, after all. All her life had been a struggle for family, and now in her old age she saw some signs that made her uneasy...."

This uneasiness in Umbertina, becomes a mental dis-ease in the third-generation character Marguerite. This conflict, which moves from immigrant grandmother, to Americanized granddaughter, to a "reItalianized" great grandaughter drives narrative. *Umbertina,* an American saga that spans four generations, can be read as the historical evolution of the Italian woman into the American woman, as the feminization of the Italian woman as she becomes the Italian/American woman. The novel is divided chronologically into three parts: Part One: Umbertina 1860–1940; Part Two: Marguerite 1927–1973; and Part Three: Tina 1950–.

The novel opens with Marguerite, the granddaughter of the immigrant Umbertina, in an Italian psychiatrist's office recounting a dream. He tells her the dream reveals her ethnic anxiety as to "whether you are American, Italian, or Italo-American," and suggests that she might begin her search for self by digging into her family's past:

> I always fantasized about my grandmother. I always thought I wanted to get back to her elementary kind of existence ... her kind of primitive strength. I've always felt that my life was wasted on abstract ideas rather than being rooted in reality; even a brutal reality would have been better than the vagueness I've been floundering in.

The novel then moves into the story of immigrant Umbertina Longobardi. She becomes Barolini's mythical mother of Italian America whom later female figures must psychologically search out and confront on their journey to self-identity. Marguerite, never knowing her grandmother's story, grows up confused as to her relationship to Italy and America, and searches for a place where her identity does not depend upon a man. She leaves her home, but a bad marriage, which her parents have annulled, sends her back. Her next attempt leads her to Italy, where she falls in love with an Italian poet, fulfilling a prediction she had made earlier in her life. All along, Marguerite is unknowingly following the advice Umbertina had once given to her daughters: "The important thing . . . is to find your place. Everything depends on that. You find your place, you work, and like planting seeds, everything grows. But you have to be watchful and stick to it." Marguerite never finds her place and the journey is continued by her daughter Tina, short for Umbertina, who completes the journey to self-fulfillment begun by her immigrant namesake.

Barolini's mythic tale of epic origins feeds the future and fuels a reinvention of ethnicity that while imprinted with the past suggests real possibilities for the future. This is a novel that presents both an historical and psychological approach to studying the impact that immigration had on the woman's psyche. No other novel is as ambitious. The recent reissue of *Umbertina* marks the twentieth anniversary of its first publication in 1979. The Feminist Press, which has reprinted out-of-print Italian American novels by Tina DeRosa and Dorothy Bryant, has once again come to the rescue of Italian American culture. This edition contains with a vital "Afterword" by critic Edvige Giunta which sketches the publishing history of the novel and sets the novel appropriately in the context of American feminist writing.

(April 1999)

Helen Barolini, *Umbertina: A Novel,* "Afterword" by Edvige Giunta" (New York: Feminist P, 1999). Pp. 453. ISBN 155861205X (paperback); 1558612041 (hardback); $18.95 (paperback).

Over the course of her literary life, Helen Barolini, author of the novels such as *Umbertina,* an essay collection *Chiaro/Scuro,* and a number of other creative works and translations, has published short fiction in journals like the *Paris Review, Cross Currents,* and in a variety of anthologies. *More Italian Hours, and Other Stories,* her latest publication, gathers fifteen of these short stories.

The collection takes its title from one of the stories and evokes the great American writer Henry James. Barolini pays polite homage to James, then asks why America has welcomed the Italian observations of Anglo-American writers and not paid similar attention to the observations of those Americans whose "experience is refracted through the particular, not much recorded, view of an Italian American."

As she states in her "Author's Note," "my time in Italia was different from

James's 'Italian Hours,' so my view is another; it extends to include also those Italians who became Americans and made us, their descendants, Italian Americans with all the special complexity that implies."

The heart of the collection "Shores of Light" reflects this connection and unmakes that connection at the same time. "Why," she writes, "has it always been the Anglo-American sensibility to Italy that is heeded and not that of Italian Americans," asks the middle-aged James scholar in Venice to give a talk at a conference. "What is the heightened meaning of Italy to those who are Italian American, not Anglo-American?"

These stories take us beyond the boundaries and traps that foreign countries place in front of tourists. As a trusty guide, Barolini takes us deep into the territory that only a descendant of a native can reach.

The weaker stories are nevertheless interesting and could have easily been published as autobiographical essays. While they seem out of place in a collection of fiction, they do bring the reader a good sense of what life has brought to Barolini and how she has responded. Some of these dramatized essays are just too heavy handed to do more than jostle one's sense of complacency. This is the case with the first two. "Seven Fishes" could have appeared in her culturally rich cookbook, *Festa*, and "La Giardinera" is a nice metaphor for how to deal with the twilight years of life.

The best stories juxtapose the Italian and the Italian American and in the conflict. Barolini shows us how an Italian mentality derives from spiritual sources deep in one's soul. Her descriptions create a tactile sense of Italy that writers like James can never accomplish. Some of these are quite functional treats of fiction that rattle like the story that names the collection, "More Italian Hours, which contains my all time favorite Barolini line: "When it became clear she wouldn't be a writer, she settled for interesting vacations." In the friction between the two Italian and Italian/American comes a sense of difference that's palpable and perhaps never capable of being reconciled.

Barolini often eschews the label of Italian/American writer because she feels that it minimizes her Americaness. Not that she is trying to distant herself from her subject matter, she just would like to be accepted as a writer on equal terms with the likes of James. And while this collection does not place her on equal footing with the master, it should be acknowledged as the place where Barolini took her stand against the greats and challenged the power they have wielded over American literature.

(November 2001)

Helen Barolini, *More Italian Hours, and Other Stories* (Boca Raton, FL: Bordighera, 2001). Pp. 175. ISBN 1884419488; $16.00 (paperback).

Joseph Bathanti

Joseph Bathanti's *East Liberty* is a novel set in the 1960s, when Pittsburgh Pirates were baseball's world champs, when everyone is singing the songs from the film *West Side Story*, when nuns are the queens of corporal punishment and single-parent families are rare. The beauty of this work is that it tells a familiar story in an unfamiliar way.

Bathanti, an award-winning poet who teaches creative writing at Appalachian State University, creates scenes like paintings. His style is a unique synthesis of impressionism and realism that distorts reality and realizes the kaleidoscopic nature of memory as it reconstructs a past that the present needs. Here is tight, concise writing that you want to read slowly so you can gaze at the images and let the sounds sink in. It's easy to see how this novel won the Carolina Novel Award.

The narrator, Robert Renzo, describes himself as "a boy who has always said he will marry his mother, even past the age when I've realized I would not." He lives with the fear that his mother, whom he refers to as Francene, will abandon him as she does from time to time: sometimes with her parents, Italian immigrants from Naples, sometimes with friends he calls uncle and aunt. His father is a vague memory that reappears in times when a hero is needed.

Bobby learns much from his grandparents. His nonna, her head wrapped in a black kerchief, speaks no English and warns him not to go near her steamer trunk filled with the bones of her ancestors who will drag him in. She also teaches him about Spacaluccio, a monster that grabs kids who wander alone too far from home. Francene tells him that Spacaluccio, who takes on the identity of the latest immigrant tragedy: a construction worker buried in concrete, or a cuckolded soldier, is "just a story made up by crazy Italians to scare their children. They are in love with misery. It is their genius, and out of it they conjure a monster. They really are the monsters. East Liberty is a monster. Its enemy is happiness; it eats children." Roberto witnesses the struggle between Francene and her parents, for control over her life as a single mother and her ability to love as an independent woman.

At times *East Liberty* is reminiscent of other great works by Italian American writers, like Gilbert Sorrentino's *Aberration of Starlight* and John Fante's *1933 Was a Bad Year*. You can really see this in Robert's passion for baseball. "She [Francene] feels I substitute baseball for religion — for God — and attributes my obsession to the fact that I do not have a father. But she is wrong. Baseball and God are the same to me." But his mother has no problem letting him into her escape from the troubles of their life.

The classic films they watch together on television feed the young boy's imagination. To Bobby, they are "good stories," and serve as "morality tales, like the Old Testament and Jesus' parables." But these romances are crashing contrasts to life on the streets of East Liberty, a Black and Italian neighborhood in Pittsburgh where if school nuns don't get you then the street gangs will. The street parables come in the form of misfits "like Mooch and Montmorrissey Hilliard, or any of the neighborhood freaks that parents point out to their children as warnings." The novel ends in a home movie reprising the characters who made up his childhood, all lifting a toast to his health. East Liberty" is one novel that you will want to read more than once.

(June 2003)

Joseph Bathanti, *East Liberty* (Simpsonville, SC: Banks Channel Books, 2001). Pp. 207. ISBN 1889199087; $21.95 (hardcover).

Adria Bernardi

Adria Bernardi, first known to *Fra Noi* readers through *Houses with Names: The Italian Immigrants of Highwood, Illinois*, has racked up a number of literary prizes that announce her arrival as a powerful voice of contemporary American letters. Some of these recent awards include: *The Missouri Review* Editor's Prize for the Essay, The Drue Heinz Literature Prize for her short story collection *In the Gathering Woods*, the Bakeless Literary Publication Prize for fiction for her novel *The Day Laid on the Altar*, and the 1999 Aniello Lauri prize for creative writing published in *Voices in Italian Americana*.

A close look at her novel, which in some ways synthesizes her earlier work on immigration and her studies of Italian culture, reveals the reasons for her success. *A Day Laid on the Altar* is set in sixteenth-century Italy, a time of renaissance art and devastating plagues, and dramatizes the lives of emigrants, the homebound, and the homeless with equal flair and dignity. At stake is the role that art plays in separating the mortal from the immortal.

You don't read this novel for the plot, because, unlike the usual historical novel, there is no narrative thread that pulls you along. Bernardi's elegant and sturdy style keeps you moving from sentence to sentence with pleasure and without distraction. The place of art in the life of the worker and the celebrity are issues that come to life as the novel opens with the story of Bartolomeo di Bartolai, a simple man who knows he must leave home to be taken seriously as an artist. His problem is that he takes too seriously his bonds to his family and so never leaves home. Strapped to the land but not daunted, he makes art on the floor of an unused barn behind the house.

Bartolai's friend, Martin de Martinelli, does leave home and finds work preparing painting surfaces for the great Tiziano. Martin leads us into the artist's life as the master painter begins to sort out his legacy. We see Titian's greatness surrounded by weakness and ruin. Succeeding chapters follow his children

Orazio, Pomponio, and Giovanna as they attempt to escape the shadows cast by their celebrity father. The last two chapters bring us first to Martin who has never realized his ambition, and finally to Bartolomeo, creating his masterpiece in a cave he's known since childhood.

A history full of story, *A Day Laid on the Altar* is a well-paced meditation on beautiful images, as found in Martin's first sight of Venice:

> His cape flutters, sinoper, a corner stretching toward the horizon, where buildings are jewels strung out on rope, a necklace made of precious stones, topaz, ruby, amber, glinting in the late-day sun, forming an enormous, wide mansion, a floating structure with outstretched wings whose threshing floor is the sea.

A Day Laid on the Altar becomes a book about the roles dedication and luck play in the making of art and in building an artist's renown. It is also about how the greatness of greatness of others can blind us to the greatness in our selves. The central metaphor of art as sacrifice and offering, implied by the novel's title, speaks equally as well to the spiritual quality of Bernardi's prose and often spills out like poetry:

> The day laid on the altar is sacrificed. It is laid upon the threshing floor, laid upon worn-out stone. The day is laid flat, like the disc of the sun, blinding and metallic. Flat, like the disk of the moon, shimmering and buffed. Face up, face down, it does not matter. The day is laid down with open palm, hardship.

We may or may not learn more about the sixteenth century or even the great Titian, but we cannot help but better understand the impact of art on the human life in this fine first novel by a writer who has placed her own work of beauty before our eyes.

(January 2001)

Adria Bernardi, *The Day Laid on the Altar* (Hanover, NH: UP of New England, 2000). Pp. 210; ISBN 1584650443; $24.95 (hardcover).

Adria Bernardi's *In the Gathering Woods* is a compilation of fourteen short stories that echo and expand on much of what she's written in her novel, *A Day Laid on the Altar*. The stories, traditional in style if not subjects, are set in a variety of places and times ranging from sixteenth and nineteenth century Italy to twentieth century north shore Chicago.

The opening, title story, reveals how a young man comes alive when his grandfather takes him mushroom gathering and teaches him how to tell which are poisonous and which are to be picked. "Waiting for Giotto," the opening of her novel works as a story and follows, taking us deep into an Italy of plagues and renaissance art. "The Child Carrier" and "The Coal Loader, Above Ground" and "Shoreline" are powerful pictures of pre- and post-immigration life that capture the difference ethnicity and class make in shaping one's world view.

In "Sunday," Bernardi takes us into a typical Italian family's Sunday dinner through the eyes of a newborn. In this way we are privy to thoughts that rarely break the surface of the usual family encounters. "Rustlings," "Straight Shot," and "A Slight Blow to the Cheek," are insights into 60s north shore suburban life of the Gimorri family that reveal the toll assimilation takes on traditional gender roles and typical ethnic expectations.

The next two stories seem strange fish out swimming out of the ethnic waters of earlier stories. "The Minnie Minoso Cure" is nice look at how a person self medicates a mental illness through regular doses of celebrity contact. "With These New Tunes" is the least successful of the bunch, but works well to set up the final stories.

"Noli Me Tangere" and "Shards" are a brew of strong fiction that touches on earlier stories and on Bernardi's wonderful novel. A young neurologist unknowingly connects to the greatness of her ancestral past by travelling to Italy for pleasure and duty.

It is easy to see how this collection earned the prestigious Drue Heinz Literature Prize for "In the Gathering Woods" is a literary monument of Bernardi's love for language and a joy to read.

(April 2001)

Adria Bernardi, *In the Gathering Woods* (Pittsburgh, PA: U of Pittsburgh P, 2000). Pp. 224; $22.50 (hardcover).

LUCIA CHIAVOLA BIRNBAUM

Lucia Chiavola Birnbaum's *dark mother: african origins and godmothers* is a collection of sitings, histories, liberation theologies, artwork, and personal offerings around the theme of the original Mother Earth. This study recalls come Birnbaum's earlier works, *Liberazione della donna: Feminism in Italy* (a 1987 American Book Award winner) and *Black Madonnas: Feminism, Religion and Politics in Italy* (winner of the 1998 Premio Internazionale di Saggistica), as it offers a compilation of data scientific and spiritual that all point to early mother-centered cultures around the world.

Birnbaum, an independent scholar who teaches graduate students at the California Institute of Integral Studies, presents genetic and archaeological evidence that support her location of the first veneration of homo sapiens was a dark mother and goes back more than 100,000 years; the dark mother's presence can be identified later on through all continents and all religions. The impetus behind this book is Birnbaum's lifelong search: "I am a sicilian/american woman recovering my suppressed Sicilian ancestry, a journey that has taken me, via a circuitous route, to Africa," she writes. She encourages us all to take a similar journey, if not by physical then by mental travel through memory: "all humans carry the memory (often preconscious) of the dark mother and her values."

More than an educator, Birnbaum is an activist who is bucking the authorities who continue to benefit from a male-centered and male-dominated society. While not always the most coherent writing, "dark mother" gathers up pieces of history from around the world to bring light to the world's "african inheritance" and the performance of the dark mothers through the saints and sinners of Europe, Asia and North America. Birnbaum pierces through the chauvinistic guise of nationalism in an attempt to call the world to peace and unity through a common reverence of women. Birnbaum traces the evolution of the pre-historic goddess from the dark mother, to the camouflaged and often whitened versions that appear not only in churches but points of political uprisings throughout the world. Birnbaum believes that the world is due for a transformation from war to peace based cultures.

While her thesis is sound, and her evidence plentiful, Birnbaum's work poses a number of problems that make *dark mothers* a more difficult book than it needs to be. There is a tendency to simply state and not analyze the various studies she brings together. At times the prose is ponderous and repetitive, as though sections had been written without others in mind. And while this is always the danger when working with one's life work, it is something a good editor would have caught. We don't need to be reminded that Sicily is her ancestral homeland. Someone dropped the ball by not providing an index that would have made it more accessible to students.

Often Birnbaum uses personal travelogue and autobiography to illustrate key arguments that require a bit more objectivity to be convincing. This is not to say that the autobiographical take is not powerful. In fact, one of the most telling sections is one written by one Lucille Birnbaum about her experiences in Berkeley during the mid-1960s. This section captures not only the historical events, but also the author's changing sense of self that led to the creation of the scholar and activist we know her as today.

dark mothers will most definitely put off anyone clinging to the belief that white people are superior, but that's the point. This book is less a study than a survey of studies, and more a scrapbook of one woman's voyages, physical and psychic in search of origins and a sense of how to make our a better world.

(March 2003)

Lucia Chiavola Birnbaum, *dark mother: african origins and godmothers* (Author's Choice iUniverse, www.iuniverse.com, 2003). $25.95 (paperback).

Mary Jo Bona

With *Claiming a Tradition: Italian American Women Writers*, Mary Jo Bona joins Olga Peragallo, Rose Basile Green, and Helen Barolini, as one of the great advocates of Italian American literature. What separates Bona from the others is her command of cultural and literary theories that help place Italian American women's writing in the context of American history. Hers is a most important contribution to the filed of American literature in general, and women's studies and Italian/American culture in particular.

Claiming a Tradition is the first book-length study of Italian/American women writers, and Bona's clear writing and lucid arguments make it accessible to the casual reader as well as the professional scholar. From the opening, there's a strong, authoritative and confident voice that guides us along.

A solid introduction places the literature in the context of American literary history and ethnic studies. Bona does an excellent job of setting up the background against which her readers are projected. She writes: "claiming a tradition for Italian American women writers is an act of assertion in the face of possible resistance." She then shows us the many sites, which generate that resistance, in mainstream American culture and from within Italian American culture itself. There is a good summary of earlier critical work on the literature so that we know we are listening to someone who has done her homework.

The bulk of the study explores elements of Italianita that Bona finds inside each of the works she reads. These include, the role of the mother, "l'ordine della famiglia," "destino," "la via vecchia," "compareggio," and "omerta." She structures her chapters by pairing texts which highlight concepts such as: family in Mari Tomasi's *Like Lesser Gods* and Mario Benasutti's *No Steady Job for Pappa*; coming-of-age in *A Cup of the Sun* and Josephine Gattuso Hendin's *The Right Thing to Do*; personal identity in Diana Cavallo's *A Bridge of Leaves* and Dorothy Byrant's *Miss Giardino*; and recovering ancestry in Helen Barolini's *Umbertina* and Tina DeRosa's *Paper Fish*.

In many cases the authors she covers have had little, if any, critical attention. We are witnessing an original contribution to the field of literary criticism and history that work advances previous thinking and scholarship. The study is well integrated study, and each chapter builds on the previous the way a narrative might build a plot, only her story is composed of critical arguments. Her organization helps up witness a tradition evolving.

Bona's keen sense of what's been missed by previous scholars stems from the thoroughness of her preparation, the precision of her execution, and her passion for the material. Based on her dissertation, *Claiming a Tradition* represents a mature rethinking and immense reworking of the ideas and the language that were ahead of their time even back then in their early stage of development. Bona, an accomplished essayist and poet, has revised her earlier writing to reflect both her continued passion for literary expression and mastery of her field.

Her methodology of pairing authors works well to bring out commonalties as well as differences. This technique advances her argument that these women are, whether they know it or not, creating a real literary tradition. Beyond giving us insight into the past, this study serves the future development of Italian/American literature.

Her final chapter "Recent Developments in Italian American Women's Literary Traditions" is a survey of contemporary writers such as Rachel Guido deVries, Renee Manfredi, Agnes Rossi and Carole Maso, and provides us with a good sense of what will be happening in the decades to come.

Claiming a Tradition is published in Sandra M. Gilbert's prestigious Ad Feminam series, which, as Gilbert tells us in her signature preface,

> is dedicated to publishing books that will use innovative as well as traditional interpretive methods in order to help readers of both sexes achieve a clearer consciousness of that neglected but powerful [female] tradition and a better understanding of that hidden history.

Bona's contribution has more than achieved this goal and will no doubt be the benchmark against which much future criticism of ethnic American women writers will be measured.

(March 2000)

Mary Jo Bona, *Claiming a Tradition: Italian American Women Writers* (Carbondale, Southern UP, 1999). Pp. 253; ISBN 0809322587; $39.95 (hardcover).

The Voices We Carry takes its title from a line of a powerful poem by Maria Mazziotti Gillan. In her poem "The Crow," Gillan writes: "We are driven women / and we'll never escape / the voices we carry within us." And the women in this collection are certainly driven. The variety of stories and the styles through which they are presented range, from the nicely nostalgic to the outright anti-sentimental.

By dividing the collection into four thematic sections, Bona has structured our reception of these diverse writers so that their stories interact with each other. I recommend reading them in the order they appear. In this way, you'll better understand why Lynn Vannucci's "An Accidental Murder" is an appropriate ending to this important anthology.

The first section, "The Recreation of Historical Lives," opens with, "Planting," a long awaited glimpse into Mary Bush's latest work. For the first time, we gain access to the world of the indentured Italians who fled southern Italy only to find themselves in similar straights in America's post-bellum South. Much of what happens comes to us through Amalia, the matriarch of this transplanted family, and Bush's keen sensibilities create a dynamic world in which no burden goes unborne and no hope is too small to grasp.

In "The Lost Era of Frank Sinatra," Rachel Guido de Vries, recreates her parents' generation in a manner reminiscent of Delmore Schwartz's powerful "In Dreams Begin Responsibilities." Like Schwartz, de Vries captures a courtship in cinematic detail, but de Vries uses an ironic sense of humor that relieves the tragic development of what will certainly become a prototype for the dysfunctional family.

Daniela Gioseffi's excerpts from "Americans: One Minute to Midnight," juxtapose perspectives of a daughter of the Sixties generation with that of an her immigrant father to create a wild read. Dorissa's experience in jail, after her boyfriend takes the Washington monument hostage, is psychologically similar to Donatuccio's experience in trans-Atlantic steerage.

The "Juniper Street Sketches" of Diana Cavallo capture in incredible detail and sensitivity the rituals, both transplanted and invented, which helped to define Italian/American culture. Cavallo is unmatched in her ability to make scenes shimmer through words, to turn memories into meaning for even the most detached reader.

Part Two, "The Intersection Between America and L'Italia," includes Lisa Ruffolo's "Southern Italy," a transformation of Black Capri into an ancient Italian through her interaction with friends, an Italian lover and the enchanting sea and landscape of Italy's south; Laura Marello's "Claiming Kin" deals with family on both sides of the Atlantic; and Dodici Azpadu's "Desert Ruins," creates a new thirst for an old, familiar past.

The highlight of Part Three, "La Famiglia in America," is Susan J. Leonardi's "Bernie Becomes a Nun," which is simultaneously a depiction of a saint's and sinner's struggle to belong to the world by separating herself from her family. Adria Bernardi, Phyllis Capello and Giovanna (Janet) Capone, all present younger protagonists growing up in a world of Barbie Dolls, G.I. Joes, historical asassinations, unfaithful parents, divorce and a stiff and stiffling Catholic Church.

The final section, "The End of a Generation," features an excerpt from Dorothy Bryant's novel, *The Test,* which is a bittersweet a testimony to the immigrant generation: sweet is the fondness of a daughter for her father, bitter is the experience of having to deal with his aging. Anne Paolucci's "Buried Treasure," is a telling portrait of a man who is only truly understood by his daughter-in-law. And Lynn Vannucci's excerpt from "Driving" is the exclamation point that finishes the collection with a flourish!

The book's cover is a telling painting by Chicago artist Christine Perri. Entitled, "The Interruption," is serves as a warning label that this book contains works-in-progress that have been interrupted, that women at work are prone to interruption, but also that an eruption is occurring among Italian/American women and that the outpouring of literature has never been better.

(November 2001)

Mary Jo Bona, ed., *The Voices We Carry: Recent Italian/American Women's Fiction*, 2nd ed. (Tonawanda, NY; Guernica Editions, 2000). ISBN 1550710990.

Peter Bondanella

With Peter Bondanella's *Hollywood Italians*, we finally have a thorough survey of the ways and means Italians have made and been made by Hollywood. Bondanella, author of the acclaimed *Italian Cinema*, and other books on Italian filmmakers, has created a veritable primer of the history of the Italian American presence in American film in an interesting and accessible style. From the earliest silent films such as *The Greaser's Gauntlet* (1907) to the HBO hit series *The Sopranos*, Bondanella gives statistics and covers the plots of all the major and many minor productions that have had anything to do with Italians. This is the overview that the field has been waiting for.

Along with *Screening Ethnicity* and *Italactors*, *Hollywood Italians* helps students and seasoned scholars alike better understand the role that ethnicity has played in the development of US cinema. Bondanella dispels the myth of stereotype by giving us the big picture in which various images of Italians have appeared. Bondanella rightly situates early Hollywood stereotypes in the tradition of their earlier historical constructions. One of those most responsible for the earliest negative images was D.W. Griffiths. Sometimes called the father of the gangster film with his *The Musketeers of Pig Alley*, made in 1915, Griffiths' *In Little Italy*, *The Violin Maker of Cremona*, and *Pippa Passes*, all made in 1909, and *Italian Blood*, made in 1911, used Italian stories riddled with stereotypical representations. Bondanella does an excellent job of explaining how these films got made, looks at audience and critical reactions, and provides us with interesting production notes on many of them.

He divides his study thematically by various characterizations. After an excellent introduction he presents "Dagos: Hollywood Histories of Emigration," which covers many of the silent films and others throughout history that have depicted the Italian experience in coming to the US "Palookas: Hollywood Italian Prize Fighters" is an interesting chapter focusing on the famous and not-so-famous films that imitated the reality of such sports heroes as Primo Carnera, Rocky Graziano, and Jake LaMotta to the fictional folk of the *Rocky* films.

One of his more interesting chapters is "Romeos: Hollywood Italian Lovers," which looks not only at Rudolph Valentino, but the film roles enacted by Frank Sinatra, Dean Martin and John Travolta, and how the supported or challenged the Latin lover stereotype. The largest section of his study focuses on the presentation of the Italian American gangsters. "Wiseguys: Hollywood Italian Gangsters," "Comic Wise Guys: Italian Gangsters Yuk It Up," and "Sopranos: The Postmodern Hollywood Italian 'Famiglia,'" all present the most thorough discussion of this stereotype to date. Arguing primarily from a basis in aesthetics as opposed to one on social activism, Bondanella sees the figure as an artistic character capable of representing the American experience as well as being abused into stereotypical nonsense.

What you won't find here is any kind of rigorous relation of the films to various critical theories, something the common reader will appreciate, but something that will no doubt frustrate the scholars looking to see these films analyzed with traditional and postmodern critical tools. However, with a sound history, solid plot summaries, and interesting accounts of production highlights, Bondanella has produced a very useful book. His timin couldn't have been better as a number of schools have begun courses in Italian American films. Bondanella has done the field and the culture a great service by taking on such a grand study. Bravo!

(January 2005)

Peter Bondanella, *Hollywood Italians: Dagos, Palookas, Romeos, Wise Guys and Sopranos* (New York: Continuum, 2004). Pp. 352; ISBN 082641544X; $29.95 (hardcover).

Dorothy Calvetti Bryant

In *Miss Giardino*, Dorothy Calvetti Bryant, dramatizes the impact that a single event can have in changing one woman's whole way of looking at her life. Anna Giardino is a retired school teacher who one Monday morning finds herself in the emergency room of a San Francisco hospital. As she struggles to remember what put her there, she begins to understand just what she's done with her life. Assuming that she must have been the victim of a mugging, the media use her as an example of how terrible life has become in the city's Mission District the area that has been Anna's home for most of her life.

The events take place over one week in chapters named after the days. Monday, Anna's in the hospital. Tuesday she goes home to slowly begin the process of remembering. The rest of the week runs along as though it was a version of Holy Week leading to the death of one Anna and the resurrection of a new Anna.

The story advances as senses spark recollections of the distant past: the touch of a dusty box, the feel of a book in hand, the sound of a familiar phrase in a friend's voice, the sight of an ex lover's nod to another man, the smell of the hospital room, all trigger sporadic memories and dreams that eventually combine to help her solve the mystery. A recurring dream, centered on a burning school, sends images into her consciousness that rebuild in her memory like photographs in a pool of developing solution. When the memory of the incident returns, Anna's guilt begins. As she faces the reality of how she was hurt, she understands the mystery of the mistakes she's made in her life.

Bryant's alternating use of personal history and imagination combine to create a wonderful structure for the novel through which Miss Giardino's past comes to us in pieces that slowly give us the whole of the puzzle of her life. Anna grows up in the 1920s, a child of an abusive immigrant father and a fearful, but loving, mother. The only one who can read English in the family, Anna's command of the language becomes her shield against her father, who stops using her name and calls her "The skinny one," "the stick," or even worse, "the American." Anna saves her Italian for her mother: "I will caress her with the easy, good-humored Piedmontese dialect, the tongue of golden sunsets and week oranges, of the place that is forever home to her."

Anna recalls former students like Willie Fortuna whose "D" would have kept him from playing sports; somehow the grade magically transforms to a C, enabling him to go on to fail his way up to becoming Director of Disaster Control for the School District. Then there's Maria Flores, whose only "B" in school came from Miss Giardino. Flores' who's replaced Anna as English teacher at the school, calls to set up a meeting at which Anna fears she might try to harm her. Anna's few friends, her sister, even her tenants all contribute to the reshaping of Anna's consciousness. What she finally remembers turns her from victim to victimizer.

As a novelist, playwright, and short story writer, Dorothy Calvetti Bryant has also been a long-time publisher of her own work. In the tradition of Mark Twain and Virginia Woolf, Dorothy, with her husband Robert, established Ata Books of Berkeley, California in 1978. Recently, the Bryants decided to turn over some of Dorothy's books to The Feminist Press for reprinting. "Miss Giardino," along with "Ella Price's Journal" and "Confessions of Madame Psyche," joins Tina DeRosa's "Paper Fish," in The Feminist Press series Contemporary Women's Fiction from Around the World.

The book's "Afterword," by Janet Zandy, is part interview, biography and scholarly essay. No one writes more sensitively about working class literature and culture than Zandy, whose own edited books, "Liberating Memory: Our Work and Our Working-Class Consciousness," and "Calling Home: Working-Class Women's Writings," have become central to working-class studies. The choice of Zandy, who's of Italian descent on her mother's side, to write this "Afterword," was a masterful move by Feminist Press director Florence Howe.

Zandy brings to light a number of issues that previous criticism has missed and gives us a sense of how the novel fits into the whole of Bryant's writings by taking the novel past the ethnic factor to make it speak to the larger issues of class and gender. "Bryant was able to draw from her own ethnic Italian background to create Anna," writes Zandy, "but the identity of Anna is too complex to fit the dominant culture's stereotypic notions of Italian Americans — as if there were no regional, class and language differences." Zandy's interpretation helps prepare a classic Italian/American novel for a new generation of readers.

(April 1998)

Dorothy Calbetti Bryant, *Miss Giardino*, Afterword by Janet Zandy (New York: Feminist P, 1997). Pp. 186; ISBN 1558611746; $11.95 (paperback).

Dorothy Bryant's *The Test* recounts ten hours in the day of a life of a middle-aged daughter trying to deal with her elderly father. The novel, first published in 1991, speaks to many of the trials soon to be faced by baby boomers as their parents reach their "golden years." With only ten hours in the life of Pat Sancavei, Bryant teaches us much about the Italian father/daughter relationship without being didactic and without taking sides. The daughter can be as manipulative and feisty as the man who helped give her life.

The Test is a brilliant meditation upon meanings and ends of life. "If, beyond the easy, sentimental stereotypes," she writes,"there is, after all, any trait that is Italian, it must be this yielding to a pure agony of grief for the end of each human life." Bryant brings out the passion and the frustration of trying to live a life for one's self without abandoning the family or one's sanity when it seems that one or the other must go.

Pat and her sister Flora spent their lives trying to get away from the man they now they must help him make it through the rest of his life. It's hard to tell if the old man is helpless or merciless, and Bryant's clean prose sets a mood that's alternately tense and relieving. Pat's daughter echoes her own thoughts when, after trying to stay with him for a while leaves in a huff saying, "He's not satisfied just to have company, Mom, he has to invade my mind. I can't have my own thoughts."

First published by ATA books in 1991, this Feminist Press reprint has a helpful and substantial "Afterword" by Barbara Horn sets the novel in the context of Bryant's other works and the literature of aging.

Dorothy Bryant, *The Test*, Afterword by Barbara Horn (New York: Feminist P, 2001). Pp. 170; $13.95 (paperback).

ANNE CALCAGNO

Don't leave home without it. No, it's not a credit card, but the latest *Travelers' Tales Guide: Italy*. This latest release strengthens the reputation of O'Reilly and Associates as the most exciting publishers of travel writing in the world. There is not a dull moment in any of these forty-eight "true stories of life on the road." Besides being a cheap way to go to Italy for the holidays, the fine writing will keep Italy alive in your mind for a long time. The entries, selected by Anne Calcagno, a fine writer herself, recount the trials and triumphs of travelling through one of the most visited countries in the world. Featured writers include the usual suspects like Tim Parks, Barbara Grizutti Harrison, and Luigi Barzini, along with a host of newer voices, and they all provide stories sacred and profane.

Like lively graffitti, excerpts from longer works appear spattered against the entries. Here you'll find classics like Lucretius, Virgil, Plautus, Dante, Shelley, Goethe, D.H. Lawrence, Henry James, and James Joyce. Throughout the book, Calcagno tosses in editorial notes like spices that clarify or highlight points.

Beyond the fine writing, *Travelers' Tales Guides: Italy* offers basic cultural information that includes "Dos and Don'ts" like using "arrivederci" rather than "ciao," to say goodbye, and "Fifteen Fun Things to Do," which advises to eat the pizza but not the mussels of Naples. A list of helpful websites and other books to read rounds out a fine volume that should in the hands of everyone who has ever been to or wanted to go to Italy. Calcagno has fashioned a treasure of travel lore and information that should make for a great gift this season.

(December 1998)

Anne Calcagno, ed., *Travelers' Tales Guides: Italy* (O'Reilly & Associates, www.oreilly.com/ttales). $17.95 (paperback).

PHILIP CANNISTRARO

Most people associate Fascism with the period of time in the late 1930s and 40s that led up to World War II. By then, Mussolini was the fanatic dictator leading Italy in search of international respect. Also by then, most Italian Americans had turned their back on Mussolini and strove to prove themselves to be good Americans.

But this was not always the case. As T-shirts in Little Italy gift shops attest, there was a time when Americans of Italian descent worked to support Mussolini's government and his idea of what was good for Italy. Often this support manifested itself in Blackshirts, blind boasting, and fighting in the streets.

Blackshirts in Little Italy: Italian Americans and Fascism, 1921–1929, is a tight little book that serves as an excellent introduction to the role that Fascism played in the lives of Italian Americans. Written by Philip Cannistraro, one of the world's leading authorities on Italian fascism, and Distinguished Professor of Italian American Studies at Queens College and the Graduate Center of the City University of New York, "Blackshirts," is accessible to the general public and serves well the seasoned scholar of Italian and American history.

Covering the period of overt display of loyalty to Italy, "Blackshirts" describes the relationship between Fascism in Italy and its proponents and sympathizers in the United States. Cannistraro's lucid historical presentation is divided into chapters on "The Origins of Italian American Fascism," "Mussolini, Fascism, and the United States," "Fascism and the 'Prominenti,'" "The Fascist League of North America," and "The Crisis of Fascism." An "Epilogue" provides an entry into the 1930s and suggests areas where more work needs to be done to tell the whole story.

Blackshirts establishes a great sense of both the infighting within the American fascist organizations and the intra-ethnic fighting between them and anti-fascist groups and leaders such as Carlo Tresca. Cannistraro's research, using both diplomatic and grassroots perspectives, covers most of the major sources on both sides of the ocean. He uses them well in recreating the events that led up to the establishment this little understood and more often ignored period of Italian American history.

(April 2000)

Philip Cannistraro, *Blackshirts in Little Italy: Italian Americans and Fascism, 1921–1929* (West Lafayette, IN: Bordighera, 1999). Pp. 124. ISBN 1884419275; $12.00 (paperback).

&

Mayday, or the 1st of May, used to belong to the workers of US and the world. It originated as a date to launch the struggle for an eight-hour work day. In 1886, a May 1st rally resulted three days later in the famous Haymarket Riot. Since then the day which came to symbolize workers' struggles to obtain rights and dignity has continued to be celebrated throughout the world except where it started. Few Americans remember the day, and a vague attempt at masking its origins has turned it into Law Day.

Like the origins of the day, so too have the radical legacy of many Italian Americans, become buried under an avalanche of assimilation, shame and ignorance. As many Italian Americans lament the shadow that organized crime has cast over the culture, few have bothered to look into those shadows to see the light that comes from the rich proletariat history in politics and labor. Thanks to the editorial work of Philip Cannistraro and Gerald Meyer, that tradition has been uncovered in over sixteen critical essays.

The essays came from presentations at a conference sponsored by the John D. Calandra Institute in 1997 that have been expanded. A powerful and thorough introductory essay by the editors reminds us:

> For Italian Americans, the experiences of grandparents and parents are replete with deafening silences that are the product, in part, of the fears and taboos that drove many first-generation immigrants to bury aspects of their past that seemed to make them somehow too Italian and not sufficiently American.

Students and scholars have much to learn from what's been uncovered by veteran historians like Rudy Vecoli in "The Making and Unmaking of the Italian American Working Class," Nunzio Pernicone's "War Among the Italian Anarchists," Paul Avrich's "Sacco and Vanzetti's Revenge," Salvatore Salerno's "Italian Anarchists and the Industrial Workers of the World," Gerald Meyer's "Italian Americans and the American Communist Party," and Gary Mormino's and George Pozzetta's "The Radical World of Ybor City, Florida."

The role of women, long downplayed in all aspects of Italian American history, has been well documented by Jennifer Guglelmo in "Donne Ribelli," Julia Lisella in "Behind the Mask: Signs of Radicalism in the Work of Rosa Zagnoni Marinoni," Mary Jo Bona's "Rooted to the Family: Italian American Women's Radical Novels," and Edvige Giunta's "Where They Come From: Italian American Women Writers as Public Intellectuals."

Forgotten heroes of the Free Speech and Civil Rights movements like Mario Savio and Fr. James Groppi are richly recalled in Gil Fagiani's "Resurrecting an Italian American Radical" and Jacki DiSalvo's "The Militant Humility of a Civil Rights Activist." Paola Sensi-Isolani explores local radical movements in San Francisco 1900–1920; The famous New York harbor strikes of 1907 and 1909 historicized by Calvin Winslow provide new contexts for reviewing films like "On the Waterfront." Charles Zappia charts the movement of the Italian locals of the International Ladies' Garment Workers Union, from radicalism to anti-communism. Donna R. Gabaccia adds a concluding essay that places all of this work in a global perspective.

While most of the essays are written by academics, they are all accessible and will reward even the most casual reader of American history. As the editors suggest, "What is at stake is both historical accuracy and Italian American self-perception." The image of the fictional gangster will shrink next to the historical portraits contained in these important essays.

(May 2005)

Philip Cannistraro and Gerald Meyer, eds., *The Lost World of Italian-American Radicalism: Politics, Labor, and Culture* (Westport, CT: Praeger, 2003). www.praeger.com; ISBN: 0–275–97892–3; $29.95 (paperback).

Mary Cappello

What flowers in the night can be as hopeful as a dream, and as dreadful as a nightmare, and Mary Cappello's memoir, *Night Bloom*, gives us a little of both as she tells us a lot of what has happened to make her who she is. The book opens with a meditation on humor that dissolves into a contemplation of fear. This shift becomes a familiar pattern of the prose throughout the memoir as her life dances in, around and through the lives of those who make her laugh and cry, stand tall and cower.

What's important to Cappello, besides of course what she's telling us, is how she tells it to us. Her prose is melodic, even when what she's saying seems self-pitying or a bit indulgent, it never sounds that way. She has a great ear for language, and the possibilities of sound composed well. This comes to us from the very beginning section, entitled "The Sweetness of Doing Nothing":

> And even though the feeling is liquid, my mother does not dissolve in this memory of the garden so much as she resolves, is resolved, finds momentary resolution in the shade of a cherry tree or as she bends to break a spring of parsley or, buoyed up by a trail of rose by her side, looks up to the sky.

Cappello's sense of poetry and pacing keeps this memoir breathing. "Memory catches and memory cuts," she writes. "Memory attaches and memory subtracts. All things swim and glitter." Swimming throughout *Night Bloom* are excerpts from a journal her mother's father kept. The juxtaposition of the voices creates a dialogue of two generations that are better known for talking about, than to, each other. She sees her grandfather's page as "an overcrowded tenement," and understands, "especially in light of my fancy theorizing, that I lack the resources, I do not have the means to value my grandfather's writing for what it is." This is a truth rarely expressed in the post-immigration literature of Italian Americans.

Her grandfather complains about the lack of heat in his home, and what was a physical lack in one generation, can become a spiritual void in another

> Warmth persists for me as an aesthetic goal — the desire to conjure warmth

from words — even when what is important to me on other levels and in other places changes. I must produce warmth with my words if I am to coax my ancestors out of their shadows, because what is most apparent about the trouble they are in is that it chills them.

When we read her grandfather's entry, "Va o mio bel pensiero in ogni dove poiche lo spazio e senza limiti," we can sense his connection to Verdi's "Nabucco," which helps us understand how the immigrant can feel captive by the restrictions of work, language, lack of range in social mobility. What Cappello teaches us through this montage of voices is that the self is the other, that we are both product and process of our family's history. Ultimately this memoir is the story about missing links due to assimilation, about love's possibilities and impossibilities, and the beauty and danger that lurk in the garden of our lives.

For Cappello, plants become a way of speaking about the unspeakable, about the fear and the abuse she experiences growing up. Her parents hide their love in their gardening. They all displace their pain, their hunger, and their ability to control their own lives by transferring touch to the plants they tend. As the gardens grow, people wither, and only the writing remains as a witness to the good and evil that is harvested.

(November 1998)

Mary Cappello, *Night Bloom: A Memoir* (Boston: Beacon, 1998). www.beacon.org. Pp. 262. ISBN 0807072168; $23 (hardcover).

Peter Carravetta

The Carravetta family's 1963 arrival in the United States from Lappano in Calabria came during what would be the last great wave of Italian emigration. Ten years later a young Peter Carravetta began a journey of his own. After earning a Bachelor's of Arts degree in English literature and creative writing at the City College of New York in 1973, he took off to study at the University of Bologna, the University of Chicago, and universities in Milan and Dallas. Carravetta completed his doctorate in Italian at New York University in 1983.

As a professor of Italian and director of the World Studies Program at Queens College, Carravetta has used his world travels as a basis for his studies, teaching and writings. Equally adept in Italian and English, well versed in philosophy and the physical sciences, he has published critical and creative writing in Italy and America. He is the founding editor of *Differentia, Review of Italian Thought* and a frequent contributor to *Voices in Italian Americana*. Until recently he has primarily been known as a cultural critic, but the poetry he's publishing these days comes from writing that he's been doing since his teenage years.

While Carravetta has previously published a number of poetry chapbooks and books of poetry in Italian, his first collection in English, *The Sun and Other Things*, published by Guernica Editions, marks a major shift in his writing career. Ranging over the past twenty-years of his life, he deals with such subjects as life, literature, linguistics, sensual and platonic love and adolescent *angst*. He anxiously reacts to the influence of classic poets as Dante, Shakespeare, and the English Romantics and the modern masters such as Joyce, Eliot, and Stevens. The entire collection is a metamorphic journey in which the poet, at home in English and Italian traditions, travels from thought to word. The result is that for Carravetta, writing becomes the sanctuary of a self besieged by forces competing for the author's attention.

His poetry is characterized by its frequent allusions to ancient Greek and Roman mythology, as well as to various traditions of Italian, British and American lyric and epic poetry. Sometimes you get the feeling you're reading Whitman's heart through Emerson's head as in the opening poem. The interaction between these cultures becomes a basis for the creation of new myths that concern life and love between two worlds. The more you know about these literary traditions, the more you are likely to get out of this poet. His are not poems about the Italian/American experience as much as they are the result of two great traditions smashing into each other through one man forming some strange hybrid of classic and contemporary cultures.

The possibilities of a hybrid come through most clearly in section XII. From "Cancionero," the penultimate section of the collection. Here Carravetta leaps out of the structures and strictures of past forms, and through a voice all his own, creates imagery that makes you think new thoughts.

One of his stylistic trademarks is frequent code switching between English and Italian; his work also includes phrases and sentences from other Romance languages such as French and Spanish. Carravetta demonstrates that he's absorbed two traditions, from the Latin through Italian, and English through American. With some interesting nods to other European Languages such as German, French, and Spanish, Carravetta's writing moves in interesting directions.

What's most impressive is his poetic range. Always ready to experiment, Carravetta creates poetry that is always challenging, even if it is sometimes too reflective of his scholarly training. Looked at as an evolution of one man's art, an experiment of a mind at work, *The Sun and Other Things*, will no doubt prove to be the fount of his future creative writings.

(September 1998)

Peter Carravetta, *The Sun and Other Things* (Toronto: Guernica Editions, 1998). Pp. 148; ISBN 1550710265; $12 (paperback).

Michael P. Carroll

Madonnas That Maim: Popular Catholicism in Italy Since the Fifteenth Century is an intriguing study of how Italian social life has changed the official Catholic Church order of worship of Christ, then the Madonna and then the Saints. It also examines the legends of vengeance that are often ignored in the emphasis on the Madonna's and the saints' beneficence.

Written by Michael P. Carroll, a professor of sociology at the University of Western Ontario and author of *The Cult of the Virgin Mary* and *Catholic Cults and Devotions*, *Madonnas* helps us understand how and why Italy is virtually the only Catholic country that has reversed the official order of worship.

Carroll, who by the way is Italian on his mother's side, opens with an excellent overview of the origins and development of these three followings and explains their impact on local, national and international cultures. "The fact that saints are local while madonnas are distant has social consequences," writes Carroll. "Precisely because madonnas transcend the local community, devotion to a madonna can pull different communities together; the local nature of a saint, by contrast, promotes religious factionalization."

In Chapter Two, Carroll, after presenting us with a fine summary of the wealth of previous scholarship, offers a corrective to the idea of the place of saints in Italian culture. He writes,

> What might come as a surprise to some readers is that Italian Catholics regard the power to correct a current misfortune of far less importance than the other power attributed to the saints — the power to protect from dangers yet to happen. This power to protect is usually what is being conveyed when a saint is called a patron. This supernatural patron lies at the core of Italian Catholicism.

Carroll clearly and often humorously illustrates his analysis with thorough historical accounts of the famous saints such as Sant'Antonio Abate, and the Church-manufactured saints such as San Zopito — an unknown whose remains received a legitimate name by the Church in response to the town of Loreto Aprutino's request for relics for their church. That the name Zopito was created by mistake made no difference in his acceptance and continued celebration by the local people.

In Chapter 3, Carroll explains that Mary's status in Catholicism is greater than in the Protestant religions because of "the experience of apparitions." He points out that the nearly 400 madonne worshipped in Italy is distinctly Italian phenomenon. In the exciting, "The Dark Side of Holiness" Carroll examines apparition accounts, literature and folklore to demonstrate that the madonnas and saints are as capable of vengeance as they are of protecting devotees from harm.

Carroll writes,

> The danger has nothing to do with the punishment of sin as defined by the Church. It derives from something much simpler: the saints and madonnas of Italy want to be worshipped, and it is toward this end, the maintenance of their own cults, that they use their great power.

As evidence of such power Carroll draws on earlier studies which identify numerous instances in which saints and madonnas have defended themselves or have punished the impious. Central to his argument is Elisabetta Grigioni's work which documents events such as "The Madonna dei Miracoli, in Lucca," in which a soldier who after losing at gambling throws the dice against an image of the Virgin and in doing so breaks his arm. Another example from Puglia is when a Turk is struck dead after trying to destroy an image of the Madonna Capreolana. The examples, to the modern reader might read like folktales, but in fact come from reference works such as the "Marian Atlas" which are considered to be reliable sources of matter-of-fact accounts.

Carroll explores the "Regional Differences" between Northern and Southern Italy in the next chapter, concluding that the differences in regional practices of Catholicism can be attributed to the lesser impact that the Council of Trent had on the parishes of Southern Italy. The difference, he says, is due to the more scattered organization of parishes in the south. "As late as 1897, Lombardia had 9 dioceses for a population of 3.5 million, while Puglia . . . had a staggering 32 dioceses for a population of only 1.5 million." After establishing the reasons for the differences, he provides a fascinating analysis of such strange practices as "Temporary Resurrections," in which dead babies were briefly brought back to life just long enough for women to baptize them.

In his discussion of the connections between magic and Catholicism (Chapter 6), Carroll debunks the notion that popular religion practiced in southern Italy was always more magical than in the north. He notes that it wasn't until the Council of Trent, 1563, that such things as invoking the saints, venerating relics and the sacred use of images were to be removed from the practice of Catholicism. So while the Church in Northern Italy was busy cleaning house, practice of magic in Southern Italy was actually on the rise. Carroll uses the blood miracle of San Gennaro, and other, less famous saints, to illustrate the magical practices of the south.

In Chapter 7, Carroll examines the practice of masochism in southern Italy and helps to explain some of the strange behavior some of us might have seen years ago such as people walking barefoot in processions, self flagellation and tongue dragging along church aisles.

In the final chapter, "The Psychology of Italian Catholicism," Carroll concludes that: "The practice of magic, the Mary cult, and the cult of the saints can be seen as functionally equivalent adaptations to . . . the dangers and hostile environment faced by Italians and the anxiety that such an environment produces." Using the psychology of Sigmund Freud and Melanie Klein, Carroll explains that people dominated by "the father-ineffective family" living in a region prone to male emigration for work and environmental disasters such as earthquakes and volcanic eruptions, create a religion that meets their unique needs. This absence of the father in the day-to-day life of the family creates "in sons a strong but strongly repressed desire for the mother," which in turn "produces a strong sense of guilt and a resultant desire for self-punishment in those sons." This, combined with a strong sense of maschismo, explains how public displays of pain can play a role in worship of the Madonna and saints.

Carroll combines thoroughly researched arguments with accessible writing to create a study that reaches well beyond academia and into the heads of those whose hearts have always believed that there was more to Italian Catholicism than meets the eye.

(May 2001)

Michael P. Carroll, *Madonnas That Maim: Popular Catholicism in Italy Since the Fifteenth Century* (Baltimore: Johns Hopkins UP, 1992). Pp. 202; ISBN 0801842999; $34.95 (hardcover).

Mark Ciabattari

Mark Ciabattari has become Italian America's premiere postmodernist. His *Dreams of an Imaginary New Yorker Named Rizzoli* (1990) and *The Literal Truth: Rizzoli Breams of Eating the Apple of Earthly Delights: Tales of Manhattan and the Hamptons* (1994) have proven his ability to create the wonderful small tales, no small feat in today's trendy big screen reality mania.

Ciabattari's latest, *Mystery of the Clay-Molded Curse of Sicily, as Revealed in Two Stories: The Urn by Mark Ciabattari and The Oil Jar by Luigi Pirandello, A Post-modern Homage to the Great Italian Modernist Pirandello*, contains the famous Pirandello story, "La giarra," masterfully translated by Maria Enrico and Ciabattari's own story about the strange behavior of a piece of Sicilian pottery.

Presented in the form of a found journal, *The Urn* follows the misfortunes of one Grimaldi, a not unpleasant peasant until the day his every movement is shadowed by a giant urn that moves about on feet of hard clay. Grimaldi is a brick maker, who unable to read or write, is more like than unlike most of his contemporaries. This ordinary worker becomes a "freak" as people begin to reason why this urn follows him about.

When things finally fall into place, we learn that reality gets squashed, repressed, eliminated, and eventually hidden only to be recovered by a later generation who can no longer can tell the difference between truth and lies and no longer cares. And it doesn't matter, for writers like Ciabattari remind us that only by imagining what can never happen can we transcend where we are and get to places we have never been.

(January 2005)

Mark Ciabattari, *Clay Creatures* (Canio's Books, 2004). Pp. 94; ISBN 1886435146; $10 (paperback).

Edward Cifelli

From his early writing in *Nation*, to his editing of poetry for the *Saturday Review*, John Ciardi gained national celebrity status as a poet. This is certainly a rare accomplishment, and one that made him a public intellectual and artist in a sense that has long been shattered by the separation of academic and public life. Author of more than forty books of poetry and criticism, Ciardi has done more to popularize poetry than perhaps any other American of Italian descent.

In 1965 he gave the world a new translation of Dante which by now has surpassed the million-copy mark in paperback. Among his accolades were election to the National Institute of Arts and Letters and to the American Academy of Arts and Letters. He was also named Fellow of the American Academy in Rome.

There was more to Ciardi than his high-profile public persona, and in "John Ciardi: A Biography" Edward Cifelli tells us how Ciardi came to say things like: "I never met an Irish priest I liked," and how the poet made the upgrading of the food served at the famous Bread Loaf Writers' Conference a condition of accepting its directorship. Using a combination of story, history, interviews, and Ciardi's own words, Cifelli shows us just how personal Ciardi's poetry actually was in a style that makes reading about the poet's life as enjoyable as reading his poetry.

Ciardi's work took him to Italy more than a few times in his life. The first time was during World War II. In 1956 he received the Rome Prize fellowship and spent the year in Italy. He also was given honorary citizenship to his mother's home town of Avellino when the mayor got word that Ciardi used the town's name in one of his poems. As an American writer of Italian descent, Ciardi refused to be categorized and alienated by his ethnicity. He used his experience and talent to carry "Italianita" out of the neighborhood and into the world of American culture where he could serve as translator of "self" and of his culture.

Cifelli, awarded a "Choice" Outstanding book award, has given us a biography that is as entertaining to read as it is informative. If you know Ciardi's poetry, here's a great way to get to know the man, and if you know neither, then Cifelli has created a great introduction.

(December 2000)

Edward Cifelli, *John Ciardi: A Biography* (Fayetteville, AK: U of Arkansas P, 1997). Pp. 557; ISBN 1557284482; $48 (hardcover).

RITA CIRESI

In her debut as a novelist, Rita Ciresi, a Flannery O'Connor award winning short story writer, turns her talented pen off the narrow streets of the short story and onto the wide open highway of the extended narrative. Fueled by humor, *Blue Italian* achieves success as a parody of the young love and young death stories that have come before.

In an interview, Ciresi told of how the novel came to be a spoof of Erich Segal's bestseller, *Love Story,* which told the story of a rich, Harvard law student falling in love with a working-class girl with a terminal illness. Ciresi's strong with dialogue, but weak when it comes to developing her characters, who seem better suited for stand-up comedy routines than for extended play in a novel. But this is hardly a problem if you able to see *Blue Italian* as a witty, parodic play on the schmaltzy Segal prototype.

While the lack of character development might be the flaw of any number of new novelists, especially those adept in the short story genre, it doesn't detract from the realization that a wise and humorous mind is at work on an issue that has occupied Italian/American feminists for decades: Can the daughter of Italian immigrants use any of her ancestral culture in creating her own American self?

As Joshua Fausty so perceptively remarked in his review (*VIA*) of Ciresi's story collection, *Mother Rocket: Stories* (1993),

> Ciresi's struggle to respond creatively to the status of Italian/American culture within American culture leads her to create a ventriloquist narrative that enables the marginalized, silenced and repressed within her to find a voice and be heard.

The characters in *Blue Italian* might become the puppets of Ciresi, but beyond ventriloquism, the characters portray the author's rich sense of humor, a sense that Italian/American writers rarely activate. That Italian/American culture can be funny seems to belong more to outsiders than insiders. Perhaps that's why Ciresi's protagonist in *Blue Italian* is better read as a critic of Italian/American culture than as any real-life representation.

The critical voice heard loud and clear in *Blue Italian* belongs to Rosa Salvatore, a second-generation daughter of Italian immigrants who is looking for a way out of the old neighborhood and the old country notions that stunt a woman's growth. What she stumbles upon in her search for freedom becomes another way of seeing herself as an Italian/American woman.

The plot centers on the courtship and marriage of Rosa to Gary Fisher. Rosa, the daughter of Italian immigrants, works in Yale's New Haven Hospital and longs to escape the fate she feels comes to any girl who marries a boy from the neighborhood, "becoming a woman who leaned out of a second-floor window, her heavy upper arms jiggling as she hung out on the clotheslines the white flags of laundry, like so many signs of surrender." Her savior comes in the person of Fisher, a Jewish American law student who volunteers in the legal counsel department of the hospital.

The juxtaposition of the Jewish and Italian characters makes for a humorous version of Marianna DeMarco Torgovnick's *Crossing Ocean Parkway,* a non-fiction account of an Italian/American daughter's attempts to break away from her Bensonhurst upbringing by marrying a Jew. The Italian/Jewish culture clash takes off when Rosa brings Gary home to meet her parents, Aldo the plumber and Antoinette, the housewife. Rosa begins to see her Pizza Beach neighborhood — a place where "people wore their poverty like a badge of honor" — through Gary's eyes, and becomes embarrassed by her working-class life upbringing and the portrait of Mussolini that hangs in her parent's home. The dinner prepared for the couple turns into a humorous interrogation in which Rosa's mother, unimpressed with Gary's status, says things like: "You go to Yale... That's a bad neighborhood."

And when Gary takes Rosa to Long Island, to meet his parents: middle-class Mimi and Artie, the eyeglasses franchise magnate, Rosa becomes self conscious of her wrinkled clothes and white shoes, and quiet about her parent's reactionary politics. But her sense of the grass being greener outside of Pizza Beach is tempered by the reality of how superficial middle class life can be, and she repels Mimi's condescension by admitting her parent's differences and clinging to her working-class values.

When Gary begins acting strange, Rosa is certain that he's having an affair, but when she finds out the other woman is "Cancer," she's totally unprepared to have pity for the man she depended on to bring her away from her upbringing. Gary's dying guides her deeper into herself as he loses the strength to make love, to make her laugh, and finally to help make her into someone else.

Like a sponge, Rosa Salvatore becomes so absorbed with others that there's little of her Italian culture that can help her, except maybe to see through her in-laws, and to observe, but not understand, the clash of classes and ethnicities. By the novel's end, Rosa Salvatore is just as divided and lost as she was at the beginning. And as nice and funny as Gary is, you want him to die, if only so that Rosa can come alive and have another chance to escape.

(February 1997)

Rita Ciresi, *Blue Italian* (Hopewell, NJ: Ecco Press, 1996). Pp. 287; ISBN 08800 15152; $22 (hardcover).

&

Rita Ciresi's first novel, *Blue Italian,* published in 1996, proved she could create humorous dialogue, but revealed that she still needed to work on developing characters who could sustain the long haul of a novel. This flaw of many new novelists, especially those adept at the short story (her story collection, *Mother Rocket,* won a prestigious Flannery O'Connor award), did not detract from a debut that revealed a humorous mind at work.

Cirsesi's early writing presented a question that has occupied Italian/American feminists for decades: Can the daughter of Italian immigrants use any of her ancestral culture in creating her own American self? *Pink Slip,* Ciresi's new novel returns to this question, and this time the author presents an answer in a well-developed novel.

Lisa Diodetto faces the traditional pressures placed on Italian American women. Marry soon, have babies quickly, and just as quickly get over the idea of ever being independent. But Lisa's too smart, and too American, to fall into that trap. Trained to be a literary type she leaves the world of publishing and picks up a pen in the communications department of Boorman Pharmaceuticals. With better pay, she begins upgrading her surroundings and her ideas of what makes for a good man.

She uses her new job in a novel she writes that ends up becoming a Potboiler reflecting her actual experiences. Between the fact of her life and the fiction of her mind, Lisa struggles to find a place to be a friend to her gay cousin, a lover to her boss, and an artist to her self. She's better with people than with words, which almost always seem to fail to bring out her true thoughts. Lisa's platonic, (or is it), love for her cousin, and her passion for her boss, come together to help her find a way of maturing in love without giving into the traditional relationships that have plagued her women ancestors. When she gets a pink slip from her boss, it's not walking papers, but a pink chemise.

Pink Slip provides all the evidence we need to see that Ciresi has overcome the weaknesses of *Blue Italian.* She has learned to listen, and not just speak, in her writing. This novel depicts a stronger character development, as this meditation of Lisa shows:

> As I drove the winding parkway, I thought there were two kinds of people in the world: those who when confronted with the worst of horrors would throw themselves on the fence, and those who would walk on their mother's bones

to keep on living. I was afraid — and relieved — to find I fell into the second category. But the minute I came to this conclusion, I was sure my jeep would wipe out. I kept looking in the rearview to see if another car was bearing down upon me, its accelerator stuck and its steering wobbly as my emotions, but all I could see in the poorly adjusted mirror was a flash of my own eyes. I was so busy looking behind I didn't pay enough attention ahead and I almost rear-ended a slow-moving Pontiac.

Ciresi's greater integration of ethnicity is reflective of how pervasive a culture can be. She shows us how ethnicity is not the sole province of a single people, or of a single style. This is also an important milestone that she has accomplished with this second novel. While *Pink Slip* is a novel about assimilation, it also teaches us that what does not change can also mix mysteriously into the American scene. The end result is that we cannot be so sure what is American and what is Italian anymore.

The originality of her voice, now matured beyond simple witty and humorous one-line quips, make this novel a pleasure to read. *Pink Slip* reveals the maturity of style and the advancement of Ciresi's craft. The humor is still there, but now our laughter is tempered by an understanding of their humanity. Rather than just making fun of Italians, she is making us all see the limitations of ethno-chauvinism. *Pink Slip* is the first Ciresi novel you just might find yourself reading twice.

(August 1999)

Rita Ciresi, *Pink Slip* (New York: Delacorte Press, 1999). ISBN 038532362X; $22.95 hardcover.

&

In 1993, Rita Ciresi's first collection of short fiction, *Mother Rocket* won the prestigious Flannery O'Connor award, giving notice that a young, new talent had arrived. Ciresi's stories were strong in voice and varied in subject matter and style, revealing her ability to capture diverse voices and visions.

Three years later, *Blue Italian*, her first novel, revealed problems that were overcome in her novel *Pink Slip* (1999). In this novel, the narrator listened and spoke not as a director but as a guide to the characters' points-of-view. *Pink Slip* revealed a maturity of style and a great advancement of Ciresi's craft as a storyteller. Her characteristic humor was there, but now she was listening to those whom she helped us laugh at, so that while we as readers may laugh at them, we also learn to feel for them.

Sometimes I Dream in Italian is Ciresi's best work yet. Composed of twelve interconnected stories, the novel centers on the actions and antics of two sisters,

Angela and Pasqualina Lupo, and their immigrant parents. Equally divided into two sections: "ragazze" and "donne," *Sometimes I Dream in Italian* recounts the girls' coming of age in a New Haven, Connecticut of the 1970s and '80s. Filled with Ciresi's characteristic humor and melancholic meditations, the stories also reveal the author's capacity to create a sense of ordinary terror that is relieved through humor.

Angel's family is ordinary and that bothers her, especially as they chase the American Dream in their unique way: "Everybody has their dreams. So the men in our family went to the track. The women entered raffles and went to bingo." And she strikes a familiar chord for those who have had to wear family hand-me-downs when she laments: "The clothes Lina wore became costumes on me."

Her mother drags her around shopping, a ritual which peaks at the butcher's where she learns how "bella figura" factors into life beyond bargaining for cheap scraps and bones. Her father "seemed like an invader" lying on the couch in his work clothes watching television, mostly the weather channel. Both are presented as comic foils against which Angel and Lina learn to become American.

Angel is also embarrassed by her neighborhood, especially by the ladies who work in the local pocketbook factory.

> When Lina and I were young, we looked upon the Pockabookies with absolute dread. Never mind Michelangelo, the Medicis, Mona Lisa and all the folks we someday would learn about during our college art-history classes. For us, being Italian meant being Pockabookie-issima. Horrors!

Angel's only escape comes when she slips into a library where she can imagine worlds beyond her own and where she gets her best lessons in being American. When she finally move out of the house, her mother stalks her through the packages she sends which contain newspaper clippings and obituaries from the old neighborhood.

In spite of the humor, there is little joy in the sisters' lives. The further they move from their parents the greater their shame becomes. Eventually it all turns into a hatred that feeds on other relationships. Angel confesses to a lover she found through the classifieds that she was never happy in childhood; he confirms her feelings by telling her he always thought they were "warped."

Sometimes I Dream perceptively captures the disintegration of an Italian family as it assimilates into a new land with new rules for behavior that the parents cannot fathom and the children cannot avoid. When Angel comments to her sister "'Sometimes I dream in Italian,' I told her, 'I'm talking, but I don't have the least idea what I mean to say,'" she is really saying that she cannot reconcile the idealized Italy to the reality of her parent's immigrant experiences that have formed her into the neurotic darling that she becomes.

(May 2001)

Rita Ciresi, *Sometimes I Dream in Italian* (New York: Delacorte Press, 2000). ISBN 0385334931; www.bantamdell.com; $23.95 hardcover.

David Citino

Our world can sometimes be too frenetic. Surrounded as we are by headlines, sound bites, and emails, this bombardment of brevity takes it toll not just on the way we think, but the way we feel. In such a world, sustained talk and thought seem to be hiding out in the attics and basements of our culture — places frequented only by students and scholars. Mention the word essay to people and they flinch — most likely from muscle memory of the times when they were told to write an essay before they were taught how to write one and had to stay up the whole night before it was due just to get "C." The good essay, someone's sustained thought on a single subject, is hard to find these days, but I can tell you where to find some.

I think poets make the best essayists — not all of them of course, but the better poets, like Felix Stefanile, Diane DiPrima, Dana Gioia, Lewis Turco, and David Citino, who tend to write some pretty dynamic essays. They don't usually write many, but the ones they do are usually gems. In *Paperwork*, Citino, Poet Laureate for The Ohio State University, has gathered essays and some poems that he's previously published about a variety of subjects throughout his career.

Especially appealing to Italian Americans will be the first two sections: "The Many Houses of Memory" and "Homage to Birds." The first essay, "The Poet in the Kitchen" evokes Helen Barolini's famous words "Mangiando, ricordo" [by eating I remember], as Citino whips up a piece as delectable as any on the subject of food, family, and memory. The phrase "mangiando, scrivo" [through eating, I write] could apply to this one. "NATO Air Base Proposed for Southern Italy," is one of the best meditations around on the relationship between southern Italy, the US, and the individual Italian American: "we're not-new and yet not-old Americans, as secular and stolid and unbelieving as our fairer-skinned neighbors and prone on occasion to feeling unassimilated, to feeling lost."

Some of the essays read more like prose poems ("The Beatification of Padre Pio" and "The Land of the Liars"); all of them, even the ones that seem written only for other poets, are not only accessible, but easy and pleasurable to read. In the next section, "A Homage to Birds," we get meditations on landscapes and animals that remind us if we take the time to really see where we are we might just be happier beings.

Citino has spent most of his life in Ohio, and writes with a such keen sense of place that what he says almos t always transcends the regional. The Cuyahoga

River, "dark, thick-muscled servant of industry to through the days of my youth ... is now reborn — holier-than-thou, like a reformed smoker" takes on the stature of the Nile in his "A Personal History of Rivers."

Known as a poet and teacher of poetry, Citino is a well respected commentator on the craft of writing poetry, and includes many of these essays in the last two sections entitled "Poetry Smells" and "Paperwork." While these may be a bit much for the general reader, they deserve inclusion for the very personal way they are written. Citino not only knows poetry of all kinds, but he cares for them all.

You can keep *Paperwork* around and dip into it now and then. The wisdom gained here does not depend on starting from page one and moving methodically to the end. Citino's brilliance comes in a single line as easily as through the accumulation of sentences.

(October 2005)

David Citino, *Paperwork* (Kent: Kent State UP, 2003). kentstateuniversitypress.com; ISBN 0873387848; $24 paperback.

Joseph Colicchio

Nicky Finucche, who pronounces his name "Finooch," runs a Wellness Center in what used to be his parents' storefront meat market. Walls once covered with four-color posters of meat types and cuts, now display black and white maps of the human mind. Where he once used to help his parents slaughter and butcher evening meals for neighborhood customers, he now listens to the problems of those very neighbors and some of their kids. Nicky's a bit out of it in terms of what is cool and hip in contemporary American life; mostly what he does is react to others. He seems to have no direction in life and is not much better good at helping lost souls find their ways through troubled times. But, for the most part, he gets by, and so do his patients.

Nicky runs a strange group therapy session that's dwindled down to a scant two members; someday it's hard to tell who's the therapist and who are the patients, and many is the day when Nicky begins, and rightly so, to doubt his abilities as a counselor. Nicky has four rules:

> Help the patients (at least the nice ones); Rule Number Two: If you can't help, pretend you can; Rule Three: If you can't pretend convincingly, pretend anyway and hope the patient pretends along with you; Rule Four: If one through three fail, shut the patient up.

Nicky is not in danger of becoming too successful.

One day, one of his patients, who just happens to be his sister's mother-in-law who has spent most of her life in depression, commits suicide, and all of a sudden Nick faces a day of reckoning that he could never have imagined. Without adequate records he cannot defend himself against his brother-in-law's charges of wrongful death; he is on the brink of losing everything he worked for. While this is the extent of a somewhat interesting plot, it's not what happens, but how it happens and how the story teller makes it happens for us, that is the treasure of this novel.

Colicchio, who was born in the Jersey City where this novel is set, spins and sputters his yarn in a great mix of Jersey street talk and standard American English. There's a rhythm to his diction that keeps us moving even when the plot stands still. More than a story about something happening, *The Trouble with Wellness*, reminds us that so much depends on the times when nothing happens, or when one thing happens that requires everyone to stop what they're doing to focus on the same event. Colicchio is able to turn place into a character that affects everyone. Central Avenue, the location of the Finucche Wellness Center, is full of people and places that would most likely be lost, or at least not feel at home, anywhere else in the world.

This is a novel composed of everyday folk who are the most unlikely heroes to step into each other's lives. It seems everyone's doing something they shouldn't be doing, and the ones who are doing what they're supposed to, are doing it all wrong. Colicchio shows us that even the losers of the world win sometimes, and what they gain, is something far beyond material wealth or public recognition. There's a peace of mind that comes from living within your weaknesses and turning them into, if not strengths, then something you can live with, a lesson that might help us all keep out of the trouble that leads away from mental wellness.

(October 2004)

Joseph Colicchio, *The Trouble with Mental Wellness* (Lanham, MD: Rowman and Littlefield, Bridge Works Publishing, 2004). www.nbnbooks.com; ISBN 1882 593820; $15.95 paperback.

Stephen Cooper

The best way to meet one of the greatest American writers of Italian descent is to pick up Stephen Cooper's, *The John Fante Reader*. More than just selections from his best works, this reader presents a veritable mosaic of Fante's life's writing. If you don't know Fante, here's a great introduction; if you do know him, then here's a way to get to know him better. From his early short stories to his latest novels, the selections are well woven by the editor into a chronology of Fante's literary life.

The first section, "Home Confessions" contains some of Fante's earliest short stories originally found in *Dago Red* (later reprinted as *Wine of Youth*) and a few others from the new collection *The Big Hunger*. There are also excerpts from *Wait Until Spring, Bandini* and *1933 Was a Bad Year*. Each selection is a powerful rendition of life in an Italian American family. Section two, "Days of Fever," covers the years from the time Fante first left home to the time when he begins to write professionally. Here we find excerpts from his novels *Ask the Dust, The Road to Los Angeles,* and *The Brotherhood of the Grape.* These are key insights in the development of Fante's writing genius.

Part Three, "A Time of Dream and Reverie," contains selections from *Dreams from Bunker Hill* and *Full of Life,* novels that reflect Fante's shift from bachelorhood to marriage. The final selection of his fiction, "I Must Remember to Face It," is composed of excerpts from his novella, *My Dog Stupid* and his novel *The Brotherhood of the Grape,* samples of work from his later years. A selection of letters, some appearing in print for the first time, provides us with a sense of the voice behind the characters and some of the fact behind the wonderful fiction.

(January 2003)

Stephen Cooper, ed., *The John Fante Reader* (New York: W. Morrow, 2002). www.harpercollins.com; ISBN 0060184965; $25.95 hardcover.

Pietro Corsi

Originally entitled *Due Rapporti* and then *La giobba*, Pietro Corsi's two long stories of the immigrant experience of Onofrio Annibalini, *contadino*, and Rob Perussi, *ex studente*, now come to us in English translation by Antonio Di Giacomantonio as *Winter in Montreal.* The novel captures the post World War II Italian immigration to Canada in the lives of two Molisani.

Onofrio's story is one of survival; his immigration experience has reduced him in social status and he has lost his self-respect. He will take any work to save face and to reclaim the respect that he has lost. But in making his choice he becomes alienated from his past as well as his paesani. In the end, Annabilini makes the transition, but as the author asks, at what price.

Perussi's story is quite different; he takes a job as an underworld messenger merely to occupy his time and by doing so loses his Old World sense of stability. Perussi doesn't need the money, but he does need to fit into his social surroundings. In order to do so, he Anglicizes his name and lies to himself and his history.

This loss of identity brings with it a boredom that forces him to confront what he has lost. And in an ironic twist, Roberto lives long enough to understand what he's done wrong and sets out to change things.

Winter in Montreal is a chronicle of immigrant experiences and thus reads closer to biography than fiction. Corsi is at his best when he relates Annibalini's story. There is a depth with the contadino that he fails to achieve with the "exstudente." His reliance on the stereotypical mafiosi to present the dilemma of Perussi offers us more of an insight into the problems encountered by the immigrant author who is still unaware of his skills as a writer and so depends on the more popular myth for his story.

But beyond the story of the characters, Corsi is also telling us about the division of every immigrant into he who wants to stay true to his traditions and he who wants to cut off all ties with his past. In seeking to establish themselves in a new society, both types cling to the notion that job will enable them to do so.

Both Onofrio and Perussi are inside Corsi as they are inside every immigrant; they leave their homeland with the expectation that life somewhere else must be better, will be better; they struggle with each other as the immigrant comes to realize that those expectations were built on false hopes; Perussi overcomes the myth, then dies; Onofrio succumbs to the myth and lives. More than characters in a story, they are both testaments to the process of destroying and rebuilding one's self-identity that the immigrant experience forces upon those who dare confront the transcultural experience.

Job is identity and for Corsi, his job as a writer forces him to assimilate. Corsi never wrote with the same expectations of making a living at it that an author like Mario Puzo did; he wrote in the hours after work and this novel originally appeared serially in a Canadian newspaper.

A "Preface" by Sante Matteo and an "Afterword" by Giose Rimanelli" situate the novel well in Italian and American literature and provide a great introduction to this established Italian writer who recently retired as a Vice President of Princess Cruises. Novels such as Corsi's *Winter in Montreal* gives us a much needed insight to what it is the immigrant writer does with the experience of a new land, a new language and a new story. Corsi succeeds in creating a story that speaks to us today in English, more than forty years after it first appeared in Italian.

(February 2001)

Pietro Corsi, *Winter in Montreal,* translated by Antonio di Giacomantonio (Toronto: Guernica Editions, 2000). ISBN 1550711172; $8(paperback).

PAOLA CORSO

Sometimes the only way to get what you know you deserve is to imagine it, and that's how many of the characters in Paola Corso's short fiction make their way through life. There's a danger when life becomes so predictable that you stop looking out of your window or in your mirror. When that happens to Corso's characters something happens to wake them up and turn them inside out. What Corso tells us is that this happens to all of us, sometimes every day, but not many of notice it. She has, and many of these stories show us how to imagine other ways of being real.

There's nothing ordinary about the everyday people you find in the ten stories of Corso's collection entitled *Giovanna's 86 Circles.* You'll swear you know people like these, when you first start reading, but what makes Corso unique as a writer is that you won't recognize them once you get to the end of the story. There's a certain slant of realism that she fashions and it skews the ordinary in strange ways. A young woman washing sheets in a hospital laundry can tell the future in the ones she folds. A woman's knitting unravels and stretches outside the house to wind its way through the neighborhood. A mayor leaks his death date to the press, and proves himself right. These are just a few of the characters that you'll meet in these unique stories.

"Yesterday's News" opens the collection with a woman taking her dead mother's clothing to a second hand clothing shop and is convinced by the clerk to keep one item that changes her life. "Between the Sheets" finds us in the laundry room of a hospital where one working tells another about her husband's illness. Things start getting weird when the window one of the washing machines turns red, and one of the worker's realizes she can see the future. "Unraveled," is a wonderful story that is a great example of how the repression of the real story by the imagination can create a tension that turns a story we've all heard before into something we want to hear again. The title story is another example of this. A young boy and girl are navigating their way through their first kisses in an abandoned farm house when the legend of the previous tenants finds its way into their lives; there are two stories here that wind their ways through each other so that you realize that sometimes it's what's left behind that matters more than what was. One of Corso's best is "The Drying Corner," in which a young girl finds a way to make her own space in her nonna's deteriorating fruit and vegetable store. This story reminds us that the young and old have much to teach each other.

Corso mines her Pittsburgh area past for all the things one needs to create fiction that both records the past and shows us that paying attention to the little things in our own lives might just helps us better see beyond the surface of it all. This message comes through clearest in "Shelf Life," in which a woman's who's considered to be crazy teaches a young girl how to live off what others ignore, and that craziness is sometimes the ability to live safely outside the normal.

Some of the stories shine brighter than the others, and you can't help but wonder if some of them were rehearsals for the more successful, if not in subject, then in style, but they all reward second and third readings, which for me, is the test of a good story. Brava!

Paola Corso, *Giovanna's 86 Circles* (Madison, WI: U of Wisconsin P, 2005). www.wisc.edu/wisconsinpress; ISBN: 0299212807; $21.95 (hardcover).

&

Author's note: What follows is part of a review that covered two poets. The second part appears in this volume under the Robert Viscusi entry.

Robert Viscusi and Paola Corso are two very different poets, at very different places in their careers, who have recently published their first full-length collections of poetry.

Not many of us still live in the neighborhoods where we were born and raised. What happens when we move away often becomes the stuff of myths that gather strength and power over the course of a lifetime, especially if that lifetime belongs to a poet. For Paola Corso, the Pittsburgh river town of Tarentum was where her father and grandfather worked in the steel mill and the place she recreates in a number of poems in *Death by Renaissance*.

Corso uses a variety of forms in this requiem for a time and place long gone. "Saturday Mornings" recalls the weekly act of dusting a home that is made possible by the very soot being wiped away: ". . . dust meant / jobs / in an industry where the blacker the better / angel's dust she called it but how could that be, / angels / dust, the color of the devil." Between the recollections of the past and the meditations how the clash between nature and industry affected her family, Corso evokes powerful images that remind us the past never stays still. The more we think about it, the more it changes us.

Corso's prose poems become mini-historical narratives, and lyrics like "The River Insider Her" can make us all remember what it's like to turn our backs but not our minds away from the place we come from. Corso's won awards for some of the poems reprinted here, and the all work as poetic versions of memoir. Historical and family black and white photos and a section of artistic photos by George Thomas Mendel, help turn these personal poems into sounds of an entire community.

(June 2005)

Paola Corso, *Death by Renaissance*, with photographs by George Thomas Mendel (Huron, OH: Bottom Dog Press, 2004). ISBN 0933087861; $12.95 (paperback).

David Cowan and John Kuenster

One of my earliest memories is of Sunday night, November 30, 1958. I was six years old. It was the weekend after Thanksgiving, and my cousins Skip, Butchie and Mary Lou Mele were visiting us. When it came time for them to leave, I threw a tantrum. I screamed, "You can't go to school tomorrow; you have to stay here." At the time I had no idea why I was so insistent. Of course, since parents don't take screaming six-year olds seriously, the Meles left.

The next day their school, Our Lady of Angels, burned. Butchie and Mary Lou survived, but my cousin Skippy was killed. When my family told me that Skippy had died in the fire, I had no idea what they meant. Was he burned? Did his body go up in smoke? Now I was no stranger to death. I had been to many funerals, and had even seen people try to throw themselves into loved-ones' graves, but never had someone so close to me in age been killed. At the wake, Skippy looked as though he was asleep, as though not a flame had touched him. My mother comforted me by telling me that he was sleeping with the angels.

No one spoke of the fire much after the funeral. Butchie turned into Fr. Carmen Mele, a Dominican priest, and Mary Lou into a nurse, then a wife and mother living in another state. My Aunt Eve and Uncle John have long since gone to meet their son. For nearly forty years I have not stopped imagining exactly how my cousin John Joseph Mele died. But a few weeks ago my imagination of this event was put to rest by a book.

David Cowan and John Kuenster's *To Sleep with the Angels: The Story of a Fire* is a haunting and thorough account of the events leading up to, through and beyond the tragic Our Lady of Angels fire. It is history told through an investigative drama that rivals the best mystery novels. Cowan and Kuenster uncover the whitewash of earlier printed reports by going back through the records, revisiting witnesses and doing the incredibly bold investigation that was not possible back in the late 1950s. They combine factual details from a variety of viewpoints to brings us back to the days when building heat was fueled by coal, when garbage was burned in incinerators, when the Prudential Building was the tallest in the city, and when the powers of the Catholic Church were supreme.

In the late 1950s the leaders of Chicago had their eyes on near-west side Italian neighborhoods for new expressways, a university and other public institutions, but no "urban renewal" project would devastate an Italian community more than the did the fire at Our Lady of Angels school.

The opening narrative sets the scene for the tragedy and slowly stirs in all the ingredients, slowly, then whips into a frenzy as the fire spreads. It is a if the fire is happening again, and we are all eye witnesses. The sensational retelling of the hurt might have been enough for a book, but the authors do more than recall a tragedy. By taking the story beyond the fire, into the investigation, to the recovery of those who were injured, and finally into present day memories of the events, Cowan and Kuenster actually contribute to the long postponed healing process. By the end of the book, you actually feel better, but only after having gone through a range of emotions from fear, horror, compassion, grief and anger.

This is revisionist history at its best, for the authors actually help us re-see the entire event: from the first spark in a cardboard garbage can, to the terror in the classrooms, and the heroic rescue efforts of local neighbors, fire department and school personnel. While the writers achieve a sense of objectivity by staying out of the way of the story and letting their incredibly detailed research and sources speak, they do not ignore their responsibility to criticize those who might have done better. Cowan and Kuenster achieve the difficult goals of "setting straight the record on the fire," of "giving voice to those who still grieve," and of "providing a sense of closure to an historical void that has remained open for nearly four decades."

I had to read this book twice. The first time, I couldn't stop reading to even think about writing this review. That two people can write as one is an accomplishment in itself. That they can weave so many disparate sources into one compelling narrative is a feat deserving of an award. I can honestly say that no book has had such a real effect on both me and my memory.

A few nights ago I dreamed that I was in the middle of the fire, in the room with my cousin's class. There was nothing I could do. But thanks to Cowan and Kuenster, for the first time I understood how, and little better why, my cousin, 91 other students and three nuns died that December 1st. When the authors quote Linda Maffiola's words, "I was told that my brother died in the school fire, which I could not comprehend at all," I know what she means. But I think we both can both better understand it after reading *To Sleep with the Angels*.

(June 1998)

David Cowan and John Keunster, *To Sleep with the Angels: The Story of a Fire* (Chicago: Ivn R. Dee, 1996). ISBN 1566631025; $25 (hardcover).

Antonio D'Alfonso

In *In Italics: In Defense of Ethnicity*, poet, novelist and publisher Antonio D'Alfonso offers thirty-two entries made up of essays, reviews, presentations, speeches, and position papers that are as much autobiography as they are critical statements on the place of the Italian/North American writer in the world of literature. If D'Alfonso's essays share a common theme, then it is that the nation as an idea, as a political home, is no place for a good writer to settle. "What links people in reality," he writes, "is not a territory or a nation but a sense of belonging to an expanded community or, if you wish, a network of scattered ghettos, where the sharing between different kinds of individuals is performed in a conscious manner, by free choice, and not by indoctrination."

D'Alfonso has been fighting indoctrination since the day he began Guernica Editions, back in 1978 when he chose to take control of the means of producing culture that challenged the status quo of both French-speaking Quebec and English speaking Canada. Since then, he's published over two-hundred titles by Italian Canadians, Italian Americans, Italian Germans, Italian Australians and Italians from all over the world.

According to D'Alfonso, the current crop of ethnic writers must avoid what Richard Gambino has termed as ethnic chauvinism and move toward Gambino's notion of creative ethnicity. What D'Alfonso advocates in his defense of ethnicity, is the transcendence of individual ethnic identity into a collective imagination which is open to everyone. This means that we need to stop harping on what it is that makes us different and begin looking for what we share. This also means ending the use of Italian American, Italian Canadian, and other such identifying phrases; He suggests we replace them all with the word "Italic," simply because it implies derivation without attachment to all the problems that come through national identification. And while D'Alfonso's quarrels with national identification concern his experiences with Canada, there are points in many of his arguments that concern not only the Italian Diaspora, but ethnic communities throughout the world.

D'Alfonso's experience, as a child of Italian immigrants from the region of Molise who settled in Montreal, Canada after World War II, informs every one of the entries. His struggle to forge a coherent self involved learning four languages, Molisano dialect,, Italian, French and English. During a period of rebellion through refutation of his ancestry, he escaped to make a film in Mexico where he tried assimilating into Mexican culture. But trips to Italy and to the United States, after his return to Canada, force him to realize that community can expand from the ghetto of national identity. By living and practicing multiculturalism, he has found a way beyond it's limits through the literary imagination, and "In Italics" maps the direction he's taken.

There is a fair amount of repetition of these experiences throughout the collection, especially when it comes to his ideas about the role of ethnicity in the pluricultural society of Canada, but the reader will understand that these writings demonstrate how an author has grown as a writer and citizen of the world. While at times, reading so many essays on the same theme is like watching grass grow, the patient reader will pick up the subtle changes that develop over time. The reward is a better understanding of the impact that ethnicity has in the development of a strong voice in Italic culture.

Whether he is giving advice to writers, to editors, to publishers or to critics, D'Alfonso is nothing if not controversial. In his most ambitious essay, "The Altar of Assimilation," he offers his plan for understanding the effects of cultural appropriation through stereotyping by organizing writing through an intricate schema. But he seems to be involved in self criticism when he writes, "for in the end the people who profit from the art works are not necessarily the artists but the producers."

In "There is No 'Proper' English," he confronts reviewers who weaken the link between writer and audience by attempting to "destroy another person's work." In "One Plus One Does Not Make Two" and "The Enduring Writer," he recounts the trial and tribulations of producing ethnic books. And if you're thinking of sending a manuscript his way, you'd better read this essay, because it spells out his publishing philosophy in the clearest language possible.

At times the controversy in his writing is the result of quick thinking and bitter responses to criticism — warranted or not; D'Alfonso's attacks are as poignant as the praise he gives to the brave artists who have become his heroes. D'Alfonso's critical voice has grown, not out of the classroom, but out of his artistic experiences as a poet, filmmaker, novelist, and his business and political experiences as a publisher. If nothing else, these essays need to be read so that a community can grow, both in support of and challenges to D'Alfonso's words.

In Italics bravely struggles for a coherency that can only be accomplished by seeing each entry, small and large, as a brick in the unfinished road that Antonio D'Alfonso has fashioned for himself out of the experiences he has endured, conquered and generated. If, as he says in "Starting at Square One," Guernica's "raison d'être" is "To be a bridge hanging from one culture to another," then "In Italics" is a document of the plans this cultural architect has designed to create an ethnic community out of the disparate voices of the Italian Diaspora.

(January 2001)

Antonio D'Alfonso, *In Italics: In Defense of Ethnicity* (Toronto: Guernica Editions, 1996). ISBN 1550710168; $18 (paperback).

&

Antonio D'Alfonso, who has established a strong reputation in international publishing — especially with his focus on Italian/North American writing — has consistently proven that he is as good a writer as he is a publisher, and his latest book should strengthen that reputation.

Based on his best-selling French-language novel, "Avril ou l'anti-passion," (VLB editeur, 1990), *Fabrizio's Passion* is a powerful parable of Italian immigrant life in post World War II Canada. D'Alfonso portrays the lives of the Notte family which begins with a couple from Campobasso who fall in love during World War II and then immigrate to Canada. The novel, a gallery of baroque portraits of the Notte family, is created through a combination of diaries, letters, play-like dialogue, and essay-type narratives. Through these forms, D'Alfonso creates a multivoiced tale of the struggle for ethnic and artistic identity.

The novel opens in 1944 in Campobasso, Italy, which is shifting from German to Allied occupation and is told through the diaries of Fabrizio's mother, Lina. When Fabrizio finds the letters his mother received from her husband in 1948, while he served in Italian military, he learns of a passion the two shared. The couple makes its way to Canada and in 1959 acquire a home. As Fabrizio touches on the meaning of each room, he is especially taken by the kitchen. "The kitchen is the heart of our family, the master room of the Italian household, the place where we eat and discuss, but also quarrel; it is the most sacred part of our home where all gives way and must be mended." And indeed, much of what happens in the book affects the entire family and either takes place or is discussed in their kitchen.

Fabrizio's passions are what make him human; and how he learns to realize what they are, where they came from and how to articulate them, is what makes this novel worth reading. In a chapter entitled "Scars" Fabrizio meditates on the meaning of the five he has on his body which he sees as signs of identity, permanent reminders of historical events which have literally left their mark on his life. All of his have come through passionate play in his early childhood, that's also when he learns that in Canada being Italian is not really being much of anything that matters: One of those scars comes when he plays with his more assimilated cousins, and while it may help him recall a wonderful summer experience, it also reminds him that:

> To be Italian is simply an aberration, something that is outdated, something to be ashamed of; whereas the Canadian is the hero I wish to emulate; It is by imitating my cousins that I will give myself a better future. Well, this way my way of running away from a reality I did not fully understand.

A number of the chapters read as prose poems, especially "First Loves," "Disamore" and "Friends and Jealousy" which are poetic essays on the trials of adolescence. The closest thing to an antagonist in this story is Fabrizio's friend Mario, who is more practical and threatens Fabrizio's early love life. Beyond the usual trials encountered while coming of age, Fabrizio finds his personal identity is uniquely challenged in Quebec where an English government, French language, and Italian ancestry all challenge the wholeness of the young Fabrizio whose psychological development is triply divided.

> Monreale confers onto me the privilege of being three persons in one. Being a strange combination of three cultures, I was able to converge my three views of this city and form a completely unique triangular (tripartite) woldview which was not always appreciated by either the francophones of the anglophones who forced me to take sides in their strife for power.

While others struggle for power, Fabrizio struggles for understanding, not only who he is, but where he comes from. Fabrizio's early passions are undefined, and he approaches life, love and art with the same confusing intensity. He knows only that he wants to a slave to something, for as Padre Schiavo, his religion teacher tells him, "In this world there is a place for only three kinds of slaves: God's slave, love's slave and in rare occasion, art's slave."

It is his contact with the classics, that Fabrizio finds his way out of his self-consciousness and into the universal relationship of art and life. He finds a way to personalize the great Greek myth of Antigone by making a film. And it is through this ancient story that he finds a way of reconciling his past with his present.

The novel ends with the wedding of his sister Lucia to a real Canadian, and the idea that the family will be renewed. The final scene, in which Fabrizio dances with the ghost of his grandmother reminds us all that the past, more than memory, can be the map of our future: "We really never free ourselves of our upbringing. Sometimes, just when we think we are about to get away from it, we realize that we are only repeating unconsciously everything that was taught to us from the beginning." D'Alfonso's meditation on passion in the life and art of Fabrizio ultimately raises the question, does the more we know about our past strengthen our need to conform or rebel, to re-enact or re-imagine?

(October 2001)

Antonio D'Alfonso, *Fabrizio's Passion* (Toronto: Guernica Editions, 2000). $15.00 paperback) by Antonio D'Alfonso is published by Guernica Editions of Toronto, Canada/ New York.

RACHEL GUIDO DEVRIES

Rachel Guido DeVries has been singing her songs for a good time now. Much of her earlier work is filled with powerful lyrics that strike back at the forces that thwart or slow her down. These are the poems you'll find in her first collection, *How to Sing to a Dago*, a book that ruffled the feathers of many in the Italian American flock. No less powerful, no less controversial are the poems you'll find in her new collection, *Gambler's Daughter*.

The poems gathered in this collection are like the bends of a river that's been running a long while. The twists and turns are not as sharp as they used to be, and they hold water that is deeper than ever. Much of what we have here are meditations on nature that reflect the things that keep the poet up at nights, that haunt her dreams. It is as though by not naming the cause of her sorrow or joy, the source becomes less mysterious.

This is evident in the imagery of "a snake's tiny mouth [that] is a crescent of teeth / that glisten, shiny as the 'rocks in the creek / under water.'" But therein lies the danger that anything can resurrect that source; "a squirrel's yowling from an old creaky tree," can evoke the memory of a child's scream, a gunshot from the woods can keep "The sheen of scared" on the poet.

It is as though DeVries has learned to see her life in the world that surrounds her. No longer must be as direct as her younger self may have demanded. And while the power of that direction can still be found in poems such as the one that gives the collection its title, there is a sense of distance that makes us see both the fear and freedom of being the "Gambler's Daughter" who has learned to love in spite of persecution, to live with losing, and to learn other ways of winning.

If you take your time, and read the collection a few times, you'll find that re-reading each of the forty-plus poems is like having a conversation with the poet. While there are many "nature" writers, whose mediations might be poetic, too many fall into the trap of speaking only to themselves. Not so with deVries; even the most personal of these poems reaches out for other human beings. It is as though by retelling the trauma, by turning experience into art, the poet relieves even as she relives the pain. And there's no self-pity about, or wide-eyed wonder at why these things happen. They have happened and the poet, having learned to live with them, now turns to art to make sense of it all.

One of the strongest poems is "Vanishing Ancestors," is a chant that celebrates even as it mourns the loss of earlier generations. "One by one the ancestors vanish, become smoke / or woozy dandelion in early spring I might gather / and sautéed with garlic become them again. Bitter / leave yielding to the bright yellow center of days." DeVries knows how to conjure up the strength of spirit taught by those who came before us and preserves their gifts in words.

What's most alluring about this new work is the precision that each poem displays. There are few loose lines and even fewer wasted words. Taught, tight, you can bounce quarters off poems like "Prayer" and "Gambler's Daughter, Two": "My mind keeps counting numbers as I sit / in meditation silent at the lake, / as though some figure might appease my soul, / or luck might hide numbers in a row."

(November 2002)

Rachel Guido DeVries, *Gambler's Daughter* (Toronto: Guernica, 2001). www.guernicaeditions.com; ISBN 1550711482; $10 (paperback).

Stephen DeFelice

In preliterate days, cultures would pass down wisdom by word of mouth in memorable ways like stories, songs, and proverbs. That's how cultural memory survived. These days, the idea of oral tradition seems to depend on the conversations surrounding the latest hit record or television show shared by friends more than families. The survival of a culture depends more and more on that which gets written down, read, and studied. One book you'll want to consider adding to your cultural library is Stephen DeFelice's *Old Italian Neighborhood Values*.

The novel, with a potentially dangerous plot of nothing more than a dinner conversation, becomes more interesting as a cultural artifact than as a literary work of art. In the tradition of Plato's *Symposium*, Dante's *Il Convivio*, and, more recently, Frank Lentricchia's *Music of the Inferno*, De Felice's dinner conversations provide a sense of spiritual renewal through a remembrance of things past. The dinner takes place on September 7, 2001, the night of *La Luna Stregata* [the witch's moon] in a New York restaurant appropriately entitled La Strega. Told by one of the participants, Lorenzo Bacala, the novel is a sustained polylogue that attempts to present a variety of perspectives on major subjects and themes of life in the United States.

In the opening section, "The Boys and the Madam," we meet Mario, the owner of La Strega who lives through his food and beverages. Miserabile is a conservative US congressmen; Mo is a self-made business man; Pignachi is a Catholic priest who believes that good will overcome evil. There's Pussey Rapper, a liberal media publisher, The Pig, a gay social worker who isn't as sentimental as the others about the old neighborhood values. Spinuzzi is a classically trained mind who's a medical doctor by trade and quite an effective amateur philosopher. Genella, the proprietor of a house of ill repute is the only woman, and gets her invitation by way of being the lover of Rocco, one of the boys until his death. While the perspectives may differ, they all come from the same childhood formed in the old Italian neighborhood of Philadelphia.

What DeFelice gives us is a sense of what it was like to grow up as witnesses to the immigrant generation. We get this all through the stages of the great meal. From the opening martini cocktails, through the peasant antipasto, the pasta, pietanza, dolce, espresso, and finally grappa, we move from casual observations about kids, families, divorce and their relationship to calcium and highways of today, to in-depth arguments about sex, politics, God, the liberal media, and many other controversial subjects.

With each discussion, we not only get a range of views through the characters, but a sense of how these subjects were dealt with in old neighborhood thinking and practice. While you never get a sense that these people, given the resources, could solve the world's problems, their attempts to make for interesting eavesdropping. A potential exclamation point is added to the event as the group meets soon after the 9/11 Attack on America to see if things have changed. Actually we get more of the same discussion, more concisely, but less dramatic.

The author is a medical doctor, founder and chairman of the Foundation for Innovation in Medicine, a nonprofit educational organization designed to accelerate medical discovery to improve our quality of life. *Old Neighborhood Italian American Values* is required reading for anyone who has grown up in a Little Italy; those who didn't will wish they had. In a time when people are leaving little Italys left and right, DeFelice's imagination has given us all a way back home.

(May 2003)

Stephen DeFelice, *Old Italian Neighborhood Values* (Bloomington, IN: 1st Books Library). ISBN (e-book) 1403362726; ISBN (paper) 1403362734; ISBN (hardcover) 1403362742; $22.50 (hardcover); $14.50 (paper).

Emilio DeGrazia

A Canticle for Bread and Stones is the fourth book by Emilio DeGrazia, a professor of English at Winona State University. His first, *Enemy Country,* published in 1984 by New Rivers Press, is a celebrated collection of stories connected by the Viet Nam war. The stories were praised by authors Tim O'Brien and Susan Sontag. DeGrazia's novella, *Billy Brazil,* was selected for a the 1990 Minnesota Voices Project award. *Kirkus Reviews* called it "Powerful and haunting — a work of great integrity." His second collection of stories, *Seventeen Grams of Soul,* won a 1995 Minnesota Book award.

A Canticle, DeGrazia's first novel, has been in the works for years, and is his first to deal directly with Italian/American culture. While it could be his most autobiographical, it never reads as a memoir. DeGrazia grew up in Dearborn, Michigan where his father worked in Ford's Rouge Plant. He earned an undergraduate degree at Albion College and his PhD from Ohio State University. Since the early 1970s, DeGrazia's publishing fiction, poetry and essays have been published in major journals, magazines and reviews. Along the way he has earned honors and awards from the Minnesota State Arts Board, the *Kansas Quarterly, Writers Choice* and Lake Superior Contemporary Writers Series.

Part celebration of the struggle of Italian immigrants, part mystery story, *A Canticle* succeeds as a plot-driven work of fiction made out of the same materials that many other writers have used to create simple, nostalgic reminiscences. DeGrazia, a seasoned professional, detours from the easy stroll down memory lane by creating a tale that drives deep into the soul of American culture.

In this novel, DeGrazia sings a swan's song for a disintegrating Little Italy that looms large in the mind as it shrinks on the streets of St. Paul, Minnesota. Drawn to Minnesota to build a cathedral, Raphael Amato, the stone artist great-grandfather of protagonist Salvatore Amato, runs into trouble caused by an American philanthropist who can change minds and neighborhoods with a wave of his cash filled hand.

Raphael's great grandson searches for meaningful work in 1970s America, as he tries to find out why his great-grandfather was fired from the job of building the great cathedral. This quest turns into a mystery that Salvatore must solve before he can go on with his life. But when traditional truths become lies, and contemporary lies become truths, Salvatore has to redesign a world in which history and art can speak to each other.

The first thing he does is try to piece together all the stories he has been told by those who have shaped his world. Storytellers Grandpa Guido, Grandma Rosina, Danko the resale shop man, Mr. Rochelle the woodworker, and Markels the history professor, and Rostopov, the Russian immigrant, all contribute to Salvatore's sense of a past that he must understand before he can face the future. As Sal listens to each of the stories and weighs their significance, he comes to understand that the America he has inherited is not the same place that drew his immigrant ancestors away from the poverty of the old country.

His college degree hasn't helped him find that white collar job his parents believed would be his by right of passage. Salvatore is anchored to working-class culture, but unlike his father, he understands the economic system and wants more than a job. For Salvatore, life is a combination of history and art; but his life, more driven by his eye for women, than his knack for earning a buck, is sustained by the books he reads and a marriage that only works in bed. He can't understand why no matter how well he and his wife Sandra are getting along, he continues to seek out attention from other women. Eventually Salvatore becomes an avenging savior when he confronts the man responsible for stealing his grandfather's business and his great-grandfather's art. But just as he reaches his goal, his marriage falls apart.

The art of DeGrazia's storytelling comes at the beginning of each chapter where a leading sentence pushes the reader on, guiding the plot in a unique way to the chapter's end. With a fine ear for the spoken word, DeGrazia weaves each chapter into a strong narrative strengthened by his understanding of the weaknesses of his most sympathetic characters. *A Canticle* reminds us that work teaches us ways of reading the world, and that each worker is a seasoned storyteller and critic of life. Full of old world folk wisdom and new world sins, this novel makes us take a good look at ourselves through the window of Italian/American culture.

In America we say "good as gold," but in Italy the saying is "buono come pane," and DeGrazia's latest work of fiction is just that, as good as honest-to-goodness homemade bread.

(August 1997)

Emilio DeGrazia, *A Canticle for Bread and Stones* (Lone Oak Press, Ltd.). $14.95 (hardcover).

Luisa Del Giudice

Sociologists have told us that the end of Italian/American culture is near. We are, according to Richard Alba, deep into the "twilight" of our ethnicity. Soon, there'll be no distinctive features enabling us to claim ethnic connections. Rather than just sit back and watch it all fade away, scholars and artists, such as Luisa Del Giudice are creating ways of reconnecting Italian Americans to their ethnic roots through the study of folklore.

Edited with a stirring introduction by Luisa Del Giudice, *Studies in Italian American Folklore* is a collection of six exemplary essays that are must reading for any student of Italian/American culture. While many of the essays are geared to students, scholars and most of all, cultural critics — especially those dealing with the relationship between oral and literate traditions — most are accessible to the general reader. The bibliography is thorough and useful and provides a detailed map for future scholarship.

This collection pays attention to regional differences, and smashes through the stereotypes of both old and new world Italian cultures to give us a better understanding of how each has affected the other. Del Giudice makes an important point when she argues that "consciousness of two worlds" requires "Italian language acquisition and "return trips of discovery" to Italy. "No Italian American can fully know himself or herself culturally until these rites of passage have taken place." Even if a trip to Italy is not in your immediate plans, this collection is an excellent first step toward achieving this self-knowledge.

In, "Tears of Blood: The Calabrian 'Villanella' and Immigrant Epiphanies," Anna L. Chairetakis, veteran ethnomusicologist, uses the "polyphonic song poem" form called "villanella" to explore the relationship of performance to community life and traditions. We can hear the Brooklyn singers through Chairetakis' fine writing as we come to understand them through her carefully researched historical and richly depicted contemporary accounts of their lives. Here is "thick description" at its best.

Luisa Del Giudice's contribution, "The 'Archvilla': An Italian Canadian Architectural Archetype," explains how structure and design choices made by Italian/Canadian homebuilders in Toronto were influenced by their cultural heritage. Del Guidice's analysis moves beyond the surface and penetrates deep into the culture of Italian political movements, such as Fascism, to describe and explain a key moment in the transition from Italian to Canadian identity.

In "Playing with Food," Sabina Magliocco, presents an exciting description and analysis of how the selection of foods for display at a Little Italy Festival in Clinton, Indiana "suggests important aspects of community identity and the dynamics of ethnic representation." Dorothy Noyes's "From the 'Paese' to the 'Patria,'" recounts as it reconsiders the effects a 1929 pilgrimage (organized by the

Sons of Italy and the Fascist regime), had on 1,400 Italian Americans. In spite of the fact that many of the travelers jumped ship in Palermo to visit families, instead of following the Fascist directed tour, Noyes argues that the Order gained power to speak for individuals and thus "The 'patria' did not abolish, but it successfully contained the 'paese;' consensus at the inner level fed consent at the outer."

In "Stereotypes as Cultural Constructs" Paola Schellenbaum analyzes "stereotypes as the product of the interrelationships between the people and those who study them. The result is a kaleidoscopic picture that takes into account cultural variability and individual creativity, as well as public and intergroup social meaning." Her analysis of fieldwork in Northern California invites us to reconsider culturally created stereotypes and their changing relationship to both common sense and a sense of common cultural heritage.

Juxtaposing his own, academic based language with the language of local Staten Island devotees of Our Lady of Mount Carmel, Joseph Sciorra helps us understand how people express differing views of their culture through the spoken, written and visual word. The result is a better understanding of the dynamic interactions of past and present, public and private worlds in which architecture such as grottoes speak in unique languages. "Multivocality and Vernacular Architecture" may sound like an academic treatise, but thanks to Sciorra's respect of and sensitivity to his informants, the essay dignifies as it examines, popular expressions of faith and Italian heritage.

Del Giudice's guidance of this publication is but one of the many ways she has contributed to the greater awareness of Italian/American folk culture. A native of Terracino, Italy and formerly of Canada, with a PhD from UCLA, Del Giudice has recently revised an earlier limited edition of "Italian Traditional Song" an anthology which gathers traditional songs from all over Italy. This publication, which includes a wonderful introductory essay, a thorough bibliography and the lyrics printed in Italian and English, will take you beyond the usual musical worlds of opera and Naples which are often the only exposure most have of Italian popular music. Included are two audio tapes containing performances of lullabies, songs of work and play, prison and protest, love songs and more. Just listening to the beautiful music can be a way of beginning the trek back to your roots; reading Del Giudice's words will help you understand why we can't afford to let this culture fade in the twilight.

(October 2001)

Luisa Del Giudice, ed., *Studies in Italian American Folklore* (Logan, UT: Utah State UP, 1993). ISBN (hardcover) 0874211670; ISBN (paper) 0874211719; $39.95 (hardcover); $19.95 (paper). "Italian Traditional Song" ($22.50) Publications Department, Instituto Italiano di Cultura, Los Angeles, CA 90024.

Don DeLillo

No matter where you were on October 3, 1951, whether you were born or not, the date forms the epicenter of a new novel that will send tremors through your sense of history, you sense of what it means to be American, and your sense of what it means to be alive on the brink of a new millennium.

That was the day Bobby Thomson hit the famous home run to win the National League pennant for the New York Giants; it was also the day the Russians test-exploded their first atom bomb. Within these events, Don DeLillo presents the past fifty years of American history through the persona of Nick Shay, son of an Italian American bookie Jimmie Costanza; Cotter Martin, the kid who left the game with the famous homerun ball; Klara Sax, who becomes a famous artist after divorcing Albert Bronzini, and a host of other characters such as J. Edgar Hoover, Jackie Gleason, and Lenny Bruce.

Garbage, art, baseball, adultery, the homeless, advertising, miracle apparitions, serial murders, civil rights, atomic bombs, air raid drills in school, rock and roll, AIDS, Jell-O, all become signposts of American history that Don DeLillo maps in *Underworld*. The little that has happened in the past fifty years of American history is writ large in DeLillo's unique script.

A novel rich in many of the stories that have become American history and legend, "Underworld" takes us under the world as we know it to where bookie-fathers disappear, where nuclear weapons are turned into hazardous waste eliminators, and to where the dead get resurrected; the result is that we can see what's going on under our noses.

The beauty of DeLillo's art is that he portrays what you might see if you weren't in such a hurry or moving in a crowd that blocks your view and shuts out so much of the world. The story is as much in the style of DeLillo's prose as it is in his characters. If you don't hear yourself in the dialogue, you will hear those you know and love. Through Albert Bronzini and Nick Costanzo Shay, DeLillo recreates life in a Bronx Little Italy that will make your mouth water for Campobasso's bread.

Less driven than his earlier novels, *Underworld* is a fascinating story that might make you wonder what you've been doing with your own life. Give me DeLillo and keep the newspaper and the encyclopedia. Whether the argument is systems vs. nature or chaos vs. order, DeLillo's diction reveals one fine mind at work. He pierces the surface of nostalgia, and takes us into the very mechanism of history the way only a writer of the highest imagination and greatest perception can. This is a story to linger over, and the author gives us the prose to make that lingering worthwhile; it is dense, poetic, "parrotic" (he's got quite an ear for street talk), and parodic. And for the first time we get more than a glimpse into what might be the more personal side of the author.

Of the little that he has revealed about his life, we know that Don DeLillo was born in 1936 to Italian immigrants and left his working class, Italian American home to attend college at Fordham, a Catholic university in New York. His early life was spent in the urban settings of the Bronx and Philadelphia where he experienced the type of neighborhoods about which he has written little until this new novel.

But DeLillo's too much the artist to spend much time on his own past. In a 1979 interview, DeLillo constantly referred to his desire to "restructure reality," to "make interesting, clear, beautiful language," and to "try to advance the art." He has achieve all three of these goals in his latest novel.

A regular question raised in much of DeLillo's work is "What does it mean to be American?" While much of contemporary American writing wrestles with this question, so little of it actually advances the art of storytelling. It is no wonder then that writers such as DeLillo don't want to be associated with any group that advocates independent consideration of an ethnic literature. But with his latest novel, DeLillo both invites us in to his Italian American sensibilities and to a better understanding of our place in this country.

Echoes of nearly all his earlier novels can be heard throughout *Underworld*, but only by the faithful DeLillo fans who have read everything he's ever written will catch it all. It is as though the earlier writings, which earned him a Guggenheim, a National Book Award, and the Pen/Faulkner Award, were all rehearsals for this performance, steps along the way for this man to become a great American writer. If you don't know DeLillo's writing, then this is the novel that will send you to read all of his others; If you do know his work, then you will want to read this more than once.

(December 1997)

Don DeLillo, *Underworld* (New York: Scribner, 1997). ISBN 0684842696; $27.50 (hardcover).

Tina De Rosa

When Tina De Rosa's novel, *Paper Fish*, was first published back in 1980, I must have bought fifty copies to give as gifts. I wrote a review in a local American Italian Historical Association newsletter calling it "an important work of art because it preserves what we must never forget." I did what I could to get the word out about this wonderful work. Unfortunately, the press that first published it went out of business, leaving the first printing to fend for itself on shelves in local bookstores. The only novel to come out of the Taylor Street area of Chicago soon disappeared from those shelves, surfacing occasionally in used bookstores and in conference conversations.

As the years went by I would send copies to editors and publishers hoping that one would see its value and reprint it. But it wasn't until I met Florence Howe of The Feminist Press in 1995 that *Paper Fish* found the publisher who would take a chance on a real literary novel. Now that the novel is beginning to reach the audience that it has always deserved, I find myself wanting to say to those people who ignored me in the past, "I told you so," but ironically, I find myself fumbling my words of praise.

Paper Fish has become such a part of me that I feel I'm too close to be objective. I've read it at least ten times over the fifteen years, and have written about it in articles and books. Rather than rely on what I had previously written about the novel, I sat down to read it as though I had never read it before. And in spite of my familiarity with the work, the novel unraveled before me as though it was brand new. There was so much I had missed during my earlier readings that I realized this is a novel which, like an exquisite liqueur, needs to be sipped, not guzzled, and like great literature, it holds up over the years. Sentences have been crafted so carefully that unless you read the novel slowly, you'll miss its connection to oral traditions and lose out on its ability to chant its story in song. "Paper Fish" is memory captured in meditation, so find a quiet place to read it.

De Rosa recalls, in a beautiful, lyric form of linguistic impressionism, the disintegration of a family and an old Italian neighborhood, but while the community shrinks and trolley tracks disappear, the protagonist, a young Carmolina Bellacasa, grows strong and finds her own image in a mirror that once reflected only her family. This story of life, death and a young girl's redemption reaches the reader's soul through poetic rendering of pictures in a gone world. And even when the world is disappearing, De Rosa never lets go.

> Next to Giovanni's house, where the little wooden home of Mrs. Consuelo had been, a dark wooden fence made a perfect square around nothing. The sunflowers still grew in Doria's garden, behind the house that wasn't there. Across the street, all the buildings were gone, so that Giovanni could sit on his stoop and look into Quincy Street a block away. Augie's grocery story was an empty frame, like a stage prop someone forgot to move. The butcher shop stood empty of its chickens. Mrs. Schiavone's butcher block shone under the sun in the alley, the blood congealed on the wood like skin.

The demise of the Italian ghetto, as De Rosa knew it, becomes a wound that heals through the writing, but remains a scar in the minds of those who remember.

Born in Chicago's Taylor Street "Little Italy," De Rosa started writing stories of her youth at the urging of Michael Anania of the University of Illinois at Chicago. Ironically, the Italian enclave displaced by the building of the university became the subject of her writing, and as a result, is preserved forever in fiction. In an interview I did with Tina more than ten years ago, she told of her reasons for writing *Paper Fish*.

I wanted the neighborhood to live again, to recreate it and so many of the people I was close to, especially my grandmother and father who had both died. I think I was haunted by it all. I wanted to make those people and that neighborhood alive again. I wanted the readers of the book to care about it, to realize that something beautiful had existed and that it was gone. Taylor Street had become a myth of terrible beauty and terrible ugliness. It was a world completed unto itself. The further I got away from it, the more I could see it as a small, beautiful, peculiar world.

As a witness to a world destroyed by urban renewal, De Rosa preserves, in mythical fashion, the memory of a time and place when immigrants, such as Grandpa Dominic and Grandma Doria Bellacasa were heroes whose tales of the old world helped to create new worlds for those who would listen.

Over the years, *Paper Fish* has become an underground classic kept alive through articles by critics such as Mary Jo Bona and in journals as far away as France. It has been taught in classrooms through, more often than not illegal, photocopying. *Paper Fish* resurfaces now to meet an audience that, more than being ready for it, is in great need of its story.

During those years the author has kept busy writing new works, the most recent of which earned her a prestigious Rona Jaffe Writers' Award in 1995. In an "Afterword," critic Edvige Giunta presents the story of "Paper Fish," both in Tina's life and in the life of American literature, and presents a case for Louise DeSalvo's quote on the book's cover in which she refers to the novel as "The best Italian-American novel by a woman of this century." As Giunta tells us in her important "Afterword," appropriately entitled "A Song from the Ghetto," "This reprint of *Paper Fish* represents a discovery as well as a recovery...."

For some readers, it is the discovery of a world never known, for others, it is the recovery of a world we might have forgotten. Already major writers and reviewers are acknowledging the beauty of De Rosa's work. Marilyn French calls it "a unique piece of work" and Rona Jaffe referred to it as: "Gorgeous writing and a generosity of spirit — a gift of love." *Kirkus Reviews* gave it a diamond review, denoting a book of outstanding quality and importance, and gave the best explanation yet of why it took 16 years to be recognized: "A novel like this — so literary yet so full of life — takes time to find a wider audience. Perhaps that time has finally come."

I think that this time *Paper Fish* will reach the audience it deserves, but more so, I hope it finds the audience that needs it most.

(October 2001)

Tina De Rosa, *Paper Fish,* afterword by Edvige Giunta (New York: Feminist Press, CUNY, 1996). ISBN 1558611452 (paper); ISBN 1558611460 (hardback); $20 (hardcover); $9.95 (paperback).

Louise DeSalvo

Louise DeSalvo, a professor of English at Hunter College in New York City, has made a career of connecting writers' lives and their works. After two powerful and original studies, *Conceived with Malice: Literature as Revenge* and *Virginia Woolf: The Impact of Childhood Sexual Abuse on Her Life and Work*, and a novel, *Casting Off*, DeSalvo turns her attention toward her own life in her latest book.

Vertigo: A Memoir is a powerful testament to the belief that reading can change your life. "It is as simple as this," she writes. "Reading, and writing about what I have read have saved my life."

Reading *Vertigo* helps us to understand why there have been so few autobiographical works by Italian/American women.

> Even as I write, though I am wary of what I am writing, I am inescapably, and Italian-American woman with origins in the working class. I come from a people who, even now, seriously distract educated women, who value family loyalty. The story I want to tell is that of how I tried to create (and am still trying to create) a life that was different from the one that was scripted for me by my culture, how, through reading, writing, meaningful work, and psychotherapy, I managed to escape disabling depression. It is the unlikely narrative of how a working-class Italian girl became a critic and writer.

This "unlikely narrative" is a verbal montage of a life lived in pieces that comes together only through writing. A mother's depression, a sister's suicide, growing up in a home with a father at war and a mother in an enclave of women managed households, form the basis for DeSalvo's early traumas. She seeks salvation in the local library and fashions her identity through rebellion and pursuit of academic excellence.

DeSalvo uses language as a "scalpel" to "exorcise" what has happened in her life. She has learned the secret of writing and how it enables the scribe to live life more fully by living it twice: She writes, "language, I have learned, by writing about this, gives birth to feeling, not the other way around."

Each chapter is a wonderful, personal essay that explores the author's feelings. Chapters such as "Fixing Things," "My Sister's Suicide" and "Combat Zones" set the scene through dramatic recollection of everyday life. In "Finding My Way," "Safe Houses," and "Colored Paper" we learn of her early experiences in school and reading the classics. "Spin the Bottle" and "Boy Crazy" tell of her early sexuality and how her "obsession with sex" made her what she wants to be "an outsider."

As a young girl, DeSalvo suffers from fainting spells, from vertigo caused by the cycle of "loving, loss, grief and mourning" both for the living and the dead. Her encounters with gender and ethnic discrimination, which she overcomes through her power over language, remind us that Italians weren't always assimilated. In "The Still Center of the Turning Wheel," she documents the education that enabled her to survive what her mother and sister could not.

Her comments on food, which form a leitmotif throughout the work, enter early: "Life, I have always believed, is too short to have even one bad meal," and are echoed in her chapter entitled "Anorexia" where she recalls her college days and her embarrassment at having nothing to say when she's asked to name her favorite meal:

> For years my mother cooked things that I believed no one should eat, things that I certainly couldn't eat. Old World things, cheap things, low-class things, things that I was sure were bad for you, things I was ashamed to say I ate, and that I certainly couldn't invite my friends over to eat. I wanted to pass for American. I wanted a hamburger.

DeSalvo's artistry lies in her deft manipulation of point-of-view. She moves from past, to present to future, covering time in what seems to be a wink of an eye. Her style whirls like an amusement park ride in dizzying fun that is laced with a sense of danger.

"Portrait of the Puttana as a Woman in Midlife" is a rewriting of the essay which appeared in *The Dream Book*. A comparison of the two shows the growth of DeSalvo's poetic sensibility, her sense of self, her confidence in her ability to say what she is, what she wants out of life. She comes off as a tough girl who's not afraid to cry: "The way I write this, the 'tough broad' tone I take, is of course, a disguise for how hurt I was, for how seriously betrayed I felt."

In "Personal Effects," DeSalvo goes through a manila envelope given to her by her father after her mother's death. The envelope contains, memorabilia: postcards, articles and poems from women's magazines. By going through the little bit her mother's saved, DeSalvo begins to understand why her mother never fulfilled her own artistic dreams. It is these pieces of other's lives, that help the author complete the puzzle of her self: "The most trivial, yet the most important personal effects of the women of my family, come together at last, and mingle in my kitchen drawers and cupboards." She has, at last fit them all into her life, first through language, then through feeling.

Vertigo joins Diane di Prima's *Memoirs of a Beatnik*, the yet-uncollected essays of Helen Barolini, as the major self-writings by American women of Italian descent. They have all dared not only to speak out, but to write their lives. The results are literary models, something DeSalvo longed for early in her life. "Though I had read scores of books, not one had been written by an Italian-American woman. I had no role model among the women of my background to urge me on. . . ." Her persistence and perseverance eventually paid off: "My work has changed my life. My work has saved my life. My life has changed my work."

Vertigo is powerful reading, a first-rate memoir that just may change your life.

(September 2001)

Louise DeSalvo, *Vertigo: A Memoir* (New York: Dutton, 1996). ISBN 05259 39083; $22.95 (hardcover).

&

Edited by Louise DeSalvo and Edvige Giunta, *Milk of Almonds: Italian American Women Writers on Food and Culture* is filled with ways to move beyond the usual distortions of women fashioned by men who could only imagine and never know what it was like to be an American woman of Italian descent. There are so many good writers in this book that simply to apply an appropriate adjective to each selection would take up more words than I get to write these reviews. The more than fifty contributors make up a virtual "who's who" and "who's new" of Italian American women authors.

After Carol Maso's tender "Rose and Pink and Round," you'll think differently about breastfeeding. Follow that with Nancy Caronia's terrifying "Go to Hell," and you get a good sense of the emotional extremes the editors have gathered in one place. Wonderful new voices included belong to Cheryl Burke, Maria Terrone, Kym Ragusa, and Rosanna Colasurdo. The heart of the collection comes through the work of veterans like Diane di Prima, Gioia Timpanelli, Maria Mazziotti Gillan, Daniela Gioseffi, Dorothy Bryant, Cris Mazza, and Mary Cappello. While each writer is well represented, the liberal sprinkling of Rosette Capotorto throughout is like a healthy dose of pepperoncino, good for the spirits and health of the whole body.

Milk of Almonds opens with a powerful introduction that is informative, historically important, and beautifully co-written by the editors. DeSalvo and Giunta present the uses, meanings, and history of almonds in Mediterranean culture in such a way as to prove this volume could have had no other title. "Cooking and eating — and also the processes by which recipes are transmitted and foods prepared, conserved, offered, or refused — are central to the work of Italian American women authors," they write as they beautifully connect the work of writing to the work of nurturing.

The selections of prose and poetry are divided into eight thematic sections that parallel the chronology of life from "Beginnings" through "Legacies." In "Beginnings" Mary Bucci Bush's "Aperitivo" is calmly shocking in a way that will make you rethink the way we use food metaphors in our references to loving children. The images of Kim Addonizio's "Beer. Milk. The Dog. My Old Man." and Rachel Guido de Vries' "Italian Grocer" will challenge any traditional photograph of the perfect Italian family.

In "Ceremonies," the familiar and new come together to bring us new ways of reading Italian American women. An excerpt from Dorothy Bryant's novel "The Test," Mary Beth Caschetta's ingenius story "The Seven Sacraments," and Edvige Giunta's rich memoir, "The 'Giara' of Memory" remind us of the how the rituals of preparing and eating foods reflect other aspects of our lives. "Awakenings" features Nancy Caronia's haunting memoir, an excerpt from Rita Ciresi's novel, "Sometimes I Dream in Italian," and "Bones, Veins, and Fat: a wonderful memoir by Cheryl Burke.

"Encounters" contains prose gems from di Prima, Timpanelli, Anges Rossi and the wonderful straight-from-the-street-talking poems of vittoria repetto. "Transformations" features Sandra Gilbert's masterfully literary "Finocchio," Adele Regina La Barre's poetic meditation on tomatoes, and Anne Calcagno's tenderly tough "Let Them Eat Cake," along with an excerpt from Flavia Alaya's controversial memoir, "Under the Rose."

"Communities" presents Adria Bernardi's rich "Sunday" and powerful prose by filmmaker Nancy Savoca. In "Passings," there is Alane Salieno Mason's touching "The Exegesis of Eathing, and in "Legacies" Maria Terrone's poetic prose and poignant poetry. The volume appropriatly ends with De Salvo's hauntingly beautiful "Cutting the Bread."

DeSalvo and Giunta have concocted a volume worthy of much attention, one that will no doubt last long after other anthologies are out-of-print or forgotten.

(April 2001)

Louise DeSalvo and Edvige Giunta, eds., *The Milk of Almonds: Italian American Women Writers on Food and Culture* (New York: Feminist Press, CUNY, 2002). ISBN (hardback) 1558613927; ISBN (paper) 1558614354; $26.95 (hardback).

Diane di Prima

In *Recollections of My Life as a Woman* Diane di Prima returns to the troubled times before she left home — when *Memoirs of a Beatnik* begins — and struggles to uncover and understand the family secrets that have haunted her. Di Prima uses memory to extend her "self" beyond the traditional constraints that have silenced earlier generations of Italian/American women.

Like many other Italian/American writers, di Prima uses the figure of the grandmother as a symbolic source from which she draws her ethnic identity. "My Life" opens with an ancestral connection. In contrast to her grandmother's fatalistic sense of realism is her grandfather's idealism. Through her grandparents, she learns, at an early age, the Italian sense of irony that enables her to envision unity in opposites: "To my child's senses, already sharpened to conflict, there was no conflict in that house. He was an atheist, she a devout Catholic, and for all intents and purposes they were one."

Di Prima's memoir is woven out of journal entries, unsent letters, accounts of dreams, quotes from other writers, poetry, stories told by her grandfather, and a variety of forms which interrupt the narrative flow to remind us that memory comes in pieces. Through it all we get a sense of the many selves that di Prima has fashioned during her life and how they continue to interact in her mind. Her autobiography, as much of her poetry, is an attempt to redefine the idea of woman through Italian/American eyes. If you know di Prima's poetry, then think of this book as the white space that surrounds those poems, those silences and the day-to-day reality out of which she fashioned her art.

Unlike her mother, who kept quite about her own "breakdown" until shortly before her death, di Prima is able to talk about her weaknesses as well as her strengths. When she confronts her siblings about their perceptions of the past, she is met with silence. As she continues to investigate and reimagine her past, she begins to form the idea that all that silence is covering childhood abuse both physical and psychological.

Fortunately for the reader, di Prima is not out to bare her wounds but to heal them. She sees writing as instrumental in healing the psychic traumas of life. A key insight comes in her identification of what she calls "immigrant fear," something similar to what Rosa Cavalleri spoke of in her as-told-to autobiography written by Marie Hall-Ets. While Rosa's fear stemmed from class divisions in the old country, di Prima's fear extends from the family into the societal strata of her life in the form of travel timetables, insurance claim forms and manifests in her "not opening the door to the census taker."

Di Prima begins to take control of her public image only when she is presented with the opportunity of going off to high school; it is the first time she is able to shape her life outside her family's reach, to "reinvent" herself. Later, by going away to college and living on her own, she is able to completely break away from the domination of her parents; yet her parent's attitudes continue to haunt her.

She leaves home for the exciting and often depressing Greenwich Village arts scene. Through her we witness the dance, painting, poetry, film, theater, performance as life, and jazz jam sessions of the 1950s and early 60s. No doubt there's more to come from this important and talented American artist of Italian descent.

(October 2001)

Diane di Prima, *Recollections of My Life as a Woman* (New York: Viking, 2001). ISBN 0670851663; $29.95 (hardback).

LAWRENCE DISTASI

2001 marks the fiftieth anniversary of the enactment of Presidential Proclamation 2526 requiring the arrest and confiscation of the property of Italian alien enemies considered "dangerous to the public health and safety of the United States." Enacted December 8, 1941, the US declared war on Italy three days later. What followed for the majority of the nation's 600,000 Italian resident aliens were minor inconveniences compared to the forced relocation of 10,000, the arrest of some 1,500 and the virtual imprisonment of 250.

For those caught up in the nation's frenzied fear of foreigners, the stories became tragic nightmares that were kept secret through silence and would have been lost to history if not for the diligent work of those who created the project "Una Storia Segreta." Some of the material that became a traveling exhibit that led to the US Government's formal acknowledgement of civil rights violations has now been preserved in a book. Editor and major contributor Lawrence DiStasi has combined the earliest published research by historian Rose Scherini, first-person accounts of those interned and their family members, oral histories from communities like Pittsburg, California, a selection from Stephen Fox's "The Unknown Internment," and a great synthesis of sources in Gloria Ricci Lothrop's "Unwelcome in Freedom's Land," into one powerful collection that sets the record straight on exactly what happened to America's Italians before, during and after World War II.

The various accounts, all woven together by Lawrence DiStasi's own contributions on the impact on Italian fishermen, life in the internment camps, and the overall effects on Italian American culture in general, create one indisputable and undeniable truth: the civil rights of American citizens were violated because of their ethnicity. One voice after another testifies to the horrible treatment meted out in the name of public safety by functionaries following orders. Each presentation defies the temptation to keep this past secret and redefines civic responsibility to include the protest of civil rights violations.

The book opens with a "Foreword" by noted feminist scholar and Italian American poet Sandra Mortola Gilbert that brings home how misguided and naïve most Americans were about this experience. DiStasi's "Introduction" provides the framework and sets the tone for the subsequent contributions. The way Italian Americans had to prove their loyalty, DiStasi writes, "was to forget what they knew, forget who they were." This forgetting, he suggests, is responsible for much of the shame and ignorance current Italian Americans might have toward their ancestral culture and helps explain why so few contemporary Americans of Italian descent speak Italian.

One of the most powerful selections is "Morto Il Camerata," in which detainee Prospero Cecconi recounts his arrest and the subsequent death of a friend he made while in custody. Rose Scherini, one of the first historians to begin documenting the internment of Italians, contributes "When Italian Americans were Enemy Aliens," which first appeared last year in the "Enemies Within: Italian and Other Internees in Canada and Abroad," and "Letters to 3024 Pierce," which the correspondence between the imprisoned Carmelo Ilacqua and his wife. Gloria Ricci Lothrop's previously published "Unwelcome in Freedom's Land," is republished here, providing an incredibly detailed and accurate history of the war time policies and their effects on Americans of Italian descent.

A helpful historical timeline and 36 photos illustrate the 28 selections and make *Una Storia Segreta* an important addition to any library that claims to contain American history.

(December 2001)

Lawrence DiStasi, ed. and introd. *Una Storia Segreta: The Secret History of Italian American Evacuation and Internement during World War II*, foreword by Sandra M. Gilbert (Berkeley, CA: Heyday Books, 2001). www.heydaybooks.com; ISBN 1890771406; $21.95 (paperback).

Louisa Ermelino

In their transformations from Italian enclaves to gentrified hot spots, Little Italys have become little more than Italian theme parks that no more resemble today's Big Italy. Recent picture books have tried to preserve the past, but a better way back is through novels like Louisa Ermelino's *The Black Madonna*. Set in New York's Greenwich Village, *Madonna* tells the story of three mammas' boys through their mothers and captures that claustrophobic, in-your-face reality of the way life in Little Italy used to be.

Nicky is the son of Teresa, whose story is set in 1948, a time when Italian immigrants had earned their Americanization through World War II. Teresa's husband works on ships, travels the world and brings back nothing but rumors when he returns. When young Nicky loses the use of his legs after a fall, Teresa turns to the Black Madonna of Viggiano and the miracles begin. Magdalena, a step-mother to Salvatore, whose real mother dies in childbirth with his twin, is a "strega" from the old country. Sal's father is matched with her when he visits his hometown. Set in 1936, this section traces the power of women through the turbulent time when a time when fascism suppressed female power. The final section takes place in 1968, a time of social uprising in the US and recounts the story of Antoinette, who had given birth to the neighborhood's largest baby, nicknamed "Jumbo." When Jumbo finally finds love, he needs all the help of his friends to keep his mother from destroying his life.

The Black Madonna features the dark force at work in the mothers as they turn their sons into defensive forces in their lives, protecting them from the men who have abandoned them for other lovers and other lives. Through these three mothers Ermelino connects us to the powers of the ancient earth mother known in Greek mythology as "Persephone," and in later Catholicism as the Black Madonna. Unfortunately the figure of the Black Madonna serves the book's cover better than it does the story. It is never really developed to its fictional potential as a political as well as a familial source of feminist strength as we know through the studies of scholars like Lucia Chiavola Birnbaum. Fortunately the storytelling is strong enough to take us beyond this flaw. To her credit, the author does explore and explain the power that women have always wielded in Italian culture.

Ermelino's got the ear for street talk and the eye for the swagger of the sons and the swabbing of the mothers as they try to keep the neighborhood as clean as their kitchens. Ermelino's come a ways since her first novel, "Joey Dee Gets Wise," which, while set in the same place, never seemed to get outside of the neighborhood. The Black Madonna is the antidote to the outsider's fantasy that we find in films like *Moonstruck* and the insider's betrayal that comes in most of the mafia stories that have both captured the nation's imagination when it comes to Italian life in New York.

This is a story that you won't want to end. How can you say goodbye to these characters "buone come pane," people you know even if you've never been near a Little Italy. I read it so fast, that to review it I had to go back and read it again, and I enjoyed it even more the second time around. Write on Louise Ermelino, give us sequels, you've recreated a generation, a cultural phenomenon that is gone, and, thanks to talented writers like you, not forgotten.

(May 2002)

Louisa Ermelino, *Black Madonnas* (New York: Simon & Schuster, 2001). www.simonsays.com; ISBN 0684871661; $23 (hardcover).

&

If Yoknapatawpha County belongs to William Faulkner then Manhattan's Little Italys of Greenwich Village and Hells Kitchen Little should go to Louisa Ermelino. She's earned them by creating three fine novels set in these places, each one better than its predecessor. From her first, *Joey Dee Gets Wise: A Story of Little Italy*, to *The Black Madonna*, to the latest, *The Sisters Mallone: Una Storia di Famiglia*, Ermelino has been exploring and explaining the places where the real power lies in Italian American culture — with the mothers.

The mother/son stories in the US have always been eclipsed by the American boy's relationship to his father. How else can you explain the success of the likes of Mario Puzo, Francis Coppola, and Martin Scorsese? Puzo realized this after his mother-centered *The Fortunate Pilgrim* failed to bring him fame and fortune enough to gamble his life away. Before he died he admitted he modeled Don Corleone after his mother. What these guys have hidden and suppressed, Ermelino uncovers and exploits.

Most writers deal with the surface of Italian American culture, where it looks like the guys are in charge. Ermelino takes us all deep into the culture through three sisters whose immigrant grandfather, born Malloni, finds himself surrounded by the Irish and does what he can to fit in, even if it means changing his name to Mallone. But as the surface hides the danger of depth, these Irish looking girls are Italian through and through and capable of any number of heroic acts.

Led by Anona, their grandmother who raised them when most of the rest of their family their parents died in the great Spanish Influenza epidemic of 1918, the sisters learn that men are useful and not necessary; Anona teaches them to get what they need by giving as little as they can. Helen, Mary, and Gracie, all grow up in an Irish controlled Hell's Kitchen of the 1920s and 30s. "Mary was tough, but Helen was flint." Both take care of their baby sister Gracie who married a pretty mamma's boy who can't stay home at night. The mystery, and the novel begins, when he winds up dead on his job down at the docks.

Ermelino's a master at turning the culture of Italian America into contemporary folklore, and the novel makes for a wonderful old neighborhood tale. Ladies like those in the St. Ann Society of Mothers form Ermelino's Greek chorus and serve as the community's conscience: "Tragedy was their entertainment. If they weren't mourning its presence, they were awaiting its arrival." And while the tragedies are plenty, they are nicely punctuated with comic relief. Ermelino is hilariously serious in her criticism of he male world of gangsters and mamma's boys, and extremely adept in her dramatization of the natural power of women. Someone should have gotten to the poor spelling of Italian dialect words like "judruls" for "citrulli" and "moltedevane's" for "morte di fame." But these minor bumps never stop the story from cruising forward to a great ending.

The Sisters Mallone has garnered great reviews, but still not a word in the great *New York Times*, and that's a shame because this book deserves the widest possible audience, if for no other reason that to take it out of the gangster genre ghetto. One misguided reviewer from New Jersey tried to say that *The Sisters Mallone* was some kind of twisted version of *The Sopranos*. That probably comes from an over emphasis on the show by both the media and Italian American activists. American audiences simply aren't familiar with real Italian women who know how to take care of themselves and each other. That's what *Sisters Mallone* is all about.

(February 2003)

Louisa Ermelino, *The Sisters Mallone: Una storia di famiglia* (New York: Simon & Schuster, 2002). www.simonsays.com; ISBN 0743223330; $23 (hardcover).

Marie Hall Ets

Rosa Cavalleri worked as a cleaning lady for the Chicago Commons Settlement House during the early 20th century. Like the majority of Italians who immigrated to America between 1880 and 1920, Rosa came from a peasant culture based on oral rather than literate traditions. She might not have been able to read or write, but she was a masterful storyteller.

Social worker Marie Hall Ets recorded Rosa's stories, and, with the help of Professor Rudolph Vecoli of the University of Minnesota's Immigrant History Research Center, published *Rosa: The Life of An Immigrant Woman* in 1970. Eventually the book went out of print. Now, thanks to the University of Wisconsin Press, Rosa's story can continue to be read by new generations. This new edition contains the original preface by Vecoli and an introductory note by Helen Barolini.

Immigrant autobiographies by women are extremely rare, and even rarer were those by Italian immigrant women. This is what makes Rosa's story so important. Rosa speaks for a whole generation of women whose stories never made it onto the pages of history. Rosa is the illegitimate daughter of a famous Italian actress whose name Rosa refuses to reveal. Abandoned at birth, Rosa spent her early years in a Catholic orphanage before being placed into a foster home. The book documents a young girl's life in an impoverished northern Italian village and her forced immigration to America to join her husband through an arranged marriage.

Rosa's entry into America is through her dual role as worker and storyteller that makes the book an important work in the growing field of working-class studies. Her narrative is filled with references to characters of Italian folklore, and as such is an important primary document to the field of ethnic American folklore studies. This is a major work for specialists in ethnic/American literature, immigration history, and women's studies. It also is made for an audience beyond the usual academics because it tells the story of a peasant immigrant who moves into the American working class.

Beyond the folktales she recounts, her narrative follows the models of folktales through her anecdotal accounts of the miracles she witnessed. Her testimony also contains important elements of social criticism common in immigrant talk, but rarely recorded in writing.

(May 2000)

Marie Hall Ets, *Rosa, The Life of an Italian Immigrant*, with foreword by Rudolph J. Veoli and Introductory note by Helen Barolini (Madison: U of Wisconsin P,

1999). ISBN 0299162540; $16.95 (paperback).

David Evanier

The new Kevin Spacey film, *Beyond the Sea,* has returned Bobby Darin to the center of American culture. While the film, which doesn't claim to be an exact biography, is a beautiful vision of the performer's life, you need to get David Evanier's biography, *Roman Candle* to see the well from which Spacey's version was drawn, especially if you're a stickler for the facts.

Born in 1936, Darin was dead by the time he was 37, having done more in less than two decades, than most singers do in five. Evanier's biography makes clear that Darin, often referred to as a Sinatra wannabe, did things in life and music that Sinatra never could.

There's some controversy as to just how Italian Darin really was. Born, Walden Robert Cassoto, his last name coming from his grandfather — described by Evanier as a small time thug, Darin grew up with a weak heart in tough New York city neighborhoods. Armed with a rough demeanor and a genius IQ, he learned to play piano, drums, and guitar.

Darin made it through the prestigious Bronx Science high school and began taking musician gigs. He formed a number of musical groups and started writing songs. One of his earliest compositions, *Splish, Splash,* gave him national attention and a recording contract. Not wanting to be known as a rock and roll artist, he began recording standards, especially songs out of the vaudeville era. He befriends old timers like George Burns and Jimmy Durante, many of whom become father figures. He has a wild dating period with Connie Francis and later marries the All-American girl, Sandra Dee, after first dating her mother.

Always in Sinatra's shadow, Darin refused to move to Sinatra's own Reprise label, when he was aksed. Instead, Darin's agent took the opportunity to have Bobby switch to Capitol Records, Sinatra's old label because Bobby was obsessed with doing things like and better than Frank. Darin once was misquoted as saying he wanted to be bigger than Sinatra, which caused a ripple through the business and led to a sitdown between the two.

Evanier does an excellent job of investigating the many secrets of the great performer's life. He vividly recreates the era of teen dances, nightclubs like the Copacabana, television variety shows, and the heyday of the Las Vegas strip. We see Bobby as he struggles and succeeds with boldness and humility. Evanier smartly steps back and lets those who knew Bobby best tell their stories, giving us many angles by which to view the man and the star. Evanier can even be poetic, as in his description of the album Bobby did with Johnny Merce: "Mercer and Darin wing it together, scatting riffing, improvising doing what's necessary; they're having a ball. They slide, they glide, they dance, they fly."

We learn how Bobby's life and his life choices were always influenced by an awareness that he would probably not live beyond the age of 30. Through commentary and criticism, Evanier takes chances that some biographer's might not, making this the book you want to read before seeing the film. At times some of the writing borders on outright cheering, but as Evanier points out, if you loved Bobby Darin, nothing could shake it. Kevin Spacey may have captured Bobby's spirit in his film, but Evanier does nothing short of capturing the man in all his fancy and with all his faults. Black and white photos and a selected guide to his recordings are included.

David Evanier, *Roman Candle: The Life of Bobby Darin* (Emmaus, PA: Rodale, 2004). www.rodalestore.com; ISBN 1594860106; $24.95 (hardcover).

&

Throughout Italian American communities across the United States, the name of Jimmy Roselli is invoked in ways usually reserved for patron saints or favorite relatives. When Jimmy's singing nearby, the neighborhoods are like ghost towns. But there are two sides to the Roselli coin presented by David Evanier in the biography *Making the Wiseguys Weep: The Jimmy Roselli Story*.

Using a variety of sources, including interviews with Roselli's friends, family, and even enemies, Evanier depicts the singer as a complex man who earned both the love and hatred he received throughout his life. Evanier provides social and historical contexts for major time periods in the singer's seven decades through classic research from Italian/American studies. The writer is at his best when he keeps his own voice in the background and lets those of Roselli's friends and family speak. Evanier does remind us that more than Sinatra, Roselli "maintained his ties to his old neighborhood and its people.... Roselli comes out of the tradition of the wandering Italian balladeer, via the street signs and the troubadours he saw at the Italian vaudeville houses of his youth in Hoboken."

Sixteen pages of photos help tell the stories of Jimmy's early days in Hoboken, New Jersey. Born Michael John Roselli on December 26, 1925. His mother died two days later and his father left the baby with his father. Jimmy grew up under the eyes of his Neapolitan grandfather and his aunts. Raised on Italian opera and vaudeville, Jimmy sang at amateur nights with his grandfather's encouraging "Canti, guaglione, canti" Sing, little guy, sing!

From school auditoriums, Roselli made his way onto the streets and even would sneak jobs in the saloons by using a shoeshine box as a part of his act. That's where he met the gangsters who would become his friends and enemies for most of his singing career. If you want the gossip and the truth behind Roselli's past and a guide for his road to success, this might be the only place to get it right now.

(June 1999)

David Evanier, *Making the Wiseguys Weep: The Jimmy Roselli Story* (New York: Farrar, Straus, and Giroux, 1998). ISBN 0374199272; $24 (hardcover).

JOHN FANTE

If the Italian immigrant experience has a presence beyond the mythic mafia of Mario Puzo, it is through the short stories and novels of John Fante. While he has never been a highly recognized American writer, by 1940, when he was 21, Fante had already published two novels *Wait Until Spring Bandini* and *Ask the Dust*, as well as half of his lifetime production of short stories in national magazines such as *The American Mercury, The Atlantic Monthly, Harper's Bazaar*, and *Scribner's Magazine*, many of which were published in his first short story collection entitled *Dago Red*. Until recently, there was little we knew about this author's life aside from what we could glean from his highly autobiographical fiction.

Through John Fante's novels and short stories, I, like many other Americans of Italian descent, came to see my grandparents and the way their children might have seen them. Much of this comes through his great Bandini novels, *Wait Until Spring, Bandini, The Road to Los Angeles, Ask the Dust,* and stories like "The Odyssey of a Wop." And later on, because of Fante, I understood why my mother recoiled at the sound of words like "dago" and "wop," "From the beginning," writes Fante," I hear my mother use the words Wop and Dago with such vigor as to denote violent distaste. She spits them out. They leap from her lips. To her, they contain the essence of poverty, squalor, filth."

One of the earliest American writers of Italian descent, Fante adapted the oral tradition of southern Italian peasants to a literary culture. His sentence structure is simple and characteristic of the language used in oral storytelling that depends on memory for the maintenance of important information. In crisp, clean, accessible language, he mingles realistic images of working-class characters with the youthful romanticism of a protagonist longing for love or the accolades of success.

Since I first discovered Fante in the mid-1970s, I have read every Fante work published. For my book on Italian American literature, he became an Italian Hemingway. He taught me that American literature is more than just what descended from the Pilgrims. Through him I learned to make sense of the drama inside the Catholic Church, to understand the sturdy pagan underpinnings of my family's fears of the "Evil Eye," and how to explain their defiance of literate authorities. Fante transformed my grandparents' broken English from sources of embarrassment into beautiful music that helps me keep their sounds in my head. Through him I hear them, as though for the first time; these resurrections have kept me sane and searching for more of Fante's work.

One of John Fante's main narrators, Arturo Bandini, was obsessed with achieving fame as a writer. In Fante's prologue to the novel, *Ask the Dust*, the voice of Bandini could be Fante's own speaking to us today from the grave:

> Am I alone now? Poof! My loneliness bears fruit, and there shall be a Los Angeles of tomorrow to remember that a Voice trod these stairs, and Benny the Gouge down on the corner of Third and Hill will weep for joy as he telleth his grandchild that he once spoke with a man of the ages. (*The Big Hunger* 148–49)

To be a great American writer, an author needs to transcend the local color, ethnic peculiarity, and develop a unique style, one that will speak to succeeding generations as powerfully as it does to his own. Like Mark Twain, John Fante's writings about the places he's lived, Colorado and Los Angeles, speak to all Americans. Fante's use of down-home American humor to tell tales of his times transcends his life. However, unlike Twain, and more like Edgar Alan Poe, Fante's strongest impact has been in Europe, where his writings continue to sell better than in the United States. Fante is one of those writers whose fame and influence are only now being acknowledged, nearly twenty years after his 1983 death. W.E.B. DuBois remarked once that "Great writers need great critics," and finally, they are arriving at Fante's works. A biography, a critical study, and an additional collection of Fante's short fiction should give the author the attention he has always deserved and convince scholars, critics and new readers that John Fante is indeed an author of the ages.

That Fante has made a place for himself in the literary histories of Los Angeles and Italian America show that his writing speaks to region and ethnicity, but does it reach beyond the regional and ethnic boundaries to matter to all of the United States and thus launch this writer into the ranks of the great American writers? What does it take to raise a writer beyond the limits of ethnic phenomenon or regional master? A good start would be a first-rate biography and a significant critical study. And if you know John Fante's work, then you've been waiting for these books; if you don't know this great American author, then the biography, the literary study, and the collection of short stories will make for a long-overdue introduction.

For nearly ten years, Stephen Cooper, a professor of English and Film at California State University, Long Beach, has been talking to Fante's surviving relatives and friends; he's also dug through the Fante papers which are not stored in a prestigious archive, but in filing cabinets on a service porch of the Fante Malibu home. Much of the biography is based on the contents of those files: letters, unpublished stories, never developed screenplays, and the bits and pieces of a literary life kept safe by Joyce Fante, the author's widow, who has overseen a renaissance of her late-husband's career.

Told as a story in 17 chapters (didn't anyone tell Cooper that the number 17 is considered by Italians to carry bad luck), *Full of Life* is a straightforward chronological accounting of the life of a man who spent his career writing about that very same life. The biography takes its title, ironically from one of Fante's least autobiographical novels, one that was made into a film starring Judy Holiday and Richard Conte. Cooper's narrative draws in a range of perspectives: from the family, there's the poetry and journal of his wife, accounts of their children, Tom Fante, the author's youngest brother; friends such as Ross B. Wills and Carey McWiliams and their writings help counter Fante's autobiographical accounts of key events and nights on the town. We see Fante as a man who, after a writing binge, would purge himself by drinking and playing with the boys. Cooper has managed to create a mosaic of the author's life that is as much puzzle as picture. Strong in his detective work, and surprisingly weak in literary analysis (something a biography does not need), Cooper makes the important connections that help us understand how the demons and muses made a Fante's life matter to others whether they knew him personally or came only as close to him as one of his pages of writing.

More interpretative than narrative, Richard Collins' *John Fante: A Literary Portrait* is best read after you have some familiarity with Fante's writing. Collins, a professor of English at Xavier University in New Orleans, attempts to connect Fante's life to his work and tries to sort out the fact from fiction, the life from legend. He does an excellent job of arguing for the writer's status as a major American writer and he identifies some of Fante's influences. Not having the same access as Cooper to Fante's papers, Collins must depend on his own instincts to distill fact from fiction. Ultimately, the study never transcends literary analysis to compete with Cooper's biography, but Collins' critical insights are considerable and commendable.

While not expressly written for an academic audience, *John Fante: A Literary Portrait* better serves those teachers and scholars who would use this literature in their criticism and classrooms than the casual reader of Fante's stories or novels. Collins' prose never drifts into the jargon that can alienate anyone not familiar with continental theories and their various interpreters, but it is none-the-less rigorous in its analysis. The book does beg for an index that would have made this well conceived study more academic-friendly.

Divided into 11 chapters, the study opens with a discussion of the major thematic concerns of Fante's work, i.e. family and religion. Collins connects ethnicity to religion to help us see how a man's upbringing can fashion the form and content of his literary and even his cinematic writings. He suggests, "Fante's familiarity with...the oral tale of his Italian-American upbringing and the confessional of the Church, was no small part of what made movie-writing or scenario-pitching so easy for Fante" (21).

From here, Collins moves chronologically through Fante's fiction, as though each story, each novel, each screenplay were an entry into an autobiographical scrapbook. The result is quite a thorough consideration of Fante's work, analyzing much from his earliest to his posthumous publications.

Collins contends that "Fante does not hide behind literature, but uses it in a more relevant and rebellious endeavor, to expose himself..." (29). Collins shows us that what Fante exposes, through the power of ironic self-mockery, is what makes for his unique contribution to American literature.

The research that Stephen Cooper did to create the biography resulted in the uncovering of a great deal of previously uncollected and unpublished fiction that has subsequently gone into *The Big Hunger*, a collection of 18 Fante stories written during Fante's formative years (1932–1959). Reading them enables us to follow the development of Fante's unique voice, observe rehearsals of materials found in his novels, and have access to selections not previously published.

The earliest, "Horselaugh on Dibber Lannon" and "The Still Small Voices," are young boys' stories reminiscent of Twain's Huck Finn. In them we can find the origins of Fante's wonderful juxtaposition of short, repetitive sentences with long, winding embedded sentences that creates a rhythm, a pace, and a style so clear the story shines through. Reading the stories in order, you can watch the writer progress from youthful struggles into mature confidence. Like home movies, these stories become a chance to once again watch the development of one of America's great writers. Cooper's notes about the stories help provide a context for understanding how they were or were not published and where they fit into the author's career.

These three books show us that we need both history and story in order to to make the search for truth worthwhile. From them, we learn that John Fante is a writer who matters today because he reminds us that there is a little bit of saint, sinner, and ethnic, in all of us Americans. Fante teaches us how to use the power of irony and self-mockery to deflate bloated egos and inflate our sense of a shared humanity. Could we possibly ask for more from a great American writer.

(*Los Angeles Times*, April 16, 2000)

Full of Life: A Biography of John Fane, by Stephen Cooper (New York: North Point Press, 2000). ISBN 0865475547; $30 (hardcover).

John Fante: A Literary Portrait, by Richard Collins (Toronto: Guernica Editions, 2000). ISBN 15507170710; $18 (paperback).

John Fante, *The Big Hunger: Stories 1932–1959*, edited by Stephen Cooper (Santa Rosa, CA: Black Sparrow Press, 2000). ISBN 1574231219 (hardcover); ISBN 1574231200 (paper); $30 (hardcover); $17 (paper).

Joe Fiorito

Sometimes an Italian American male does not become a man until his father dies. He may seem to be a man to others, but to himself, as long as he is in his father's presence, he will defer to the power and the mystery of the elder, even to the detriment of his own life. When a middle-aged Joe Fiorito finds himself at his father's deathbed, he begins recalling his father's life, and writes his way to his own manhood in *The Closer We Are to Dying*.

In this memoir, Fiorito captures the dignity of a father's life as it ends. The writer moves through his own childhood, young adulthood, and fatherhood recalling the stories his father tells and has told about his own life; they are quite different lives. While the father has not spent much time trying to understand his life, he has spent a good deal of it relating stories to his son, who then must make sense of it all so that he doesn't repeat his father's mistakes. At the same time Joe comes to accept his father's life, sins and all. Joe learns that in order to forgive his father he must understand why his father lived as he did. By listening to and then writing down his father's stories Joe comes to understanding and forgiveness.

Each chapter covers a day of hospital visits. Joe takes the night shift so the rest of the family can get some sleep. There is no relief in death; through all the pain we come to learn that even in the life of a miserable drunk, there is beauty, passion, hope, and joy. His father, Dusty Fiorito is a mailman and professional musician in a small town in Canada; Dusty's drinking anchors him to a place where dreams will never come true, and yet he never stops dreaming.

This is powerfully written and at times downright poetic, and yet is not an easy book to read, at least not for the soul. Fiorito doesn't pull any punches nor does he leave us any room for ducking from reality. The shift between the painful observations of his father's deteriorating condition and the rich and colorful scenes from his family's past create a chiaro/scuro effect that keeps the story from straying into a nostalgic no-man's land. It is not only the stories, but the telling of the stories that make this an exciting memoir. Fiorito's a master of sentences that build roads to new places in the mind: "A patina of confusion dulled certain details. There were missing pieces and inexplicable facts. Some of the tales were as improbable as opera. And there was a darkness in the way my father told a story which fired my imagination."

They say the light is brightest right before it is extinguished and we can say the same for Dusty Fiorito's life. In his son's hands, Dusty's mundane, miserable life becomes honorable and memorable. If you like Russell Baker, then Joe Fiorito is going to please you much. Like Baker, he never steps on the characters he creates; he lets them live the lives they've created without judging them, even when we can't do anything but hate them. If you don't know Baker, then start with Fiorito and he'll take you to the same places where reality stays with you like a toothache, and you learn to live with it in spite of the pain.

(April 2004)

Joe Fiorito, *The Closer We Are to Dying* (New York, Picador USA, 2000). ISBN 0312261365.

Anthony Fragola

All seven stories in Anthony Fragola's *Feast of the Dead* revolve around the interaction between a young boy and his immigrant grandparents. Fragola, a playwright and professor of broadcasting and cinema at the University of North Carolina at Greensboro, has been publishing his fiction for a while. But this is the first time his stories have been collected in one place.

The collections title story introduces the grandmother, who becomes the young man's guide through the old country ways. When she takes him to six o'clock mass on "La festa dei morti," or "All Souls Days," the chanting of the old women in black turns into a wail for the dead.

> The women's throats were instruments of the dead, lamenting their departure from the world and the families they left behind. Hearing those unearthly sounds, I understand that the dead could only live within us. During the Feast of the Dead they not only came to visit, but also to inhabit our bodies and souls.

Much of the narrative in the following stories follows a similar pattern. Grandma does something strange, the boy learns why, and thus we all learn about Italian American culture. "In My Grandmother's Bed," Fragola takes us into the mind of a young man who doesn't understand the flirtation going on between his widowed grandmother and Mr. Strano. The young boy begins to imagine himself as his grandfather, and in true adolescent fashion, fears the separation from her that will come if she marries this man. When he tells her that if she marries him or anyone, she won't see him anymore, the grandmother remarks, "Bravo, . . . You're just like your grandfather. Maybe worse."

"La Strega" is the closet Fragola comes to crafting a pure folktale. Told as a story within a story, "La Strega" opens with a friend of the grandmother warning the young boy that he must be wary of women. "A woman can be a madonna or a witch. You can't always tell." Her words set the young boy's imagination spinning. He follows his story only to realize that perhaps the storyteller is the witch.

"Ceci-Nuts" is the closest we get to seeing the little Italy of Syracuse,where most of these stories are set. Fragola presents us with a realization that those of us who have grown up and out of a Little Italy often have, that what is happening here, though familiar and sometimes boring, is probably a lot more important than we can even know. With an anthropologist's eye, Fragola thickly describes the surroundings

"The Evil Eye" how many of us still follow the sayings, believe the superstitions, because of some haunting experience in childhood. This story brings us through the young boy's conversion to believing in the power of malocchio and the need to learn how to confront it.

In "The Garden" we finally get a chance to meet the infamous grandfather. Can't relate to his son, so reaches out to the grandson, in desperation of leaving something behind. "In Exile" the finale, and longest, begins the work of a novel, of travelling back to Italy and meeting relatives who are better left to the imagination, and local people whom he will forever carry in his heart and head.

While presented as fiction, these might have had more impact as memoir. But that's just a feeling I have, and not meant at all to detract from the effect that this fine collection has. Fragola's strength as a writer lies in his ability to catch a conversation just right. Each of these stories could be a scene in a powerful film about the impact the past has on the present. If resurrection is human through art, then Fragola has achieved the rare ability to bring back his dead to tell us that until we learn to celebrate death, we may never know how to live.

(October 1998)

Anthony Fragola, *Feast of the Dead* (Toronto: Guernica Editions, 1998). ISBN 1550710362; $15 (paperback).

REMO FRANCESCHINI

No matter how we try to shake it off, the mafia seems to stick to the public image of us like cheap cannoli filling to fingers in the summertime. Even our own writers and filmmakers seem enchanted with characters like Capone, Bonanno and Gotti. While few of us have spent much time worrying about all this, there is one man who has spent more than half his life listening to what wiseguys were saying and gathed evidence to put many of them away.

In *A Matter of Honor: One Cop's Lifelong Pursuit of John Gotti and the Mob*, Remo Franceschini, retired New York Police Department lieutenant and former commanding officer of the Queens District Attorney's detective squad, recounts his thirty-five year career in law enforcement. Much of that career was spent gathering evidence on the hoodlums and thugs who the media has made into mythic heroes. In this book, he dispels that myth and details the actions that turned gangsters into prisoners.

"These guys are treated like movie stars," he writes.

> A combination of *Godfather* pictures, the mobsters' own swagger, and the public's fascination with guys who get away with it have made organized crime figures into romantic heroes. They're not. They're killers. And it's been a matter of honor with me to expose them and put them away.

Franceschini was born in 1932. His father's family immigrated from San Martino, near Parma, Italy and his mother's family from Sicily. He grew up in the Bronx, "in plain view of both organized crime and law enforcement" which forced many of his peers to make a choice between one or the other. His godfather, while involved in a number of illegal activities centered on horse racing, remained on the fringes of gangster organizations. At 17, Franceschini, who knew he "was never going into the mob," joined the Air Force.

A Matter of Honor, opens with Franceschini's 1957 entry into the New York Police Department after a seven-year military career. As a beat cop, Franceschini became a hero when he and his partner survived a subway gun battle; they were awarded the Police Combat Cross award. His career took off and soon he was made a detective. This was a time when the police controlled the streets. According to Franceschini, police lost their advantage over criminals with the 1961 Supreme Court ruling in "Mapp v. Ohio" requiring probable cause for searches.

In the early 1960s, when not much was known about the Mob, Franceschini found himself in the middle of things as a member of New York's Central Investigation Bureau. While today's technology has greatly reduced the hazards of infiltrating and monitoring gangster hangouts, Franceschini, a virtual pioneer in the wiretap business, faced danger and tells an incredibly spine tingling story of breaking into John Gotti's club to install "bugs" while Gotti soldiers stood outside on the street.

From information gathered through these devices, Franceschini, began to piece together a pattern to the crime he was investigating. He became one of the first to propose the idea that this crime was organized into the now familiar boss to "capo" to solider hierarchy. While early arrests affected this structure, it would not be until the RICOH act was passed that bosses like Gotti became vulnerable. By then, Franceschini headed Queens District Attorney John Santucci's detective squad.   For a brief period during the turbulent sixties, the police backed off the Mob to concentrate on subversive groups like the S.D.S. Weathermen and the Black Panthers. Franceschini led investigations that prevented revolutionary violence, yet he was not blind to the possibility of violating innocent people's civil rights. He strongly protested surveillance of dissenting groups which, while holding different views, posed no threat to public safety.

Franceschini also recounts his experience with Chinese and Columbian gangs and in one chapter goes into great detail of how he was able to use a barmaid's testimony to bring down a number of crime bosses. The book ends with his insights into the future of organized crime which he likens to a rat hole, "if you shine a flashlight . . . you won't have a lot of activity. Flick off the light and the place starts to scurry."

Reading this book is like standing on a street corner, listening to a great storyteller. Franceschini never lapses into braggadocio and can maintain suspense even in the briefest of anecdotes. More than a memoir, Franceschini's book tells the story of how the hard work of one man made a difference. It is a book that should inspire us all to believe that we are not powerless to change our society.

A Matter of Honor is an occasion for Italian Americans to be proud. Franceschini, who retired in 1991, should be honored as a national Italian/American man-of-the-year for his monumental dedication to damaging organized crime and for writing a strong antidote to the media created stereotype that has plagued us for too long.

(October 1998)

Remo Franceschini, *A Matter of Honor: One Cop's Lifelong Pursuit of John Gotti and the Mob* (New York: Simon & Schuster, 1993). ISBN 0671739476; $22 (hardcover).

Richard Gambino

Over twenty years ago, a book was published that broke a number of barriers set up around Italian American culture. *Blood of My Blood: The Dilemma of Italian-Americans* was Richard Gambino's attempt to document and explain the place of Italian Americans in a United States that was beginning to respond to the challenge of organized minority cultures which eventually led to what we today call multiculturalism. Published in the wake of *The Godfather* novel and film, *Blood of My Blood* was first non-fiction bestseller to challenge the gangster stereotype image of Italians in America.

Until the publication of this book, very little of Italian/American culture had been interpreted by its own intellectuals. Jerre Mangione's *Mount Allegro*, which first appeared in 1943 and has never been out-of-print, was one exception, but Mangione's memoir never attempted to survey the whole of Italian American life in the United States the way that Gambindo did in *Blood of My Blood*.

Using an interdisciplinary approach, Gambino blended census statistics, personal anecdotes, passages from Italian and Italian American literature, psychology and history into a landscape portrait of Italians in America. The result was a stunningly unique document that has served as a beacon, drawing many into the serious study of Italian American culture. At that time, 1974, Gambino was a key figure in the avant-garde of white ethnic, working class studies. The book launched Gambino's career as a professor of Italian/American studies and he went on to establish an Italian/American studies program at Queens College. Recently Queens College, the beneficiary of a landmark legal battle fought by the John D. Calandra Institute, appointed Professor Philip Cannistraro as "Distinguished Professor of Italian American Studies."

Guernica Editions' republication of *Blood of My Blood* has made this important study available to a new generation of readers. In rereading the book, I found it to be more New York centric than I remembered it to be. I also noticed a distinct absence of any discussion on the Italian American participation in areas such as the US labor movement. But its importance as a key study in Italian American culture is not diminished by these retrospective realizations.

Since it first appeared, too few serious responses to *Blood of My Blood* have appeared. I hope that this reprint will provide the occasion for serious readers to critique Gambino's ideas of "Manliness" and "Womanliness" and especially his explanations as to how and why Italian Americans and African Americans can see the world so differently.

Gambino's work has evolved since the publication of this book, but without a new preface or an Afterword that would have enabled the author to update his own work and, more importantly, survey the development of Italian American studies since the 1970s, I'm afraid new readers will not know this. But this is more a missed opportunity than a flaw of the republication of a book that has become an important primer to Italian American history and the evolution of Italian American identity. My point here is that a community of intellectuals have grown up around this important book and its republication will generate new responses.

(August 2001)

Richard Gambino, *Blood of My Blood: The Dilemma of the Italian-Americans* (Toronto: Guernica Editions, 1996). ISBN 1550710370; $15 (paperback).

Anthony Giardina

Anthony Giardina's *The Country of Marriage* is a collection of his short stories that have appeared in such top shelf venues as *Esquire, Gentlemen's Quarterly, Harper's,* and *The New York Times Sunday Magazine.* Giardina, an established playwright and novelist, leaves behind the familiar ethnic turf covered in *Men with Debts* and *A Boy's Pretensions,* in pursuit of more mainstream characters and universal situations. Along the way he has bloomed as a literary stylist.

Giardina celebrates the tragic and the comic of day-to-day routines of marriages in nine stories. Each story explores a different angle of marriage, a subject that has well served writers such as Gustave Flaubert, D. H. Lawrence, and John Cheever, but one that most contemporary writers seem to avoid. Through a wide range of voices, experiences, and emotions evoked through impeccably appropriate diction, visually striking gestures, and characters' innermost thoughts, Giardina shows us marriage American style as though it was the sun slipping through a crack in a black wooden door.

"I Live in Yonville" is a meditation on the wonders of the mundane by a manwho lives small in his life and large in his imagination through his reading of classic Flaubert and Turgenev novels. He gets a kick out of telling someone at a party that he lives in "Yonville," and even if you don't know where Yonville is, the story will teach you something about being satisfied with your lot in life. However, if you know that Yonville is a fictional town in "Madame Bovary" you're likely to get more out of the story.

In "Days with Cecilia," a man who knows his wife is cheating on him does nothing for fear of breaking up his relationship with his daugther, to whom he has devoted his quiet and desperate life. The reserve in the narrator's tone and language creates a tension that evens out the wrinkles of his wounded marriage. "I fed Cecilia and felt my wife's presence, and thought of the spurned economist under the shower.... In my mind's eye, the water became hot metal..., and there was a soldering gun in my hand." Once "quite the couple... quite the doers-of-things together," the birth of Cecilia signaled, "the end of our romance." So why doesn't he confront his cheating wife? Because, "No one, even in this unlikely age, is fond of divorce. The notions persists that certain people belong together, and I am content to believe this is so for us." Whether it's a resignation, a rationalization, or a time bomb ticking away, the reasoning is enough to make you wonder if sometimes you can't have it all your way.

A bomb does explode inside one young husband in "The Lake," in which a fireman recounts his role in the murder of his buddy's wife. Giardina takes you so close into relationships that he distorts the perspective from which we might separate good from evil. The simplicity of the terror presented through the horror of boredom is haunting. Giardina shows how even the suggestion of disloyalty can lead to trouble in a dysfunctional relationship.

When a divorced man is forced to return to live with his parents, he finds out that he's never really grown up. "Love, Your Parents" is a story that reminds us there is nothing sicker than those who think they're more normal than others. And in "The Cut of His Jib," Giardina presents a story that should be required reading for every Italian American who's ever left the grey concrete of the urban ghetto for the green lawns of the suburbs. When lawyer Matt Romano, "whose good looks... bore a faint whiff of the criminal," moves into the suburban scene onto a street where most of the neighbors are Italian American, he learns that there are rules to assimilation. Erasing his difference becomes the goal of the group. Through a fifteen-year-old narrator, Giardina captures a key moment that is rarely observed: "Perhaps when you are fifteen, you only watch; it is your principal task, whatever other functions your body might be performing. It is your obsession to figure out the world." When Matt says, "I like the cut of his jib" in reference to a man who's a business cheat, the young observer notices the discomfort in the other men.

> It was not language any of them would ever have used; he had brought it form somewhere else, and held it before them like a sign of his dual citizenship, his ability to escape their little world, if it came to that. They all know this: they were antagonists at heart.

Over the course of the rest of the story we observe the subtle pressure the adults put on this man to conform to the dismay of the young boy who, "had needed, very badly, to see him as someone capable of breaking free of this world, if he only chose...."

In "The Secret Life," the infidelity of Theo Augarten builds to the last sentence without relief. That Giardina can sustain the dramatic tension is a literary achievement of a master storyteller. "The Challenge of the Poet" uses a female's point-of-view to examine the effect of too much leisure time on the upper middle class to show us that while you might have the time to imagine, you can't always have what you imagine. "The Second Act" rewrites the life of F. Scott and Zelda Fitzgerald into an elegant "what if" cameo story of sorts. It is a nice thoughtful story; the more you know about Scott and Zelda, the more you will appreciate it. Who was Richard Egan, and why should we care? In "The Films of Richard Egan," Giardina answers those questions by taking us through sketches of a famous character actor's career as it eclipses oblivion.

Just as all of the stories in *The Country of Marriage*, "The Films of Richard Egan" tells us how much fun problems can be when they belong to other people.

(May 1998)

Anthony Giardina, *The Country of Marriage* (New York: Random House, 1997). ISBN 0679456287; $22 (hardcover).

Maria Gillan and Edvige Giunta

When most Americans think east coast Italian, they think, New York. That, and perhaps the setting of the hit series *The Sopranos* are just a couple of the reasons that Jennifer Gillan, Maria Mazziotti Gillan, and Edvige Giunta, teamed up to produce *Italian American Writers on New Jersey: A Poetry and Prose Anthology.*

Gathered here, for the first time ever, are accomplished writers of yesterday and today who have either come from or used New Jersey as a subject in their work. Divided into four sections: "Looking Back," "Blending In," "Crossing Bridges," and "Changing Directions," the anthology takes us beyond the borders of the stereotypical Italian American experience of New Jersey that we usually get from other media. They also combine to take "The Garden State" out of the shadows usually cast by its big, tough neighbor New "The Apple" York.

More than forty writers are represented in poetry, drama, essays, short fiction and book excerpts. While many of the selections are reprints, especially from the more well known writers such as Louise DeSalvo (*Vertigo*), Gay Talese (*Unto the Sons*), Pietro di Donato (*Three Circles of Light*), Diane di Prima (*Recollections of My Life as a Woman*), Carole Maso (*Ghost Dance*), Tom Perrotta (*Bad Haircut*), and Maria Gillan from her various books of poetry, together they combine to creat,e a new way of seeing both the state of writing and writing about the state. A nice surprise comes through the newer voices of Marisa Trubiano, June Avignone, and David Della Ferra.

While the emphasis is on the contemporary, the editors have dipped into the historical well to come up with some wonderful blasts from the past in through worker writers such as organizers Maria Barbieri and Maria Roda, mill worker Josephine Stifano and Arturo Giovannitti, the poet who helped organize the famous Lawrence Mill strike of 1912.

(May 2004)

Jennifer Gillan, Maria Mazziotti Gillan, and Edvige Giunta, eds., *Italian American Writers on New Jersey: An Anthology of Poetry and Prose* (New Brunswick, NJ: Rutgers UP, 2003). ISBN 0813533163 (hardback); ISBN 0813533171 (paperback); $21.95 (paperback).

MARIA MAZZIOTTI GILLAN

The hardest working woman in the poetry business has got to be Maria Gillan. Last year's recipient of the Order Sons of Italy in America, New York State Lodge's annual award for achievement in writing, Gillan is director of creative writing at the State University of New York at Binghamton, director of the Poetry Center at Passaic County Community College, editor of *The Paterson Literary Review*. On top of all this she travels to readings and workshops throughout the country.

Recently Garrison Keillor read poetry from her new book, *Italian Women in Black Dresses*, on his national radio program and the book quickly sold out of its first printing. While this is no surprise — Gillan's work has always sold pretty well and she has often been heard on national radio shows — it does point to a new level of appreciation of her work that is long overdue.

Italian Women picks up on the autobiographical themes of her previous collections, but Gillan isn't simply giving us more of the same. This new writing extends those themes further and in new directions. This collection reflects a greater sense of movement beyond the self, beyond the old neighborhood, beyond the ethnic focus of much of her earlier work. Many of the poems here represent Gillan's constant struggle to renew herself through her work.

While you might be able to say that some of her earlier work was not as precise or tight as it should or could have been, you would be hard pressed to make a case with these poems. This collection represents her ability to transcend earlier writing faults. If there is a fault to this collection it is one of excess. There is simply too much in one place.

The book opens with the title poem that sets up the author as one of those powers of the old neighborhood. She can relate to them now: "I dress now all in black like the old ladies / of my childhood, the old ladies who watched // our movements and reported to our mothers / if we did anything wrong...." These women were both caretakers of the community and witnesses to everything. In the historical drama of life, they serve the role of the chorus in Greek theater. And this is the major function of Gillan's new book: it bears witness to history and helps build a community of those who share memories similar to hers.

Much of what we have in this new book are memories of times good and bad. Most of those come through everyday images of family life past and present that creates for us a familiar world of Sunday dinners, backyard picnics, or just sitting around the kitchen. In and around the family home Gillan finds all she needs to present variations on the tragedies and comedies of life. Her poems are deceivingly simple, as though they were bare trees; you don't realize how stunning they can be without their leaves until you see them defy the steel grey of a winter sky. And Gillan's poetry defies both ornate garishness of style and overly lofty content.

This is not to say that there are not problem areas in this new book. One image, "peach slices gleaming in the red wine" gets repeated in two back-to-back poems, but is this a sign of excess or could it be a recurring image that brings comfort? Hard to say, but perhaps more careful selection would have helped to increase the impact of some of these poems. She also includes a number of prose poems that seem to be either unfinished memoir pieces or poems that have exploded by trying to do too much.

(November 2003)

Maria Mazziotti Gillan, *Italian Women in Black Dresses* (Tonawanda, NY: Guernica Editions, 2002). www.guernicaeditions.com; ISBN 1550711563; $13 (paperback).

&

Parole Scritte — *June*

Since the early 1980s, Maria Mazziotti Gillan has been a driving force of Italian/American literature. As director of the Poetry Center at Passaic County Community College and editor of *Footwork: The Paterson Literary Review*, she has continually promoted Italian/American poets and included them in readings and publications. Her dedication to Italian/American literature is unparalleled and has earned her the nickname, "The Godmother" of Italian/American poetry.

Besides creating opportunities for writers to read and be read, she has produced an impressive body of writing that has earned her honors such as the prestigious "Walt Whitman" and "Sri Chinmoy" prizes as well as a number of New Jersey State Council on the Arts awards. Her poetry was selected for the 1985 "Editor's Choice" award and was nominated for a Pushcart Prize.

If you've missed her earlier publications, *Flowers from the Tree of Night* (1982), *Winter Light* (1985), *The Weather of Old Seasons* (1989), and *Taking Back My Name* (1991), you can get the best of those collections along with her more recent work in *Where I Come From*, published this year [1995] by Guernica Editions.

This collection contains sixty poems characterized by a directness and simplicity of language that masks the complex thoughts behind them. Gillan creates a sense of what Lawrence Ferlinghetti calls, "public surface," that invites the reader into the poet's world to share in the joys and sorrows of her experiences. Gillan creates family portraits, still life images and lyrical narratives that are as haunting and powerful as they are sensitive and soothing.

Through poems such as "Arturo," "Growing Up Italian," "The Crow," "Public School No. 18," "In Memory We Are Walking," and "Columbus and the Road to Glory," Gillan dramatizes both the pride and shame of being Italian American. In "Betrayals," she captures the irony of having children feel about us as we felt about the immigrant generation.

While the places of her past may have changed, whether paved over by cement or cemeteries, they are captured forever in her words, as in her poem "Oak Place Musings":

> Today I mourn tomatoes ripening in our immigrant gardens,
> the pattern of sun on walls of old brick mills,
> a time when each day opened like a morning glory.
> Some days when I look at my hand, I imagine
> it is still stained gold.

Gillan is wise with the knowledge of an old country midwife, and what she knows about life, love, death and grief, she teaches us through her poignant poetry. She writes about the lessons she has learned from life, of how to love, to let go, and to lose, and by doing so to have even more. Whether it is one of her children leaving home, or a relative leaving this world, Gillan has the ability to keep the experience, the person alive, especially through her prose poems, which are crafted like miniature films.

Gillan believes that the future of Italian/American literature looks bright, but she warns of a number of problems that need to be solved. "One of the obstacles that we have got to overcome," she says, "is this sense of sole ownership of any territory, this belief that person 'A' is the one and only poet, or fiction writer or essayist who can represent Italian Americans. Perhaps this happens because there's so little space in the mainstream for Italian/American writers. But If we are ever going anywhere we have to start saying, if I push an Italian/American writer, then I'm pushing all Italian/American writers. This has got to happen in reviews, in conferences, in publications, in all the ways that we gather, network and disseminate our work."

But establishing an Italian/American identity and recognition of the contribution of Italian American writers is but one of this poet's goals. She has become a major player in the national poetry scene with the publication of *Unsettling America: An Anthology of Contemporary Multicultural Poetry*. With her daughter Jennifer Gillan, Maria edited this major anthology that is being used in literature courses throughout the country. This anthology represents the great diversity of cultures that have contributed to the development of American poetry, and challenges the myths and stereotypes that for years have kept racial and ethnic groups divided.

Like the anthology, Gillan's latest book delves deep into the author's self and history to give us all a better sense of where she comes from and in a way, a better sense of where we all have come from. In a very poetic "Afterword," Diane di Prima, calls the collection, "a journey home to ourselves, our ancestral customs and beliefs, and outward, to whatever possibilities await.

(June 2001)

Maria Mazziotti Gillan, *Where I Come From: Selected and New Poems* (New York: Guernica Editions, 1995). ISBN: 1550710052; $13 (paperback)

Marria Mazziotti Gillan and Jennifer Gillan, eds., *Unsettling America: An Anthology of Contemporary Multicultural Poetry* (New York: Penguin Books, 1994). ISBN 0670851701 (hardcover); ISBN 014023778X (paperback); $13.95 (paperback).

&

Maria Mazziotti Gillan's latest book, *Things My Mother Told Me,* is a mix of poems and prose memories. The writings move chronologically, from mediations on her great-grandmother, whom she could only imagine, through her own motherhood. They conclude with her arrival at grandmotherhood.

Gillan, founder and director of the Poetry Center at Passaic County Community College, is editor of the *Paterson Literary Review* and co-editor of acclaimed anthologies, *Unsettling America, Identity Lessons,* and the forthcoming *Growing Up Ethnic in America.* She spends a great deal of time traveling the country giving readings, and recently was visiting poet in the Graduate School at the State University of New York at Binghampton.

Once again, this poet has succeeded in capturing the essence of a culture by looking into her own soul. From the shame learned as a child of immigrants comes the powerful "Learning Silence," in which a child, terrorized by a teacher's attitudes towards Italians, learns to desire the perfection found in the infamous "Dick and Jane" books.

The early entries wind through adolescent ecstasies and disappointmentsas in "Glittering as We Fall," "The Surprise Party," "Training Bra," and "First Dance at the CYO," through the turning points of self awareness as a woman, as a human, as a sexual creature, best reflected in "Zia Concetta and Her Whalebone Corset." "Marilyn Monroe and My Sister" is a lament of difference that reveals the power mainstream models of beauty have to check a young girl's self esteem, leading her to wishing, "Oh I wanted to walk like her, my hips swinging, but I looked from Marilyn to my sister as we sat in the Fabian theater, and I saw that there was a sexy musk about them. I knew they were born knowing a secret I would never know."

In "The Moment I Knew My Life Had Changed," Gillan presents an epiphany that made her realize that she could be her own person.

> My life, turning away from the constricted word
> of the 19th Street tenement, formed a line
> almost perpendicular to that old life,
> I moved toward it, breathed in this new air,
> racing toward a world filled with poems and
> music and books that freed me from everything
> that could have chained me to the ground.

But while reading and writing enabled her to break chains that bound her to a past that suppressed her spirit, through art she fashions new chains from which others break away, as she shows us in "My Son Tells Me Not to Wear My Poet's Clothes:" "My son tells me not to war my poet's clothes. "They're weird," he says. He wants me to look like a mail-order catalogue grandmother. . . . My son does not say it out loud, but I know he things I'm the wrong kind of mother, that I should act my age, give up poetry...."

Heavy with the responsibilities and realities of family, "Things My Mother Told Me," charts a woman's life in a concise and creative memoir. A strong tone of mortality pervades the collection that is sung by a voice we have come to trust. Gillan proves that she can take what life gives her and turn the results into art.

The author stops at the threshold between each stage of life from child, to wife, to mother, to grandmother, looks back at what happened, and captures the lessons in powerful and sometimes painful recollections.

Her meditations uncover all the traps laid and the tricks played to keep women weak. But Gillan shows how she broke away from tradition and grabbed control of her self by synthesizing the roles of mother and artist. While some of the poems are more effective than others, usually because they are more finished, all of them are worth reading for the insight they give to this multifaceted artist.

(February 1999)

Maria Mazziotti Gillan, *Things My Mother Told Me* (Toronto: Guernica Editiions, 1999). ISBN 1550710214; $13 (paperback).

Daniela Gioseffi

As a poet, essayist and novelist, Daniela Gioseffi, has proven to be a strong and steady voice in the struggle for social justice in the United States. Since the beginning of her career as a writer and multi-media performer, she has been just as committed to exploring the place of women in Italian/American culture.

Her comic, feminist novel, *The Great American Belly Dance* (1977) dealt with an Italian/American woman's search for meaning and dignity through a return to an ancient dance ritual. Like the themes explored in her first novel, much of Gioseffi's writing deals with the dual dilemma of being doubly distanced from mainstream culture through gender and ethnicity, and presents the struggle of a woman to overcome these man-made barriers with the goal of establishing her own voice in a public space.

Gioseffi's poetry, stories, essays, and criticism have appeared in literary magazines such as *The Paris Review, Antaeus,* and the *Nation,* and anthologies such as *Kaleidoscope: Stories from the American Experience, The Dream Book,* and Ishmael Reed's anthology, *Multi-America: Essays on Cultural Wars and Cultural Peace.*

Two anthologies she edited have won prizes: the American Book Award for *Women Against War: International Voices* (Simon and Schuster 1988), and a Ploughshares Fund for World Peace grant for *On Prejudice: Multicultural Voices for Tolerance* (Anchor Doubleday 1993). Over the past few years, Gioseffi has been collecting her earlier writings: her poetry in *Word Wounds and Water Flowers* (*VIA* FOLIOS 1995), and now her stories in *In Bed with the Exotic Enemy*.

One of the problems a prolific writer such as Gioseffi has when going through a life's worth of published work is choosing just what to put into a book and what to leave out. Her latest book reflects this problem in both its scope and style.

More than the art of fiction, these stories, for the most part, are better suited for the memoir, for they evoke the art of living a life shaped by unwavering moral convictions in the pursuit of social and personal justice and equality. That which is not always accepted by others, must nevertheless be respected, seems to be the recurring theme in these stories. As a storyteller, Gioseffi is nothing if not political, and while not all these stories succeed aesthetically, most of them challenge the faulty thinking that leads to dehumanizing behavior.

To understand Gioseffi's work, you must see beyond the stereotypical notion of the generation that came of age in the 1960s. We might have been inarticulate at times, but the passion was strong and the frustration often hissed like steam from a pressure cooker. The forces that led to mass protest for civil rights often shrunk individual pride enough to create communities of activists who made things happen. The experience of uniting diversity in the pursuit of justice helped us all to re-examine traditional immigrant as well as media-made American cultural values.

Gioseffi's collection of sixteen stories and one novella is characterized by a variety of voices, which, at times sing the blues, opera arias, and off-beat show tunes in the key of history and politics. Here and there you'll find the best of Gioseffi's sense of poetry and wild imagery, but they are more often than not overlooked by a wandering narrator who is sometimes engaging as in her classic "Rosa in Television Land, and other times lecturing, as in "The Bleeding Mimosa," "The Exotic Enemy" "Beyond the Spit of Hate," and "Learning American Grammar."

Among the best of Gioseffi's stories is "Daffodil Dollars," a lyrical, urban folktale about a dwarf who has created a charming way of turning his difference to an advantage, scamming people out of a few bucks in the process. In "Mrs. Prism's First Death" and the bizarre "The Psychic Touch," the author puts her reading of D. H. Lawrence drawing out the sensuality of a woman repressed by men, and a man repressed by his own natural deformity. Many of the other stories, such as "Marital Bliss," "The Fat Lady and the Snake Charmer," work more as scenes, than full blown fictions. "The Capitulation" seems to be a an overgrown prose poem, that with some careful editing might have been more powerful.

While the collection falters in achieving a satisfactory sense of aesthetics, it does provide us with a map of the course Gioseffi's career has run over the past twenty years, a career that might better be reflected through a powerful, memoir, than through this collection of some of her literary stops along the way.

(July 1997)

Daniela Gioseffi, *In Bed with the Exotic Enemy: Stories and Novella* (Greensboro, NC: Avisson Press, 1997). ISBN 1888105178; $25 (hardcover).

EDVIGE GIUNTA

If the personal is political, then Edvige Giunta's first book should prove that she is one savvy cultural politician. With one book, she has managed to bring light to many American women writers of Italian descent and, at the same time establish herself as one of the leading critics of ethnic women's writing in the United States.

Writing with an Accent: Contemporary Italian American Women Authors collects much of what this leading critic has previously published on Italian American women writers. Included are her afterwords to the reprints of Tina DeRosa's *Paper Fish* and Helen Barolini's *Umbertina,* an essay on Agnes Rossi and Nancy Savoca first appearing in *The Canadian Journal of Italian Studies,* papers delivered at the 1996 and 1997 conferences of the American Italian Historical Association and gathered in the proceedings, and a number of other essays, book chapters and reviews.

Giunta is able to avoid the traps of a simple recollection of previous work by weaving the pieces with a strong thread of personal memoir. From her acknowledgements through to the last word of her epilogue, she connects the works of the writers she has read by looping their contributions with hers. Many of these writers have depended on Giunta for public exposure, and she continues to support them. While each chapter may focus on a different writer, Giunta, ever conscious of the collective nature of the women's writing community, reminds us that the work of one, is the work of many. She typically includes Louise DeSalvo, Mary Cappello, Maria Mazziotti Gillan, Rosette Capotorto, Kym Ragusa, Nancy Savoca, Nancy Caronia, in many of her chapters.

It's impossible to categorize this book. Criticism? Memoir? It is both, and more. This hybrid of forms jumps genres as Giunta connects her life-story with the stories that have captured her critical attention. She left her Sicilian home in 1984 to study English literature at the University of Miami. Under the guidance of the eminent scholar and critic John Paul Russo, she completed a dissertation on James Joyce and went on to teach at Union College and New Jersey State University.

What is criticism, what is memory, what is fact? and what fact is invented? What is invention, what is recollection? These are some of the questions raised in this work. There is no doubt that this style of writing has enabled the author to come into her self. You won't be able to tell this by reading her book. It is her speech, and not her writing style, that betrays her bi-culturality. Her dedication to the writing of Italian American women signals an embrace of that accent that lesser critics have avoided. "A hybrid, an inhabitant of cultural borders, I am one of those who feel at home and in exile on both sides of the border," she writes in a fluency and flawlessness that escapes many natives.

One of the limits of this juxtaposition of history, criticism, and memoir Is that we too often learn more about the writer than the written: something we expect in the memoir, but not in scholarship. But Giunta finds honor in defiance of tradition. "Accent is the function of two languages in relation; it is a sign of disjunction, but also of connection: It marks being Sicilian and Italian, Italian and American," she writes from somewhere in the middle of it all, creating a bridge between the cultures she considers. It is literary history of a personal nature — a microscopic look at a movement from the front row seat.

This book is a triumphal monument to her dedication to the accented subjects of her writing. Risking banishment to the shadows and side-streets of literary and cultural discourse, Giunta's work owes a debt to that of Olga Peragallo, Rose Basile Green, Helen Barolini, Mary Jo Bona, Mary Frances Pippino, and Mary Ann Mannino, and earns unique status for connecting these writers to both Italian and American traditions that enrich us all. And while it is not a monograph, it deserves the serious consideration by readers of all ethnic literatures.

(August 2002)

Edvige Giunta, *Writing with an Accent: Contemporary Italian American Women Writers* (New York: Palgrave, 2002). ISBN 0312221258 (hardback); ISBN 0312294697 (paperback); $18.95 (paperback).

JENNIFER GUGLIELMO AND SALVATORE SALERNO

These 18 essays, counting co-editor Jennifer Guglielmo's introduction, comprise some of the best thinking these days about Italian Americans and their relationship to the ideas of race in US society. Not always academic, but always intriguing, the collection covers the historical ground well. From the uses of the word "wop" to the innovations of Italian American hip hop, *Are Italians White?* disrupts the stereotypical view of Italian American racism and connects the power of ye old-fashioned white-skinned privilege to American ethnicity.

In part one, "Learning the U.S. Color Line," Louis DeSalvo mediates on her grandmother's naturalization papers and find that she was listed as "Color: White/ Complexion: Dark." Case studies are presented by leading immigration historian Donna Gabaccia, Vincenza Scarpaci, and Thomas Guglielmo. Part two, "Radicalism and Race," features historical studies such as Caroline Waldron Merithew's look at the 1895 Spring Valley, Illinois race riot and co-editor Salvatore Salerno's keen analysis of the role Italian radicals played in exposing and attempting to dismantle the US racial hierarchy. An unexpected treat is rapper Manifest's look at the experience of an Italian American in the contemporary world of US hip hop.

Part three, "Whiteness, Violence, and the Urban Crisis," features two strong historical looks at Italian Americans on both sides of the racial divide: Gerald Meyer on post-war Italian Harlem and Stefano Luconi on Frank Rizzo and Philadelphia. The highlight here is the IAWA award winning essay "Italians against Racism," by Joseph Sciorra. A final section, "Toward a Black Italian Imaginary," brings us the perspectives of black Italian Americans film maker, Kim Ragusa, actor Giancarlo Esposito (through a fine article by John Gennari), and poet Ronnie Mae Painter. The final word is given to one of the pioneers of whiteness studies, David Roediger.

Some of the essays try to definitively set the record that Italians are and have always been white, while others argue that we weren't always white. Whatever's your belief there's no doubt the essays here will challenge your thinking.

(July 2004)

Jennifer Giuglielmo and Salvatore Salerno, eds., *Are Italians White? How Race is Made in America* (New York: Routledge, 2003). www.routledge-ny.com; ISBN 0415934508 (hardback); ISBN 0415934516 (paperback); $19.95 (paperback).

Thomas Guglielmo

Humbert Nelli, Rudy Vecoli, and Dom Candeloro, move over. There's a new kid in town doing history on Italians in Chicago and he's created a book that anyone dealing with the subject must read. *White on Arrival: Italians, Race, Color and Power in Chicago, 1890–1945* is Thomas Guglielmo's masterwork of research full of original insight into the way Italians positioned themselves (and were positioned by larger forces) among the various social and political issues surrounding race.

Guglielmo traces the history back to the late nineteenth century when there were less than 10,000 Italians in the city. Here he does a fine job of identifying the Italian settlements in and around the city and dispels the myth that any of the Little Italys was exclusively Italian. He argues that they were all "neighborhoods in motion, continually experience tremendous turnover from constant immigration and return migration."

Guglielmo sees race as a construction designed to create unfair power advantages. To him race is about where people and groups are placed in society and the what happens because of those placements. He agrees that Italians may have been discriminated for being part of the Italian "race," but they also were able to benefit in many ways from the privileges given to them as members of the "white" race. Guglielmo calls for Italians to see the advantages given to them in terms of political rights and socio-economic opportunities, denied to African Americans, as no different from things like Affirmative Action and welfare.

He does an excellent job of presenting the larger picture of how race was used by the US immigration authorities to identify groups and to set up criteria for prioritizing acceptance of northern European immigrants. At the local level Guglielmo finds "a racial antagonism that was both ideological and embedded in the social structure of Chicago." He also brings out the racism of leaders such as Father Luigi Giambasiani, of St. Philip Benizi Church. While the antagonism may have been strong, there were never "sustained or systematic" challenges to the color of Italians. Often, Italians did not see themselves as white, nor were they always seen as white by others, but the system never formally labeled them so.

While the focus is on attitudes of race, Guglielmo, presents an excellent history of other aspects of Italian life in Chicago. He looks into the legendary stories of Italian participation in organized crime to show how the acts of a few gangsters were blown out of proportion to send the message out that "Italians — and particularly Sicilians — were a criminally inclined, dangerous, sinister lot." Guglielmo's research disputes the basis for such biased thinking.

From the race riots of 1919 to developments in Europe, Guglielmo presents the social and scientific actions that lead to the passing of the 1924 Johnson-Reed bill which reduced the number of southern and eastern European immigrants allowed into the US Italians did react with protests through groups such as the Chicago Committee of American Citizens of Italian Extraction, but could not exert enough pressure to change the legislation. He also looks to the development of fascism and the attempts of Italy to colonize Ethiopia (1935) to see what effect that had on African and Italian American relations.

One of his findings is that Italian participation in politics was more as Italians than as being white. The lack of political power was due, in no small part, to the Italians failure to vote as individuals and to gather the vote as an identifiable interest group. Guglielmo's study is a long awaited addition to the history of Chicago's Italians.

(July 2004)

Thomas Guglielmo, *White on Arrival: Italians, Race, Color and Power in Chicago, 1890–1945* (New York: Oxford UP, 2003). www.oup.com; ISBN 0195155432; $45 (hardover).

JOSEPHINE GATTUSO HENDIN

First published in 1988, Josephine Gattuso Hendin's *The Right Thing to Do* earned an American Book Award, and not much later was out-of-print before it could reach a large audience. Now, thanks to The Feminist Press of The City University of New York, Hendin's critically acclaimed story of a young woman growing out of the shadow of her immigrant father is now available in an affordable edition that should be in everyone's home library.

The daughter of a Sicilian immigrant father and a Neapolitan mother, Hendin uses much of her own background and experience to recreate the New York neighborhoods where the novel is set. Through rich dialogue and a driving narrative, *The Right Thing to Do* reaches beyond autobiography to teach us all about how the old world and new world cultures can hurt and help each other.

The novel vividly presents the drama of a young women's attempts to make her own way outside of her family and her father's expectations. Nino Giardello, a Sicilian immigrant shadows his daughter Gina whenever she leaves and when she hugs her American boyfriend, he becomes furious at her defiance of his authority. As Gina rebels, her father weakens in health. As as he moves closer to death, she comes closer to understanding his life and the legacy she will inherit.

An "Afterword," written by Mary Jo Bona, a professor of Italian American Studies at SUNY-Stony Brook, and author of *Claiming a Tradition, Italian American Women Writers,* situates the writing appropriately in American literary tradition, offers key biographical information, and presents an illuminating reading. The novel, she tells us, "offers a very contemporary awareness of the potential power of an ethnic past to provide a compass in an increasingly pathless world."

This is a novel that I have read a number of times, and it continues to hold my interest because in both style and story, Hendin has created a book that will no doubt remain among the best of American ethnic literature and among the classics of Italian American literature.

(March 2000)

Josephine Gattuso Hendin, *The Right Thing to Do,* with afterword by Mary Jo Bona (New York: Feminist Press, CUNY, 1999). www.feministpress.org; ISBN 1558612203; $13.95 (paperback).

CARMINE BIAGIO IANACCE

In 1966, a man without any formal education sat down and wrote a memoir about a major turning point in his life-the year 1906 when he came to America. That man was Carmine Biagio Ianacce and his book, *La scoperta dell'America* is finally available in an English translation. Translated with an Afterword by William Boelhower (a noted scholar of immigrant autobiography who teaches at the University of Padua), *The Discovery of America* creates public history through his personal story.

This memoir belongs to everyone with immigrant ancestors. This string of stories begins in 1900 and provides us with a good sense of life and the behavior of those courting in a turn-of-the-century southern Italian village called Cavouti, near Naples. From here the book moves on to the story of those who went to and returned from the United States. There are any number of stories of family and friends found within the larger story of Ianacce's immigrant experience. Like good folktales, they all teach listeners about how to live their lives. The author's wisdom is expressed in an honesty rarely found in immigrant memoirs: "There are three things that a man desires more than anything else in life and which he then unfailingly regrets: getting married, assuming his father's responsbilities, and them wishing him dead."

At the age of 75, Ianacce looks back on the years 1906–1907 and tells the stories of work and workers' stories as if the reader was sitting across the table. From jobs on the railroad to life in American boarding houses, Ianacce's stories bring us to an understand of what the immigrant experience did to our ancestors. The memoir ends with the author's return to Italy and his search for a wife.

A biographical foreword written the author's grandson, Professor Mario Mignone, Director of the Center for Italian Studies at the State University of New York at Stony Brook, gives us a sense of where this book fits into the author's life and fills out the author's life beyond the memoir.

(November 2000)

Carmine Biagio Ianacce, *La scoperta dell'America: Un'autobiografia*; William Boelhower, trans., *The Discovery of America: An Autogiography*; a bilingual edition (West Lafayette, IN: Bordighera, 2000). $12 (paperback).

Luciano Iorizzo

With all the talk these days being about fictional mafiosi like the Sopranos, it's a doubtful that anyone can find something new to say about the American gangster. But while all the buzz is about, this just may be the perfect time to take another look at the man who started it all. Al Capone, didn't live a long life; he died at the age of 48 after a long prison term, but the life he did live cast an incredible shadow that Italian Americans are still trying to avoid. Always considered to be the prototype for the American gangster, this legendary criminal has been the subject of many books, fiction and non-fiction alike. Some of the earlier biographies were nothing more than compilations of news stories and rumors spread by Big Al's friends and enemies.

In 1930, Fred Pasley published the sympathetic *Al Capone: The Biography of a Self-Made Man,* John K. Kobler, *Capone: The Life and World of Al Capone* in 1971; The 1990s bought Laurence Bergreen's "Capone: The Man and the Era," 1994, Tom Stockdale's *The Life and Times of Al Capone,* in 1998, and Robert J. Schoenberg's *Mr. Capone,* in 2001 just to name the most prominent. Many films have been based on his life: the earliest, *Al Capone,* by Allied Artists appeared the same year that gave us *Little Caesar,* and *Scarface.* Other documentaries continued to be produced, in 1975, and an A&E Biography in 1997; these are just a few. Capone's life and the stories that come from it have become a veritable industry of their own. Amazingly, as thorough as some of these accounts are, none brings Capone's Italianness to the fore, and perhaps that's why veteran scholar Luciano Iorizzo turned to the subject.

Iorizzo, Professor Emeritus of History at SUNY-Oswego, is a former president of the American Italian Historical Association, and editor of that organization's third conference proceedings, *An Inquiry into Organized Crime.* With Salvatore Mondello he authored *The Italian Americans* and has published numerous articles on Italian Americans in American history and politics. Iorizzo was an activist and instrumental in the Mario Cuomo campaigns for governor of New York.

Iorizzo's *Al Capone: A Biography* situates Capone's story within the framework of the active corruption in American society that Capone stepped into and "organized" better than anyone had previously imagined. Iorizzo's has created a cultural history in which Capone's life can be understood better than any previous biography. Without any loyalty to the man or the myth, Iorizzo's investigation reveals the intricacies of organized crime that help us understand how one man could have achieved such legendary status . He shows us that there was nothing innately Italian about Capone's rise to power, nor was their anything special about his ethnicity that enabled him to maintain his power.

He achieves what he sets out to do, provide "a perspective which included Italian American history and Organized Crime." Previous books totally ignored anything but the facts of Capone's Italian background. None looked into the depth of Italian immigration to the US and the experience of immigrants that might send someone like Capone into a life of crime. Iorizzo points to a US media audience prepared to distrust and dislike Italian immigrants long before Capone was born: "Official government studies and scholarly reports had identified them as prone to criminality, especially violent crime, and as strikebreakers opposing the labor movement in America."

Iorizzo reminds us that Capone's infamous career of crime, based on extortion, murder and who knows what other horrendous acts, actually ended through the commission of a white collar crime, one that "seldom leads to incarceration." In fact, as Iorizzo points out, the trial against Capone was built on intimidation and inaccuracies on the part of the US government. Capone, more a media made man, than any other of the infamous criminals, had to be stopped by any means. Once he stepped into the Chicago spotlight with a smile, everything bad that happened in that city was in some way attributed to him. Iorizzo tells of the role the infamous "Secret Six," played in nailing Capone. These rich Chicagoans financially backed the Chicago Crime Commission and supported the IRS; and once they had him in court, they wouldn't let him go.

Iorizzo provides us with a concise biography, the whole book including the index is no more than 130 pages, that includes a helpful timeline, a glossary of names and events, and a useful, though incomplete bibliography — for some reason the names of the books' publishers have not been included. But that's a small flaw that doesn't keep this book from being a necessary addition to every library. His writing is always clear and accessible to all. While the biography is primarily geared for young researchers who are usually drawn to such legendary criminal figures, it will serve the seasoned scholar well. I would rather have a young student find Iorizzo's book than any of the others. At least then he or she would see that being Italian was a fact of birth, and not something that factored into the making of the most famous gangster ever.

(*Voices in Italian Americana* 2005)

Luciano Iorizzo, *Al Capone: A Biography* (Westport, CT: Greenwood Press, 2003). ISBN 0313323178; $29.95 (hardcover).

Salvatore La Gumina

One investment that will definitely pay dividends for generations to come is *The Italian American Experience: An Encylopedia*. Created by the leading scholars in Italian American culture, this collection, edited by Salvatore J. LaGumina,

Frank J. Cavaioli, Salvatore Primeggia, and Joseph A. Varacalli, is the first, one-stop source for general information about America's Italians.

Over 160 contributors who compile a virtual who's who of Italian American studies have dedicated years of research for this volume. Experts in social sciences, humanities and sciences combine to make this quite a reliable resource. Beyond the usual shorter entries, the editors have included longer essays on such major topics as, the fine arts, discrimination, film, folklore, labor, language, literature, music, organizations, organized crime, religion, social class, theater, world wars, wine, and women in religion, work and transition. Each article is followed by a bibliography; Illustrated with photographs and important, easy-to-read tables, the volume is well indexed for easy location of information making it a convenient and useful reference tool.

Whether you're a student researching for a paper, an expert looking for background information, or just someone wanting to fill in blanks of knowledge about your culture, *The Italian American Encyclopedia* has something for you. This is the first comprehensive account of the Italian experience in the United States with hundreds of short biographies of invididuals from Catherine M. Abate to Joseph Zappulla (including such leading figures in the arts as Frank Sinatra, Joseph Stella, Connie Francis and Helen Barolini); More than 700 pages contain thousands of entries on topics big and small.

While the editors caution that this is not a perfect work, (their concept of America is restricted to the United States, leaving out the great populations of Canada and South and Latin Americas), you can be sure that this is a foundation upon which future scholars will depend as they reshape the world's knowledge of the experiences of America's Italians. There should be a copy of *The Italian American Experience* in every private and public library and in the home of anyone interested in the incredibly rich and complex story of the Americans of Italian descent.

(June 2001)

Salvatore La Gumina, et al, eds., *The Italian American Experience: An Encyclopedia* (New York: Garland, 200). www.garlandpub.com; ISBN 0815307136; $100 (hardcover).

&

If you've ever prayed to St. Anthony to help you find something you lost, or called out to any one of the hundreds of saints in time of need, then you'll want to make sure you take a look at a new book, *The Saints in the Lives of Italian Americans: An Interdisciplinary Investigation*.

The Saints explores the role that the saints have played and continue to play in Italian American culture. Edited by veteran scholars of Italian Americana, Joseph Varacalli and Salvatore LaGumina (Nassau Community College), Salvatore Primeggia (Adelphi University) and Donald D'Elia (SUNY at New Paltz), the volume contains fourteen essays that are accessible to most everyone.

The foreword by Mario Mignone of SUNY Stony Brook opens the door to the pre-Christian origins of the saints of Southern Italy. Varacalli's essay presents seven reasons for why saints should be studied today, and covers the ground from the insights we get to Italian culture to the understanding we can gain of assimilation to American culture.

Monsignor Stephen DiGiovanni's brief who's who of Italian saints and devotions is a good memory prompt. Mary Elizabeth Brown, Salvatore Primeggia, John Quinn, and Richard Renoff provide historical overviews that are must readings for anyone trying to see the general picture. LaGumina's contribution takes a look at the relationship between the saints and the suburbs of Long Island. More specific theological, psychological and philosophical analyses follow and lead into the most controversial essay of them all.

In "The Saints in the Lives of Italian-American Catholics: Toward a Realistic Multiculturalism," Varacalli goes after not only the WASP society that never really welcomed Italian Catholicism, but also, what he calls, "the radical multiculturalism among Italian-Americans" that "undermine[s] some of the key pillars of Italian-American... and American... life." His broad indictment of everything left of the Pope's right hand begs some specific finger pointing which might have turned his commentary into an argument.

Mary Elizabeth Brown's concluding bibliographical essay is a helpful guide to subject resources and a look to possibilities for future studies. Controversial and insightful, *The Saints* belongs in the personal as well as the public library.

(July 1999)

Salvatore La Gumina, et al., eds., *The Saints in the Lives of Italian Americans: An Interdisciplinary Investigation* (Stony Brook, NY: Forum Italicum, 1999). ISBN 1893127141; $20 (paperback).

&

When's the last time you were called a "wop" a "dago" a "guinea" to your face? Chances are a long time ago if at all, but these words once appeared regularly in the major media. Today we are more likely to find cases such as a professor in California who who has been, behind his back, publicly called a "dago radical" and a "wop" by his university's president.

Such behavior is inexcusable and no doubt fed by the more than a century of discrimination and prejudice against Italians in this country. For years I have been documenting arguments about this discrimination against Italian Americans from one book that was published in 1973. When I present these arguments, people, even Italian Americans, look at me like I made this stuff up. When I tell them where I got my evidence, they laugh in disbelief. Finally that documentation can be in the hands of everyone who has ever challenged my facts. I am referring to *Wop! A Documentary History of Anti-Italian Discrimination*.

Once again, Guernica editions has come to the rescue of another vital document of Italian/American history. This paperback publication of Salvatore J. La Gumina's commentary on the articles and excerpts he's compiled from major national publications is a rich resource that should be in every library in the world and in every Italian/American household.

Divided into seven sections, the entries proceed chronologically from "Pre-1880," to "The Maturation of Anti-Italianism" (1880–1890); two chapters covering the years (1890–1914) "Xenophobia During the High Tide of Italian Immigration" and "Roman Catholicism as an Obstacle to Assimilation;" "The Establishment's Solution to the 'Foreign Problem'" (1914–1930); Anti-Italianism in the Vortex of Economic and Political Turmoil (1930–1945)," and finally "The Post-World War II Period: Ongoing Problems."

LaGumina reproduces a few political cartoons that provide a good indication why we are still trying to shake the stereotypes planted more than a century ago. In such prominent places as the New York Times appeared outrageous and unsubstantiated claims such as: "Italians of the lower order have always distinguished themselves as beggars. They seem to beg, many of them for the pure pleasure of begging, and this national habit is extremely humiliating to the better classes."

Another entry from an article that appeared in the popular *Century Magazine* tells us:

> That the Mediterranean peoples are morally below the races of northern Europe is a certain as any social fact. Even when they were dirty, ferocious barbarians, these blonds were truth-tellers. Be it pride or awkwardness or lack of imagination of fair-play sense, something has held them back from the nimble lying of the Southern races.

These examples are among the tamer of the hundreds of article excerpts chosen by LaGumina to represent the incredible discrimination faced by Italians in this country. As good as this book is, I would be remiss if I didn't point out some of the problems with this second edition.

While LaGumina has provided preface which points to contemporary problems faced by Italian Americans, this republication should have been a great opportunity to update the bibliography, which LaGumina, a co-editor of the forthcoming *Italian American Encyclopedia* and Professor Emeritus of Nassau Community College in Long Island, should have at his fingertips. The volume's layout is inconsistent in terms of what's in and not in Italics which makes it difficult to tell where LaGumina's commentary ends and the original document begins. Another problem is that many of these entries are excerpts, so the original contexts are not there to consult.

These problems do not prohibit the use of any of the material gathered by LaGumina. *Wop!* is indispensable for future research. You get the feeling that this is just the surface of what's out there. You can't take too much of this at one sitting. It is not the kind of book you read from cover to cover. Sometimes just a few pages is enough to give you acida.

When you're feeling on top of the world, pick it up and it will remind you that you're probably standing on the shoulders of those in this book who've lifted you there.

(June 1999)

Salvatore La Gumina, *Wop! A Documentary History of Anti-Italian Discrimination* (Toronto: Guerinca Editions, 1999). ISBN 1550710478; $18 (hardcover).

Marisa Labozzetta

We last heard from Marisa Labozzetta a few years ago when she published her first novel, *Stay with Me, Lella,* which received good reviews. Now, her long awaited fiction follow-up appears in a story collection. From the title you might think that *At the Copa* has something to do with Manhattan night life, but none of the ten short stories have anything to do with nightclubs. A major theme throughout the collection is the difference between the inside and outside of the lives her characters lead in New England suburbs.

"When Michael is Away" is an anatomy of a relationship headed for a crash landing once a woman's husband returns home from one of his many trips. While he's gone, his wife tells us about the life she lives that he would abhor. The mantra-like repetition of the story's title throughout is key to building up a rhythm and a tension out of her everyday thoughts. The prose here sings a crazy song of impending independence.

The title story, "At the Copa," features Vita, who makes everyone's life better but her own. She had wanted to be a social worker, but listened to her mother and "So at thirty-nine, Vita was just as her mother had been: living with her mother, working as a seamstress." She's works at bathing suit factory called the Cabana Club. When Rosie the saleswoman doesn't show up one day, Vita excels beyond her everyone's expectations, but not her own, and in the end we get the sense that she is about to figure out what's been keeping her down all these years.

Most of the stories are set in suburbia with interesting twists. "The Knife Lady" explores a mother's fantasy as she imagines the life of the woman who has sold her an expensive set of knives. More predictable, yet quite interesting, is "Offsides" in which the author presents a soccer coach and reveals that his interest in coaching a young girls team goes deeper than teaching them to play the game, and "Future Games" in which a young girls learns to act like her deceiving parents.

In "Tooth Healer," a dentist takes a closer look at a preacher who supposedly can solve dental problems through the laying of hands. While he leaves thinking he has the proof that this guy's a phony, he encounters a woman in need who makes him realize that he can be just as manipulative with his scientific knowledge and ability to heal. "Making the Wine" presents a woman with a debilitating disease who has had to learn to depend on her husband for everything, and keeps him alive in her mind after his death.

Most of the stories here deftly explore the complex nature of relationships and debunk notions of true and everlasting love. Stories like "Surprise," "After Victory," and "Ticket to Ride," in different ways show how satisfaction doesn't always come through routine and loyalty. In most active minds there is always a longing that moves beyond what we've settled for and can take our lives in surprising directions. These stories do a great job in showing us that there's more to life than what we tell others, and that no matter how together our lives might be, there's always the possibility that something can unravel it all at any moment.

Even the most tragic stories float on a solid sense of humor that erupts now and then into a full scale belly laugh. Labozzetta is an astute observer of life who knows that outside of life's silver linings are roaring thunderstorms, hurricanes and all sorts of unpredictable phenomena.

(November 2007)

Maria Labozzetta, *At the Copa* (Tonawanda, NY: Guernica Editions, 2006). www.guernicaeditions.com; ISBN 1550712594; $18 (paperback).

&

In the early 1950s, when St. Christopher had his place on car dashboards, little Italys like Brooklyn's Bensonhurst were places where even an orphan could feel at home. This is the time and setting for *Stay With Me, Lella*, a first novel by Marissa Labozzetta, which centers around the DiGiacomo family. When the couple who adopted her die in a fire, ten-year old Stella Maglio is sent to live with Carla and Johnny DiGiacomo, and serves as a mother's helper.

Lella becomes a Cinderella of sorts, devoting her life to making the DiGiacomos' lives easier. She becomes a surrogate mother to the children, and lives her love life vicariously through Carla, who feels she was made for a better life than just being a traditional "Mamma Mia." As the author writes: "While the postwar boom of motherhood suited most women Carla's age, for Carla, parenting was a disillusionment."

Carla uses cigarette smoke as a way of irritating those who get in her way. Just as Carla struggles to find her way out from under the men in her life, Lella is busy trying to find her way into the lives of everyone; while Lella is picking up the pieces of the DiGiacomo home and nursing a terrible crush she has on Johnny, fate is dealing the DiGiacomos one ironic turn after another through public incidents and accidents.

Lella's story is based on the one she was told and a number of stories That get tangled up in hers. Somewhere in the midst of the rumors and the versions of truth lie the explanations; however, no story is quite as true as Lella thinks, and this makes for a series of interesting twists and turns.

Through the course of the novel, Lella becomes the catalyst through which everyone's emotions get filtered. She's there for the kids when their mother is distant; she's at Johnny's side when his wife isn't, and she's there for Dolores when she gets in trouble at school, and comforts Frankie as he grows up. All this makes for a bizarre series of events that reflects the fare real life often serves up.

Labozzetta gives us a good sense of New York Italian life in the 1950s and 60s. Stylistically she's at her best when delivering dialogue. As in life, what characters say is so rarely what should be said, and even more rarely is it reflected in what is done. Labozzeta's ear is keen and she creates characters with voices that make us turn our heads in recognition, both in joy and sorrow.

Against the strong dialogue, the novel's narration is uneven and often weak, as in this description of the neighborhood: "With fewer people on the street than on Johnny and Carla's block, it was quiet. Away from the bustling commercial end of the avenue, it boasted of a park on its corner, albeit cement paved." Labozzetta skills are better than this, and it makes you wonder if some of this just never got edited.

Ultimately, *Stay with Me Lella* never becomes more than a series of well-intentioned coming-of-age sketches in the life of a rather unique character. Labozzetta never decides what to do with the inner workings of Lella's mind, and so much of the story must come to us through a narrator who is sympathetic to a fault and who often seems to be an extension of Stella.

While couched in realism, the novel could serve as a folktale of sorts about a new kind of Italian/American woman, one who craves a traditional role but never gets the chance to have her own family. But the style and the substance set out by Labozzetta doesn't go far enough in any one direction to realize this possibility. Still, there is plenty of life in this work of fiction that should help the novel earn its way onto your autumn reading list.

(September 1999)

Marisa Labozzetta, *Stay With Me, Lella* (Toronto: Guernica, 1999). 1550710761; $13 (paper).

Victoria Lancelotta

Victoria Lancelotta's *Here in the World* contains 13 pieces of short fiction that you can't call stories in the traditional sense, but you've got to read them if you want to find out what's new in American fiction. While all of the selections disturb the usual world of storytelling, few of them disappoint. Lancelotta is a relatively new writer, though most of these fictions have seen print in major journals and reviews. She has developed a great ability to imagine a way to bring light into the darker recesses of our minds. Lancelotta's fictional worlds are macabre, not in the gothic or psychic but in the physical sense. She has a talent for conjuring up haunting everyday images in the backyard, the bedroom (usually in or out of windows), or in the kitchen. In "Festival" and "Nice Girl" we see the ability of memory to indict and convict those who destroy innocents and mould the guilty.

A slight hint of the author's ethnicity comes through mostly in food scenes or a grandmother sitings, as in "Spice" and "The Gift." Lancelotta's narrators often come up with words of wisdom that make us all nod and wished we'd have thought of things like: "In bars, 'possibility' becomes concrete, tangible with the power of faith. The air is thick with it. We all believe that we will leave somehow better than when we came, more real, more solid — that we will inhabit the world with a greater density, that someone will look at us and make us something new." Lancelotta makes fiction new and exciting in this collection that is a bright omen for a young talent.

(October 2001)

Victoria Lancelotta, *Here in the World* (Washington, DC: Counterpoint, 2000). ISBN 1582430993; $23 (hardcover).

Maria Laurino

"Were you always an Italian?" once asked Mario Cuomo of Maria Laurino, author of a collection of essays which now bears that question as its title. Cuomo, in his witty way, was being critical of Laurino's ambivalence about her Italian ancestry. And while the author shook her head no, she has since used that occasion as to come to terms with her Italian ancestry.

Perhaps a better question for Cuomo to have asked might have been, What kinds of Italian have you been? The essays in this book, subtitled "Ancestors and Other Icons of Italian America," all feature a different stage in Laurino's development from being self-conscious to being in touch with the sub-conscious of what it means to call oneself an Italian American.

The nine essays, many of them occasional and previously published in a variety of mainstream venues, combine cultural history, travel sketches, feature journalism, and personal meditations to present the evolution of a consciousness shaped by shame and ignorance and changed by the knowledge and confidence that comes with age and experience.

The longer essays are framed by two at the beginning and end that are both called "Beginnings." This should be the first indication that we are invited to observe the development of an identity that will continue to change long after this book has gone paperback. All the essays serve as charms on a literary bracelet, each with its own cache of memories that say one thing to the author and often something quite different to the reader.

As though to antagonize, if not confuse the issue of representation of Italian Americana, Laurino has *Sopranos* creator David Chase backcover-blurb the book. Chase's reaction shows his own unfamiliarity with the great literature produced by earlier Italian Americans and sets up a reason to and a way of reading the essays in their printed order.

In the earlier essays, especially "Scents," "Tainted Soil," "Clothes," and "Rome," Laurino reveals her position deep in the shallow end of Italian culture. In these we find an identity built on the fear of being connected to the "Ginzo Gang" boys who, "Olive-skinned and muscular... were sexy in their crudeness; and their faint gasoline scent and oiled-down hair defined the image of Italian Americans in our school."

Her inability to translate a native Italian's pronunciation of the word "ships," which she reads as "sheeps," reveals a lack of contact with the contemporary Italy and a knowledge of things Italian that has yet to transcend the Armani, Versace, and Gucci shops. Her discussion of ethnic self hatred and cultural misunderstandings come close to Marianna DeMarco Torgovnick's similar laments in "Crossing Ocean Parkway;" however, Laurino finds a way to use her past to reinvent herself as a strong Italian American woman.

The best writing comes toward the end. "Bensonhurst," "Work," and "Ancestors" are both heartfelt, head strong, and stylistically sound. Sentences like "Rage has found a secure home under the shingled roofs of Bensonhurst's row houses" and "But my identity as an Italian-American of southern Italian descent can now be based on actual heritage, not on what I wanted to be, whether an eastern European Jew in high school or northern Italian later in life," evidence how much she grows as a writer as the essays progress. It is as though she is sculpting her very identity out of words and the more she works, the better she sees and is seen.

The book is really a journey from the outside in, from the superficial concerns with how Italian looks on the body to how it sees from the soul. The later essays do not have the earlier whiny tone that comes with the naivete, but Laurino could have most definitely benefited by earlier consultation with the writings of Diane Di Prima, Helen Barolini, Louise DeSalvo and the critical studies of Mary Jo Bona and Gloria Nardini, writers who have considered similar issues before her and successfully created ways of defining Italian American culture that defy earlier attempts. In this way the talents of this fine writer would have been challenged to push Italian American-ness to even more complex levels of meaning.

(December 2001)

Maria Laurino, *Were You Always an Italian: Ancestors and Other Icons of Italian America* (New York: Norton, 2000). www.wwnorton.com; ISBN 0393049302; $23.95 (hardcover).

Frank Lentricchia

Frank Lentricchia's strange, new novel defies much of what can be called traditional and all of what is known as commercial fiction. *Lucchesi and the Whale* is really an anti-story that makes for tough, but rewarding reading, especially if you are familiar with American literature.

In his acknowledgements Lentricchia points to a few academic studies, novels by Don DeLillo, and Herman Melville's *Moby-Dick* as sources of his inspiration for this new, macabre tale of a strange academic's search for truth. No doubt the tendency for some readers familiar with Lentricchia's criticism will be to dwell on the critical end of the Lentricchia literary spectrum and not welcome his as a fiction writer. But with this work especially, Lentricchia shows us that there's no writer like a reader, and few readers are as thoroughly literary as he.

The center of the fiction is one Thomas Lucchesi, an academic personality, all wrapped up in his writing. Lucchesi talks mostly to himself, and when he does speak to others, it's as though he is lecturing. Through this character Lentricchia presents us with what has become common in his fiction, a man alone in the world. He observes the fractured portions of his life as they crash into each other, as though he viewed his world through a kaleidoscope.

Lucchesi and the Whale is the best of what can be called the anti-novels. There is no plot, nothing that would artificially jump-start a reading binge of this 113-page fiction. While we can't call it a novel, it is a novel approach to writing. What Lentricchia offers is writing that liberates the reader from the leash-like tuggings of plot. This writing is a story in itself.

Lucchesi opens with a section entitled, "The Nostalgic Man in Crisis." Here we meet Thomas Lucchesi, a man with a peculiar condition; he is with book. When he can't write, he can't breathe, that's when he seeks inspiration in the strangest places. Sometimes he finds it at the bedside of the dying, mostly his close friends, but he'll take any dying acquaintance in a pinch. By confronting others' deaths, he defies his own, and in that moment gains enough power to fuel a few writing sessions.

The following section, "High Blood Pleasure," presents the origins of Lucchesi the artist and includes a fabulous "sit-down" section with the gangster Thomas "Three Finger Brown" Lucchese, who serves as the artist's distorted reflection in an ethnic mirror. In "Writer in Residence" Lucchesi is dismissed from his college teaching and confesses "I have not much enjoyed life outside the page."

Without a job, Lucchesi is able to devote his time to "Chasing Melville," the name of the next section which presents a wild reading of the famous "portly tome of prose fiction." Like Melville, Lucchesi is made of books. Both authors share the great burden of the heavy whiteness, symbolized by the great whale, that haunts every reading/writing moment of their existence. Somewhere in the fog of his reading he finds what he believes is the great novel's secret meaning.

In "Sex and Wittgenstein," Lucchesi, an "amateur philosopher," constantly risks absurdity as he stalks B.F. Norman, a "distinguished American scholar of [Ludwig] Wittgenstein" who finds Lucchesi to be "darkly gifted." The same can be said for Lentricchia whose wordplay on the dark side of the mind forges a new way of reading and writing.

We have seen the dark side emerge in his previous fictions, but in this new work, we come to understand that like Edgar Alan Poe, Lentricchia is fascinated with the grotesque, and *Lucchesi and the Whale* takes us into the grottos where secret artists once practiced their trade by light of fire, where visions come to loners and sacred visitations to the holy.

(April 2001)

Frank Lentricchia, *Lucchesi and the Whale* (Durham, NC: Duke UP, 2001). www.dukeupress.edu; ISBN 082232654X; $17.95 (hardcover).

&

In *The Music of the Inferno,* Robert Tagliaferro, an orphan child of unknown racial background makes a grim discovery shortly after his eighteenth birthday causing him to leave his hometown of Utica, New York. The young man takes refuge in a bookstore in New York City. There, he reads his way through the shelves and through his life as he maintains the store. His book learning replaces his family, as he tells us: "In the absence of my father, I acquired knowledge. My knowledge is my memory."

Robert becomes a composite of all that he's absorbed through his studies. Along the way he has kept notebooks, "containing in a minute script illegible to all but himself the fruits of forty-two years of research in the history of Utica and New York state, from the coming of the Dutch to the present." Forty-two years later, he returns to Utica, where the people do not read books, to put that memory to use.

A man who knows the past, who knows what has been erased, repressed, or forgotten, can be a very dangerous man, especially when he has been hurt by those who have created the history he has studied. Robert, who sees himself as, "An ethnic freak in this fair city of such clear ethnic divisions," has, "come back to return the pain."

Going home can be hell, and in this revision of returning Lentricchia penetrates the dark recesses of a Little Italy to reveal the sins of Utica's "immigrant merchant princes" who have shaped the city's economy and thus, its history. In the process Robert begins to change everyone's sense of Utica's past. He meets Alex Lucas, who should have been Alessandro Lucca, grandson of one of the original Italian immigrants whose behavior brought the family enough shame to make them change their name.

Lucas helps Robert (hiding behind a new name), connect to the town's leading Italians and secures him an invitation to the group's regular dinner meeting. The group includes men like Albert Cesso, Professor Louis Ayoub, Sebastian Spina, decendants from Utica's first immigrants; these contemporary powerbrokers meet in Joe's cellar with a gangster boss named Paternostra whom everyone calls, behind his back, "Our Mother."

The sights conjured in this inferno are gruesome and, as those in the great work of Dante, are directly connected to the sinners actions. The novel brings us a vision of darkness that is as exhilarating as it is disturbing; it is the destruction, if not the deconstruction, of the mafioso prototype, and the destroyer is the intellectual, "a man made of words."

The Music of the Inferno, an unconventional tale by Frank Lentricchia, author of the autofiction *The Edge of Night*, and the novellas *Johnny Critelli* and *The Knifemen*, doubles as a paen to the creators of the conventional canon. Here you can find verbal monuments to Lentricchia's literary heroes. There's word play inspired by James Joyce, a dark cloud that hovers over each scene that could have come out of the heart of Joseph Conrad, and the dramatic persistence of Samuel Beckett. The sentence structure, which often eliminates, while implying, the subject, comes across like stage directions. At times they go on like Faulkner, or stop short of breath, like Edgar Allen Poe.

Beyond the setting, Utica contributes much to the making of *The Music of the Inferno*. The illustrations and ink sketches (including a map of East Utica) were created by Robert Cimbalo, Lentricchia's boyhood friend and art teacher at Utica

College; the typesetting and covers printed in Utica.

This is a book about the end of a world, about the relevance of books, of the place of modernism in a postmodern world, about the matter of facts and the purpose of ethnic identity. The inferno of Joe's Restaurant rewrites the hells of Dante, Milton, and Sartre, so that hell becomes the way the past sits in your mind. Redemption happens only through the revolutionary act of revising without reliving that past.

(December 1999)

Frank Lentricchia, *The Music of the Inferno: A Novel* (Albany: SUNY P, 1999). www.sunypress.edu; ISBN 0791443477 (hardcover); 0791443485 (paperback); $24.50 (hardcover).

Billy Lombardo

Winner of the G.S. Sharat Chandra Prize for Short Fiction, *The Logic of a Rose* brings together eight Chicago stories by Billy Lombardo, and all but the title story have appeared in such publications as *Story Quarterly, Other Voices,* and *River Oak Review.*

Lombardo tells new stories about the old Chicago Bridgeport neighborhood of the 1970s, home of the mayor, Chicago White Sox, Dressel's bakery and the Bellapani family. Petey, along with his mother and father, who delivers for Dressel's on the weekends, is the focus of most of the stories, and his coming of age in the city is as good as any you've read before. At his best, Lombardo reads like a nice Nelson Alrgen; he creates a character whose wisdom comes not from the tough breaks in life, but from breaking through the tough things life throws his way. Everyone, whether suburban or city bred can relate to these meditations on ordinary occurrences.

When you belong to the working class, your job is you and mostly what you have to talk about. But Lombardo's characters are always more than their jobs. Learning how to work, how to do things the right way, whether it's mopping a floor or delivering papers is a training ground for learning to live right.

A first-sucker punch in the stomach, the accidental hurting of a playmate, the reactive violence, the terror of a fire out of control and the peace of a neighbor's welcome, are all portrayed by Lombardo with the patience of a painter of miniatures. "Nickels" will take you back to the times when kids and adults pitched pennies and everyone kept an eye out for neighbors' kids. "Blessed is the Fruit" uses the life and death of a cherry tree planted by the neighbors, the Romanos, to explain how old cultures can renew and old neighborhood. When "The Wallace Playlot," where boys can be boys without parents around, disappears one summer, no one is there to save the neighborhood from the new housing that will change it forever.

In "The Hills of Laura" we learn that there are things in life that one must experience even if it's only through others. With "Mrs. Higgins's Heart and the Smell of Fire," Lombardo masters the way sensory perception gives birth to language; smells are stories and the fire of Dressel's bakery, which destroys Petey's family apartment and nearly takes them with it, leaves them with a story to tell and a smell that won't let them forget it

The title story, "The Logic of a Rose," a beautiful account of first love and how a strange birthmark can turn in to a treasure. In "The Thing about Swing" we move away from Petey, though we might see the protagonist of this story as Petey later in life. College boy Danny has a system for washing his clothes in the local laundromat that works well until a co-ed interferes. Danny and the girl check each other out only to realize that this is not the first time they have met.

The Logic of a Rose: Chicago Stories is a refreshingly new look at a way of living that has shaped a whole generation. Lombardo's prose is flawlessly disciplined so that what it doesn't give you, you learn to take from it. Endings, for example, are frayed, the way life really is. There are no neatly knotted bows atop these stories. And while you may have lived all this before, you haven't read it the way Lombardo tells it.

(November 2005)

Billy Lombardo, *The Logic of a Rose: Chicago Stories* (Kansas City, MO: BkMk P, 2005). http://cas.umkc.edu/bkmk/; ISBN 1886157502; $15.95 (paperback).

Martino Marazzi

Like the early Little Italy detective characters he has written about, Martino Marazzi has uncovered the mystery of some of the earliest writings by Italians living in the US. *Voices of Italian America: A History of Early Italian American Literature with a Critical Anthology*, is a treasure of the sometimes lost, but more often ignored, writings by Italian Americans. This book begins to fill a long-ignored void in the area of immigrant writing in Italian in the United States.

Essentially, *Voices* is a translation of his earlier study *Misteri di Little Italy*, but it is more valuable than its earlier incarnation as it includes more research and, most exciting of all, original writings with some translations from the Italian. Marazzi's original Italian has been adeptly translated by Ann Goldstein; thanks to her some of the earliest literature produced by Americans of Italian descent is, for the first time ever, made available to those who do not read Italian.

There are writers new and old, famous and forgotten. Anthology sections that contain samples of each author discussed follow Marazzi's essays, and each author is properly introduced. These sections contain examples from the great mystery stories of Bernadino Ciambelli and Menotti Pellegrino, along with works most experts in the field have yet to see. The essays and introductions provide us with a context through which we can better understand each selection. Here we find obscure writers such as Dora Colonna and Caterina Avella, Italo Stanco, and many, many more. Section titles are: "The Novel of the Italian in America," "Stowaway on Board: Ezio Taddei," "The New World of the Second Generation: Pietro di Donato and John Fante," "Poetry of Italian Americans," "Prose of Testimony: The Color Line," "At Ellis Island," and "Italian Americans and American Writers."

Marazzi found new material to include by well known writers John Fante and Pietro di Donato. Most interesting in the collection is a number of works written from a proletarian perspective. We know the poetry of Arturo Giovannitti and Ricardo Cordiffero, but what about the verse of Simplicio Righi, Efrem Baroletti, and Alfredo Borgianini? Thanks to Marazzi, these voices can now enter into discussions of our Italian American pasts.

Perhaps the most original section is "Prose of Testimony: The Color Line," in which Marazzi presents a powerful essay that collects racial references he found in some of these early writings. He includes a rather controversial article in which Giuseppe Prezzolini, a professor of Italian at Columbia University in the 50s and 60s, analyzes black/white relations in the US.

Above all Marazzi is an excellent literary detective and journalist. This work will no doubt enable the development of serious criticism on this earliest of Italian American literature. Here we have the work that is essentially the foundations of all the earlier studies of Italian American writing. He has found what other scholars have either missed or avoided. *Voices of Italian America* is a must purchase for all libraries, and required reading for all scholars in the area of Italian and Italian American studies; it is also something that could be used in advanced high school, undergraduate and graduate classrooms that deal with immigrant and especially Italian American immigrant literatures. Beyond the obvious academic service he's done, Marazzi, has put together a superb collection of stories, novel excerpts, journalism and poetry that will serve the general reader as well as the student and scholar.

(March 2005)

Martino Marazzi, *Voices of Italian America: A History of Early Italian American Literature with a Critical Anthology*, transl. Ann Goldstein (Madison: Fairleigh Dickinson UP, 2004). ISBN 0838640168; $55 (hardcover).

Leo Luke Marcello

What Leo Luke Marcello captures in *Nothing Grows in One Place Forever: Poems of a Sicilian American,* a collection of sixty poems, is the essence of how immigrant culture evolves into ethnic culture. His carefully crafted poems chart the stages of assimilation and its impact on his personal and professional lives with bittersweet passion.

Marcello, a native of Louisiana and professor in the Department of Languages of McNeese State University, is the author of *The Secret Proximity of Everywhere, Blackrobe's Love Letters,* and *Silent Film.* He has earned such awards as the Shearman Fellowship, a Shearman Endowed Professorship, a grant from the Louisiana Endowment for the Humanities and the Deep South Writers' Competition. His new book is a major contribution to Italian American literature.

Nothing Grows in One Place Forever serves as a poetic memoir. Most of the poems are united by powerful themes of Sicilian immigrant culture. Divided into six sections, it opens with "Immigrants" which presents a family's founding myths through poetic snap shots of immigrant ancestors. "Anna and the Great Storm," a powerful narrative poem in nine parts, tells of how grandmother Anna had crossed the ocean as a child by herself, leading her brother and sisters, of how she survived the great Galveston hurricane of 1900, of "The Ax Man's" destruction, and of Anna own death.

In "Family History" we're given glimpses of the interactions of a nuclear family, a father's burning leaves and walk though an old Italian deli, a mother's life in cameo stills, a brother's lost ring, memories of a sister — all remind us that a scattered family must rely on the past to continue relationships, as Marcello tells us in "Among Cherry Blossoms": "Things happen/ We grow old in different cities,/ our lives filling to the brim./ We didn't foresee the hard miles,/ the wrinkled years and scarred hearts, maps creased and refolded into fringe,/ or the joy of the longed-for and found."

In "Relatives and Friends," the poet moves the storytelling outside the home and into the neighborhood where everyday events of uncles and aunts and neighbors become monumental memories of snowcones and St. Joseph Days gone by. "Students in Worlds That No Longer Exist," bring us a look at people from a more professional perspective, and in "Love Lessons," we get poetic observations on everyday occurrences. The final section, "Last Words," seems to be a category for what might seem to be miscellaneous poems that don't fit the collection's theme, but it actually contains one of the poet's most powerful poems.

The last lines of "A Fig Tree" are a powerful comment on the impact that immigration has on future generations: "plant your own cutting wherever you want, / ... nothing grows in one place forever" is the advice an uncle gives to his nephew. This uncle serves as a bridge between his immigrant grandparents and the more

Americanized generation of his children. As such, he becomes the historian who preserves the past and the storyteller who ignites the imagination of new generations.

In a simple language, with carefully formed lines, Marcello crafts poetry reminiscent of the great work of Joseph Tusiani and Felix Stefanile who know that careful observation is powerful interpretation. The strongest imagination depends on the input of sensory perceptions, and whether he's grating cheese or waiting in a café, the poet's busy turning the objective into the subjective, the other into the self.

The result is the creation of a poetry that shows how an individual shaped by a culture can grow with the power to reshape that culture into something new. If culture finds stability in place, then perhaps the new place for Italian/American culture resides in the land of ideas, of art, of imagination, and the work of Leo Marcello will help us all feel at home in this new land.

(November 1999)

Leo Luke Marcello, *Nothing Grows in One Place Forever: Poems of a Sicilian American* (St. Louis, MO: time Being Books, 1998). www.timebeing.com; ISBN 15680 90366 (hardcover); 1568090374 (paperback); $22.00 (hardcover); $14.50 (paperback).

Elizabeth Messina

If you thought you knew the Italian American women at all, you've got another think coming when you pick up *In Our Own Voices*. Elizabeth Messina has gathered an incredible array of leading thinkers of Italian American culture into one powerful volume. This publication contains criticism and scholarship that speaks to a wide variety of disciplines covering Italian and Italian American cultures; sociology, psychology, history, literature, art, film, and anthropology are all well represented by excellent essays on topics as diverse as labor studies, literature, stereotypes, and joke-telling.

After a thorough introduction by Messina that provides an historical and social orientation to the works included, we get 19 essays and 2 interviews, all of which represent the leading edge of intellectual thought about the cultural and historical work done by and about Italian and Italian American women. Not since Helen Barolini's *The Dream Book,* have we had such a diverse collection of critical voices dealing with the exploration of what it meant, means, and will mean to be Italian and Italian American women.

Messina divides the book into eight sections. "Women and Social Resistance" features two essays that recover important moments in the history of Italy that have been overlooked in traditional sources. Laura E. Ruberto's essay on northern Italian women rice workers and their relationship to work and the partisan efforts and Elda Gentili Zappi's look at women during the great Risorgimento, serve as apt entries to the typically ignored history of Italian women. "Sexism, Racism, and the Law," features Mary Gibson's compelling essay on the incarceration of Italian women during the turn of the 19th century and two informative essays on the famous figure of Maria Barbella, an child of immigrants who was the first woman to be sentenced to die in the electric chair. In "Italian American as Geneological Archivists," we get Michele Fazio's wonder into her family's silence around Raimondo Fazio, a radical activist and Rudolph Vecoli's documentary of the facts surrounding this controversial figure who's story was lost for years until Fazio started asking questions.

One of the strongest sections of the book is "Italian American Women's Literary History," which contains new essays by leading scholars in the field including Josephine Gattuso Hendin and Mary Jo Bona, and the innovative work of Annette Wheeler Cafarelli that brings attention to the loss of history as she recovers some of that overlooked past. These are all required reading for anyone doing work on Italian American women writers. The following section, "Italian Women and Their Literary History," features an historical essay by Antonia Arslan and a powerful, more personal, consideration of southern Italian women writers.

At the book's center is "Italian American Women Artists," featuring beautiful color plates of some of the works discussed in an essay written by sculptor Nanzy Azara, painter Joanne Mattera and art historian Flavia Rando. "Cinematic Representations" includes Robert Marchesani's notes on the mother-son relationship in Italian culture as portrayed by poet and filmmaker Pier Paolo Pasolini and documented in the *60 Minutes'* piece on "Mammoni" along with Dawn Esposito's look at the Italian American women in the films of Spike Lee. We also get two interviews, with critic Camille Paglia and filmmaker Christine Nochese. The final section, "Gender, Ethnicity and Bella Figura," brings us Gloria Nardini's study of joke telling in the women's auxiliary of an Italian American Club, Mary Ann Amannino's study of women and community in fiction, and memoirst Flavia Alaya's exploration of America's love-hate relationship with the Italian immigrants and their evolution into *The Sopranos*. All in all, there's enough new thought here to take up hours of great reading and thinking. Messina is to be applauded heartily for gathering such diversity in one place.

Elizabeth Messina, ed., *In Our Own Voices: Multidisciplinary Perspectives on Italian and Italian American Women* (Boca Raton, FL: Bordighera P, 2003). ISBN 1884419585; $25 (paperback).

Ben Morreale

Sicily: The Hallowed Land is a tricky memoir of novelist and historian Ben Morreale. Best known for *La Storia* — a history of Italian America he wrote with the late Jerre Mangione — Morreale breaks the rules of the traditional memoir by taking us beyond the life of one man to recount the lives of Don Baldassare's offspring. Born in Racalmuto, Sicily, Baldassare, the author's grandfather and namesake, is the origin of this history that spans a century and two continents.

After an opening in first person which sets up the historical evolution of Sicily and his role as a participant observer of the story he is telling, Morreale, once accused of creating a novel that was "more Anthropology than a novel," shifts into a third-person narration that is more like a novel than the typical memoir. In this way, the author can step back and let us see things before he was born. He can use information gathered by others to recreate scenes he could never have witnessed.

In "Point of Departure" we come to know Raffaelli, the only one of Don Baldassare's family not to come to America and through him the story "The Time of the Green Mice," when times got so rough that hungry people began to hallucinate. That un-fed hunger drove them away from their homes like refugees in wartime. Those who lost their jobs at the faltering sulphur mines, those who gave up on the Fasci Siciliani, headed for the one land that promised good pay for hard work.

In "Don Baldassare," Morreale presents the struggles of a family of some means to come to terms with forces larger than themselves which were driving them like winds to places they never dreamed of. Morreale uses traditional songs of work, of protest, of prayer, to demonstrate the rugged responses of workers as they struggled to keep their families fed and together.

Those familiar with Morreale's earlier writings will find the historical counterparts to the material used in his novel *Monday, Tuesday, Never Come Sunday* in the sections entitled "Lu Rabbi Schwartz," which deal with the family's early attempts to assilimate in New York's lower east side neighborhood called "lu Vaticanu." Bennie's godfather, Don Arrigo, we first saw in the novel *A Few Virtuous Men*.

Joy and grief, the search for work, for shelter, the traditional customs of Sicilian wakes and funerals and dealings with the evil are all recreated in "'*Malanni*' or Hard Times." The book is peopled with characters such as Bastiano through which we are shown how pro-Fascist sympathies were cultivated and manifested in the immigrant colonies. "The Depression hastened the assimilation of Sicilians. The families from Racalmuto were no exception. Hard times made them give up the idea of ever returning to Sicily. They were in America to stay. The malanni had to be accomodated to in an American way."

The author's two identities, as Baldassare DeMarco Morreale and Benny Moreli, is the difference between Sicily and the United States, the true subject of this memoir. Once called "the hollow land" by a Greek geographer because of how fertile it was, Sicily becomes, in Morreale's hand, full of stories that are as explanatory for the individual as they are puzzling for the people.

> Sicily was fading, was not part of these impressionable years. Sicily remained behind in an age of innocence, a land without the disturbances of puberty and because of its innocence, it took on an aura of wholeness, the purity of a lost world. America became reality, reason, materialism. Siciily took on an importance which, as Sciascia was to remark later, "his parents never invested in it."

The memoir closes with a dialogue between Bennie and Turiddru Sinatra who claims he is famous Frank's cousin. Entitled "Ava Gardner's Brother-in-Law," this final section shifts from the reportage to a more philosophic argument ala Plato: This debate of what is better life in Sicily or in the US is really an argument within the author, who enriched by both cultures is unable to align himself with one more than the other.

There's only one complaint: *Sicily* could have used one more screening by the copy editor to eliminate the irritating, but not fatal, errors that occasionally halt the flow of the narrative. Other than that we have an interesting stretch of a memoir to add to the growing story of Sicilians in the US.

(September 2000)

Ben Morreale, *Sicily, the Hallowed Land: A Memoir* (Brooklyn, NY: Legas, 2000). ISBN 1881901238; $18 (paperback).

&

The Loss of the Miraculous by Ben Morreale is a rich meditation on the the ways we win and lose love in our lives. The ideal contemplated in the writing is the balance between sensual and spiritual, between the mixed up world of free love in the United States and the straight-laced romantic spirit of Sicily in which public behavior in the pursuit of love is shaped by centuries of tradition.

Lacking a traditional plot, the novel forms as 117 lyrical entries built around the lives of the narrator, a few of his buddies, and a mysterious Sicilian painter as they all encounter one woman whose independence both turns her into an object of desire and an agent of despair. Jean is a woman who the narrator tells us, "at twenty-three had lived a dozen lives of anyone in my Mediterranean town, and because of her unawareness of her own gluttony for life, had harmed and transformed everyone she touched." As the needle that guides the narrative thread, she unites disparate elements through her search for satisfaction.

In his latest novel, Morreale abandons the traditional forms of his earlier works and weaves threads of stories. These carefully crafted pastoral portraits, mystery vignettes and allusive anecdotes, create visions and versions of physical and spiritual love in the United States and Sicily of the 1960s and 70s, two worlds that have contrasted in nearly all of Morreale's writings.

Morreale is a novelist, playwright and professor Emeritus of State University of New York in Plattsburgh. Born in Manhattan, in what is now known as the Roosevelt Park area on New York's lower east side, his parents came from Racalmuto, a small town near Agrigento in Sicily. His mother's people were poor farmers and his father's side of the family were impoverished sulfur mine owners. Turn-of-century accidents and a steep drop of sulfur prices forced the whole family to emigrate. But they'd often return to Sicily and much of Morreale's sense of life comes from the experiences of two diverse cultures.

Morreale's first novel, *The Seventh Saracen* (1958) tells the story of a Sicilian American's return to the birthplace of his parents. *A Few Virtuous Men*, his second novel, published in 1973 and translated into Italian, was a literary thriller about Sicily and what it is like to live on the other side of the Mafia. *Monday Tuesday Never Come Sunday* (1977) is about growing up Sicilian in Brooklyn."

In *The Loss*, Morreale paints two parallel worlds, which while separated by oceans live together in the mind of the narrator who is in a quandary about how to deal with love. Raised in a Mediterranean town, where expression and fantasy are curtailed by prescribed codes, the narrator is exposed to the unleashed urges of his friends in their attempts to satisfy sexual appetites without destructive consequences.

Caught between two different cultures, the narrator wonders: "Can there be lyricism in a town where there are no donkeys, mules or horses — in a town where there are no animals but pets?" Made from experiences in both worlds, and belonging to neither, the narrator hovers between the two, commenting on the action in both. This is a great device that enables us to understand both in cultures new ways. The ideal contemplated is the balance between sensual and spiritual, between the mixed up world of free love in the United States and the straight-laced romance of Sicily in which public behavior is shaped by centuries of tradition.

The Loss of the Miraculous, published shortly after the death of Ben's own love Linda Rogers Morreale, is filled with wisdom ancient and new as it touches many sign posts on the road of life. When an old friend of the narrator falls for the young Jean, the narrator mediates on the process of aging: "memory remains, a seed blown from mind to mind and place to place, to skip along the gloss of time, to stretch and break, to settle in the kitchen light among the tables and chairs and waits to bloom." For Morreale, these seeds blossom into fields of story.

It is thoughts in words such as these that make Morreale's contribution to the literature of love unique as he makes us all see love in a different light: "Love is a promise, love is a hope, love is hope of growing better to perfection, love is a willingness to sacrifice, love is an expectation that death will be conquered."

Since most of his earlier work is out of print, this novel might be your introduction a wonderful American storyteller.

(June 1997)

Ben Morreale, *The Loss of the Miraculous* (Toronto: Guernica Editions, 1997). ISBN 1550710192; $13 (paperback).

GLORIA NARDINI

In *"Che Bella Figura!" The Power of Performance in an Italian Ladies' Club in Chicago*, Gloria Nardini, a lecturer at the University of Illinois at Chicago, describes and analyzes the activities of the Colandia Club (a pseudonym for a real Italian American club). Nardini gathered her information while serving as the club's recording secretary, but this recorder took more than just the minutes of meetings. As a participant and observer Nardini launched a unique study of the role that "fare figura" plays in the way Italians behave in public.

Nardini contends that at work in the interaction of this bilingual and bicultural women's club, are many "communicative strategies" that have not previously been explored. She suggests that by understanding how the idea of "fare bella figura" works, we can better understand how women "indirectly assert themselves in order to claim power." Her work here helps turn outsiders into insiders, and contributes to the better understand of how being Italian makes one a different type of American.

The opening chapter is her greatest contribution to the understanding of the impact Italian culture has on those who immigrated to the United States. In it she explores the notion of "fare bella figura." Nardini has scoured dictionaries old and new and brings us ideas from authors dead and living to arrive at a working definition of this code of Italian behavior.

Most of the book is dedicated to the description and analysis of a single meeting in which the women's auxiliary of the group confronts the president of the men's association. By isolating this single event, Nardini reveals the cultural drama that can appear in everyday encounters and teaches us it means to be an Italian living in America. This meeting, according to Nardini, "can be viewed as an especially public performance of 'bella figura.'"

"*Che Bella Figura*" is a slight revision of Nardini's doctoral dissertation, and as such it still speaks more clearly to its original audience. The jargon of the field might be an obstacle for some, as readers are expected to know words such as "emic" and "etic." But these are found mostly in the book's second chapter in which Nardini presents the framework of her study and connects it to earlier work done in relevant academic disciplines. You can skim this chapter and still learn much about the way "bella figura" is constructed and maintained from the others.

The reader may wonder why Nardini doesn't see these participants as Italian Americans, in spite of the fact that the club's "State of Purpose" urges its members to "cooperate in worthy endeavors fostering of a spirit of civic pride" that will "preserve the American traditions to which the club is committed." What's Italian, what's Italian American is difficult to separate, but she does so without much hesitation. But no matter what you may think and how you might argue with the ideas, the material is always clearly presented.

"Che Bella Figura!" is written in a lively and always engaging style in a strong, authoritative voice. Nardini's insights into reading Italian women's culture through language and behavior are remarkably unique. She provides an excellent demonstration of the analysis of how language and culture work together to reveal the strange in the familiar, and teaches how to locate the drama in the mundane.

Most importantly, Nardini's study enlarges our notions of "bella figura," and opens the way for future applications to Italian American culture. It also expands our awareness of how indirection is used in Italian culture to maintain and monitor one's "figura." *"Che Bella Figura"* has broken new ground and has paved the way for others to examine the role that "bella figura" plays in the expression of Italian culture in America. It will be interesting to see how others employ Nardini's ideas to explore the uses of "figura" in music, literature, film, theater and other cultural products.

(July 1999)

Gloria Nardini, *"Che Bella Figura!": The Power of Performance in an Italian Ladies' Club in Chicago* (Albany, NY: SUNY P, 1999). www.sunypress.edu; ISBN 07914 40915 (hardback); 0791440923 (paperback).

Michael Palma

They say it takes a poet to translate poetry, but until now, it's been tough to find the poetry of award-winning translator Michael Palma. Palma's work as a translator is well known. His translations of over 150 Italian poems have appeared in major journals like *Paris Review, Grand Street,* and *Poetry,* and in a number of anthologies. He's co-edited *New Italian Poet* with Dana Gioia, and the poetry of Luciano Erba with Alfredo de Palchi. His current work includes translations of Dante's *Inferno* and the poetry of Franco Buffoni and Paolo Valesio.

It's not that Palma hasn't published his poetry. On the contrary, his work has appeared in journals and collected in two chapbooks, *The Egg Shape* and *Antibodies.* But finally, with *A Fortune in Gold,* we have an entire volume of Palma's own poetry. What Palma does best is play with words in a memorable way. Even in the most challenging of poems, on the most serious of subjects, Palma never let's us forget that he is playing with a language we thought we all knew so well. And after reading Palma we get to know it just a little bit better.

A Fortune in Gold contains over forty poems divided into three sections. The first presents some of the lighter fare, the second, the more bizarre, or what I call the bawdy and bloody lyrical, and the third, the more historical narratives.

The poems, all done up in formalist attire, cover a variety of subjects traditional and not, in moods ranging from serious to downright silly. Palma's poetry rhymes and when it doesn't, it still sings like poetry used to. Equally adept at depicting the real in "Cats" who "love themselves with your hand," and the surreal in "The Patron Saint of California" who "Wears both of his eyes/On one side of his face," Palma is exceptional at placing the bizarre alongside the normal as he does so well in "With Boughs of Holly," a twisted Christmas ballad.

Blood, in image and spirit, works as a leitmotif throughout the book. Whether it is the blood shared by family or that coursing through a men chasing love in "Women," "Not All the Blood of Goats" and "The Grateful Heart," or that dripping in accidental imagery in "Counting My Corpses," blood becomes a signal to both begin and end life.

Palma uses history and contemporary news to shout and twist about life in his time. In "Give Us This Day," his summary of our "Daily News" reminds us how little we can contain in the course of a day. "All the Conquerors" shows us how connected historical violence is to growing notions of nation and the repetition of hurt transferred through human and mechanical imagery. What makes Palma so exciting is how seriously he doesn't take himself. He leaves us with "Poetry won't save us in the end, / Love won't save us / And not Jesus. In the End / We will die and be translated. / Everything says itself / Without meaning to."

Even Palma's most opaque work is accessible in ways that counter the trend of academic poetry. To read Palma is to recognize the masters who have teased and tempted him to try to outdo them. We see the ghost of William Carlos Williams in the imagery of "In Time" and "I Wanted to Write." We touch the pulse of Henry David in "After Thoreau," a poem that leaps from the famous observation that "most men lead lives of quite desperation" to conclude "All indications show where / All pathways bring them nowhere. / Too schooled to suffer needs, / How quietly men go where / Their desperation leads."

(February 2002)

Michael Palma, *A Fortune in Gold* (Gradiva Publications, 2000). $13 (paperback).

Vincent Panella

While many of us know the "Ides of March," (no, not the Chicago rock band of "I'm Your Vehicle" fame) as that fateful time of Julius Caesar's demise, there's not much known about the days before he was leading Roman legions and ruling the Roman empire. From an incident mentioned in passing by Roman historians Plutarch and Suetonius, Vincent Panella has crafted a novel that not only creates not only a feeling of being there, but a feeling of what it might have been like to actually be Caesar himself.

Written in Caesar's own voice, *Cutter's Island: Caesar in Captivity* is a series of diary entries about the kidnapping of a twenty-five year old Caesar on his way to study oratory under the great Apollonius Molon in Rhodes. The kidnapping and ransom of rich boys was a common occurrence on the seaways between Rome and Greece. Chief among those who rebel against Roman rule are the pirates who perform services for enemies like King Mithridates.

Along the way his ship is boarded by pirates led by a one-handed Cilician called "Cutter," a nickname earned by his reputation for lopping extremities of his enemies, and Caesar is taken prisoner. While in captivity on an island controlled by the pirates, Caesar is afforded the luxuries appropriate to his potential ransom and gets things like writing materials that enable him to record not only his reactions but also his reflections on his past.

During this time he rethinks his place in the world and makes plans for his future. "I'll need to remember this: that the gods don't live in one place and man in another. In some form, the gods are within the thinking man, and the sense of justice once espouses much be divine-based."

Panella, a master of ancient psychology, reveals many levels of Caesar's development as a young tactical thinker learning how to manipulate language and men. This tale of captivity, ransom, and revenge is told through writing that is disarmingly simple and compelling. If you've ever had to translate passages from Caesar's writings you'll recognize Panella's great familiarity with Caesar's ability to make poetry out of simple, direct language.

To Panella's credit he develops Caesar's nemesis equally so that by the end we understand the compassion Caesar shows as he orders the death of Cutter and his men. From a section (the book's longest) devoted to Cutter telling Caesar his own story, Panella shows not only his skill as a creator of great imagery, but his ability to show that the actions of those who seem the most insane are actually skewed attempts to balance the extremes of their lives.

> So I was a street pirate, but my idols were the sea dogs, those men with ears and noses spiked with jewelry, fingers sheathed with old and precious stones. Their purple and gold-trimmed galleys defied your state most openly, and operated with the approval of provincial governors by exploiting their greed.

Don't be surprised if you see *Cutter's Island* translated for the screen in a few years. The opportunity to play a great historical figure at such a pivotal point in his development should have a Leonardo DiCaprio or Johnny Depp drooling all the way to the auditions.

Cutter's Island is a bold and successful work that raises the question: Where has Panella been since the 1979 publication of his memoir *The Other Side: Growing Up Italian in America*? This journalist and freelance magazine writer, who teaches writing at Vermont Law School, could only have been busy honing his skills, for this novel is not only, as reviewer Steven Pressfield put it, "a perfect flawless gem, without a false note anywhere," but a model for how to imagine history into being.

(March 2001)

Vincent Panella, *Cutter's Island: Caesar in Captivity* (Chicago, IL: Academy Chicago Publishers, 2000). www.academychicago.com; ISBN 0897334841; $23 (hardcover).

Paul Paolicelli

In *Dances with Luigi*, award winning television journalist Paul Paolicelli took off in search of his Italian roots and came back with a heartwarming story of one man's recovery of a past that changed his identity. In his new book, *Under the Southern Sun*, subtitled *Stories of the Real Italy and the Americans It Created*, Paolicelli reports the results of a second journey he made to find out what those immigrants carried with them and what they've left behind.

Writing this book has brought him in contact with the likes of Sam Patti, cultural broker and coffee impresario in Pittsburgh, Walter Wolff, holocaust survivor rescued by Italians, theater and cultural maven Lionel Bottari and other colorful characters whose stories represent a range of southern Italian legacies. Paolicelli nicely wraps his personal story in the larger history of others and the result is a complex reflection of reality that works. This is especially well done in "U figlio di Giovanni" which recounts an earlier time he and two Italian American US Army buddies camp through Italy and end up at a family reunion.

Paolicelli's journey begins and ends with Matera, in Basilicata, birthplace of his paternal grandparents and writers like Carlo Levi. He meets journalists, public officials and servants, pensione owners, all of whom contribute to the author's education. He is at his best describing what he sees, and his meditations upon the land and the people are often quite exquisite. Much of what he learns comes from conversations; in fact, he reminds us that in Italy conversation is an art that rivals cooking and the renaissance arts. His best work comes when he stands back and lets people like Frank Capra's nephew say to us: "Southerners had to be more intelligent because they had more need, and need builds the mind as much as formal schooling" and the immigrants "brought values, not valuables" to America. It is these values that Paolicelli draws out so well from the people he interviews.

He's at his weakest when he tries to extend his observations into sociological truths and philosophical conclusions about culture. His energy and enthusiasm sometimes take him further than his research into unsupported generalizations like: "Rome is one of the world's most beautiful cities, and aside form the motorists and graffiti, still one of the most polite and innocent on earth." Makes us wonder if he's ever been anywhere in Rome outside the Vatican. With insights into the plight of southern Italians somewhat clouded by nostalgia and limited by his method of gathering information, Paolicelli suffers a bit from the Gay Talese syndrome: an energetic journalist eager to report an untold story generalizes from personal experience.

The questions he formulates are good ones, and sometimes what he doesn't find out tells us as much about Italy as what he does, for example with the Valentino museum that is never open. The journey ends with a powerful conclusion of how the old world is changing. Village life and dialects disappearing as the youth leave home in search of work and excitement. The small worlds that created those values are losing ground to a standardization that is creeping in. New Italy, sends "sofas, not sons" to America these days as it takes its place among the strongest economic powers of the world.

In the end Paolicelli has found a home in two worlds. He suggests we all return to Italy because you can't find this stuff in the US and never will. Who knows, it might not be there the next time he goes to Italy, but he should. He's got the prizewinning knack for a good story, and the ability to let it come through his writing.

Paul Paolicelli, *Under the Southern Sun: Stories of the Real Italy and the Americans It Created* (New York: St. Martin's P, 2003). www.stmartins.com; ISBN 031228 7658; $24.95 (hardcover).

&

If you missed *Dances with Luigi* in hardcover, don't let it get by you now that it's in paperback. Paul Paolicelli tells a story that most grandchildren of the early immigrants have experienced and one that most everyone will enjoy. Whether you've been back to the old country or not, this book will teach you something about yourself and your relation to the generations that came before you.

Paolicelli pursues his past with a passion that many have but few are able to channel into such powerful prose. The secret to his success lies in his ability to turn an eye skilled by years of writing news onto the canvas of contemporary Italy and to search for the records and recollections of his namesake's existence. Instead of news reporting, he must now do historical research and biographical storytelling. He's up to the task and the process becomes quite an adventure.

In his mid-forties and without his own nuclear family, Paolicelli, a Houston television news producer, receives a job-related windfall of cash and decides to take some time off to "get back to something spiritually important." He chooses Rome and plans to educate himself. He starts by studying the language and quickly gets drawn into the lives of locals, like his neighbor Luigi, who, (roughly the same age), takes him along on his forays into the weekend singles scene at a local dance hall.

In search of more, Paolicelli travels to his grandparents' birthplaces and comes upon old friends and long lost relatives who all try to help him learn about his grandfather. He knows his grandfather lived and died in a tragic work accident in Pittsburgh, but can't find a legal document to prove that the man was born, baptized or married.

He remembers seeing documentary films made of his grandfather's visits to Italy (a couple times at Mussolini's invitation), but the films have long disintegrated because no one thought to preserve them, so he takes it upon himself to reconstruct his grandfather's life. It's a frustrating journey, as he writes, "It seemed for every answer I found I had twice the amount of questions," but Paolicellli is determined.

During the first couple of years he makes friends, loses family back home, and never gets close to finding the information he thought he wanted to get him his very own Italian citizenship, but now needs in order to make sense of his life. He gets comfortable with the language, then realizes that he really needs to know dialects. The author comes to realization that he must never stop learning.

His friend Luigi, and a few other native Italians, help guide him through some of the stickier situations that would have stymied most anyone trying to go it solo. This memoir is plotted like a detective novel. This story of one man and his family draws us strangers in so that we feel that this is our life. If you've ever been back to what they used to call "the old country," then you know just how new Italy can be. Paolicelli learns that though he might have been called Italian in his US neighborhood, he has never been more American than during this trip. But he has become a changed American.

He stumbles on the reasons why traditions in Italy are sturdier than in the US and witnesses the crumbling of many of the rituals that have enabled him to trace his identity back a couple of centuries along his ancestral line. Along the way, he might have learned to dance, but he has more importantly remembered how to play the songs to help others dance as well.

(April 2002)

Paul Paolicelli, *Dances with Luigi: a Grandson's Determined Quest to Comprehend Italy and the Italians* (New York: St. Martin's P, 2000). ISBN: 0312251822; $14.95 (paperback).

JOSEPH PAPALEO

To know Joe Papaleo's writing is to know some of the best of Italian American literature. To not know him is, well, shame on you, as my mother used to say; you don't know what's good for you. Russell Banks compares him to Nelson Algren; Grace Paley says all his stories are "a great pleasure to read," and most everyone agrees that he's a major American voice of Italian descent.

Papaleo's a veteran, publishing regularly long before, during and after the 1990s renaissance of Italian American literature. The author of two novels *All the Comforts* and *Out of Place,* his stories have appeared in such mainstream magazines as the *New Yorker, Harper's, Paris Review,* and many others. Recently retired after over 30 years of teaching literature and writing at Sarah Lawrence College, he has spent his time fine tuning his fiction. *Italian Stories* is the first result of his concentrated time at the writing table.

Prior to the fiction he gives us a "Prologue for an Ethnic Life," that serves as both introduction and warning that what you are about to read is the whole truth and some of it will not be believable. This is the beauty of Papaleo's work; you get the feeling that it's real and that it relates to life as we know it, but then along comes something in the work: a character, a scene, a string of catchy prose, and you're reminded that this writing can't even begin to capture the complexities of this thing called living. What's marvelous is that Papaleo doesn't let that bother him. He keeps at it. Struggling to have his say about it all.

While not all of the twenty-six stories have the same protagonist, we get a sense of the evolution of one man's life as we read the collection from beginning to end. The stories are divided into three sections that serve as stages dramatizing the life and death of Little Italy and the rise of a man from street kid to Florida retiree.

"Immigrant Epiphanies" contains stories that are sometimes no more than slices of life that come right at you, then slip away like fierce split-finger curve balls. In "Kidnap" a ransom note arrives before the crime occurs, forcing the family to do its best through the worst of the characters of Little Italy, the relative who's connected. Most of these stories are really reminiscences of times gone captured through a brilliant nostalgia that is neither sweet nor sour. As the children "drink America," and get drunk on change, the old timers struggle to stay connected to their children and to the values that shaped their visions and gave them the strength to leave the old country in the first place. If you remember family rosary recitals in the home, the old-timers and their broken English, then these stories will combine to strike a chord of recognition and longing.

"Losing the Bronx," could mean many things, but most of all it means losing the old neighborhood as the immigrants lose their need to protect each other from the invading American culture. Overcome by assimilation, Papaleos shows us that as the Italians leave the Bronx, they lose much of what used to make them historical people. Confrontations between old and young, black and white, make up most of the conflicts in this section as the once solid Little Italys give way to the big U.S.A.

The most challenging and experimental stories come in "Blendings and Losses." "The Last Sabbatical," is a swan song to an academic career. "Twenty-Nince Steps Toward Re-adhesion," is a meditation on how traveling to and home from Italy ("a country where the size of things does not shrink me" can cause a man's spirit to unravel. And finally the days of retirement in Florida come to a man who is not used to palm trees and geriatric perspectives.

(October 2002)

Joseph Papaleo, *Italian Stories* (Chicago: Dalkey Archive P, 2002). www.dalkeyarchive.com; ISBN 1564783065; $14.50 (paperback).

David Prete

Talk about books that read themselves, David Prete's debut novel, *Say That to My Face*, is one that you read so quickly you'll want to go back to the beginning and do it all again. What you'll learn is that there are many ways of being Italian American and that Prete has captured a most interesting version in language that comes from the streets and stays in your ears long after the pages have stopped turning.

Since when he was a kid, pretty boy Joey Frascone got pretty much what he wanted and so little of what he really needed. He and his sister come from a family broken when Joey was just a year old. That's when they moved from the Bronx to his mother's parents' home in nearby suburban Yonkers. Set in a time of "Big Wheels" cruising down suburban sidewalks of a neighborhood terrorized by the famous Son of Sam, the stories that comprise this coming-of-age novel are powerful distillations of everyday life that arrive with all the peace of the mundane and leave you thinking about how close some of us can come to living truly desperate lives.

The best of this effect happens when his divorced parents find themselves playing softball on opposite teams. Mom hits the ball back to Dad at the pitcher's mound. "Mom didn't run and Dad didn't throw. They both just stood there for a moment looking very surprised, looking very young, looking as thought they forgot, for one moment, what the rules of the game had always been."

We understand how boys grow up to be just like their dad's when we hear his father say, "A guy needs the kind of things he can keep his feelings out of." The in-between life of the suburbs comes through clearly when we read,

> we had a view of the Manhattan skyline. Presiding over the skyline made us feel

like we were actually doing something with our time, other than killing half a night and a full case of beer. It made us feel like we were almost in New York City, therefore almost productive, almost important, almost worldly and almost even wise.

Joey ends us a high school dropout, whose idea of college is a bartending job in the city. This happens after an earlier attempt to escape the neighborhood by traveling with two buddies cross country ends up with none of them talking to each other. When he returns, he leaves the neighborhood and finds a woman in Manhattan who forces him to confront his inability to love. "No one had ever turned me inside out with such ease." She forces him to begin searching for the reason he's unhappy. He takes a shot at getting ahead the easy way, by smuggling drugs from Jamaica. The lesson he learns along the way is how useless is the undeveloped mind.

At the novel's end, Joey finds himself in the strange position of having to take care of his Aunt Connie, who has hosted memorable neighborhood barbeques. Connie has put up with a wiseguy husband who beats her and anyone else who gets in his way until he finds Jesus in jail and attempts to change everyone's life, and so she's had just about enough of being a traditional mater dolorosa and is ready to break some taboos.

You've got to buy this book, because we want to encourage Prete to continue writing. He's got a talent that could take his work to the screen with the possibilities of removing the gangster shadow that's been hiding the best of our culture for too long.

(June 2004)

David Prete, *Say That to My Face: Fiction* (New York: Norton, 2003). www.wwnorton.com; ISBN 0393057984; $23.95 (hardcover).

Stanislao Pugliese

Carlo Rosselli, a St. Francis of the antifascists, was born into a wealthy Jewish Italian family in 1899, refused to live within his privileges, and devoted his life to seeking justice and liberty for all oppressed by fascism. Using his brains and his family's resources, he designed, led and financed one of the strongest antifascist movements in Europe. Unlike St. Francis, Carlo Rosselli would give his life for his beliefs.

The development of a man and his mind is a difficult task to capture in words, but in *Carlo Rosselli: Socialist Heretic and Antifascist Exile*, the first book in English on Rosselli, Stanislao Pugliese, Assistant Professor of History at Hofstra University, makes that task look easy. On the surface, *Carlo Rosselli*, winner of the 2000 Premio Internazionale Ignazio Silone, is an academic book. But the more you read, the more you can read, as Pugliese writes to educate as well as analyze, and the book becomes accessible to anyone interested in early 20th century Italy.

Well grounded in pre- and post-fascist history, *Rosselli* helps us to see the rise and fall of fascism in the context of Italian history. At times, the writing helps move the story along the lines of a mystery novel. From the "Introduction," you know that the protagonist and his brother will be murdered by fascist thugs, but the strong identification Pugliese creates between the reader and Rosselli forces you to root for a different outcome. Scattered throughout are scenes of escapes, trials, flights and the smuggling of antifascists and illegal writings across the Italian border into France and Switzerland. Rosselli was a man who believed that ideas should be enacted. As he develops his ideas, his risks increase; first he risks his his reputation through his creation of newspapers, then his life through assisting in the escape Filippo Turati.

Pugliese presents a fine analysis of Rosselli's work in comparison to those whom he read and those who read him. The author does a superb scholar's job in explicating of Rosselli's writings and by historicizing its reception. Beyond the scholar's job of helping us understand Rosselli's ideas, Pugliese fulfills the biographer's responsibility of making a life ended more than sixty years ago matter to us today.

Chapter One, entitled "Younger Brothers," recounts the early years of this young man born to a musicologist father and a mother who was a noted author. Both parent's families had been involved in the Risorgimento, and "saw their emancipation directly tide to the Risorgimento and the Enlightenment, liberating Italy and her Jews from the rule of both the Austrians and the papal authorities."

In "Autocritica," Pugliese presents Rosselli's earliest work as a professor and a cultural critic. We observe Rosselli's reactions to the repealing of every liberal freedom once enjoyed by the Italian people as Mussolini's regime begins to take over the minds and bodies of the Italians, forcing its critics underground.

Chapter Three, "Liberal Socialism," focuses on the arrest, trial, and confinement of Rosselli. During this period Rosselli pens his major critique of Marxism and develops the ideas that will brand him a heretic by the socialists. While describing the past and interpreting the uses and abuses of political thinkers such as Karl Marx, Pugliese speaks to the relevance of that thought to today's world, enabling Rosselli's story to transcend historical curiosity.

"Justice and Liberty," the largest chapter of the book follows Rosselli's flight into exile and explains how and why he was considered to be such a dangerous threat to the Italian fascists. A discussion of Rosselli's wife helps illuminate the overshadowed role that women played in the anti-fascist movement, "The Tragic Hero" presents the murder of the Rosselli brothers and the subsequent search for justice after the fall of the fascist rule. A conclusion connects events of Rosselli's life and death to the end of the war and the beginning of Italian democracy.

Though he could only experience his liberty in exile and justice in his words, Rosselli, by those words and actions inspired others not only to defeat fascism, but to fashion the Italian democracy that rose after the end of the war.

(May 2000)

Stanislao Pugliese, *Carlo Rosselli: Socialist Heretic and Antifascist Exile* (Cambridge, MA: Harvard UP, 1999). ISBN 0674000536; $35 (hardcover).

Mario Puzo

From his first novel, *Dark Arena*, to his last, Puzo's work has consistently been focused on the role that family plays in the way individual's face their lot in life. After his best work, *The Fortunate Pilgrim*, left him as poor as he'd ever been, he turned the family towards more interesting things like organized crime. Puzo's obsession with the family in nowhere more evident than in what we think is the author's final word on the subject.

The Family, a novel that he'd been working on for 20 years, and finally completed after his death by his companion, novelist Carol Gino, takes us deep inside the Borgias, one of the most powerful families in the history of Western civilization. Headed by Rodrigo, who would become Pope Alexander VI, the Borgias, originally of Spanish origin, became one of the most powerful and influential families during the Italian Renaissance.

Through their good deeds and bad, they fostered the arts, controlled the Catholic Church, made strides in unifying Italy, and ultimately created their own demise. There's treachery, debauchery, honor, glory, and blood and guts enough to satisfy the romantic, but the news is not so good for the realist.

Puzo uses facts when they fit his artistic needs and abandons them whenever he chooses. So don't read this looking for historical accuracy. You might find there's a sense of emotional reality relayed somewhere, but then you'd have to have a good imagination. Better to read it as a story, like a made-for-television film, loosely based on historical records, but mostly there to entertain and sell advertising. So what's being sold here? Obviously the connection between Puzo and his gangsters, why else would the cover's only blurb come from Nick *Wiseguy* Pileggi. In any case, Puzo's final novel is an interesting use of Renaissance history and might be worth the price of the paperback.

(December 2003)

Maria Puzo, *The Family: A Novel* (New York: Regan Books, 2001). www.reganbooks.com; ISBN 0060394455; $27 (hardcover).

DAVID A.J. RICHARDS

When the US House of Representatives passed, by acclamation, House Resolution 2442, on the 10th of last November, it was the first time that the national government recognized the violation of the civil liberties of Italian Americans. This victory for civil rights in general, might need greater explanation to be useful to today's Italian Americans.

Italian American: The Racializing of an Ethnic Identity, by David A.J. Richards, should help explain what this resolution and other significant historical events have done to create the American of Italian descent. Richards, a professor of law at New York University and director of that school's Program for the Study of Law, Philosophy and Critical Theory, proposes

> American racism could not have had the durability or the political power it has had, either in the popular understanding of American culture or in the corruption of constitutional ideals of universal human rights, unless new immigrants, themselves often regarded as racially inferior, had been drawn into accepting and supporting many of the terms of American racism.

Richards, a grandson of Italian immigrants who came from the hill towns of Campania, writes in order to shed light on how American racism kept Italian Americans from knowing "both their own traditions in Italy and the very real struggles of their grandparents against injustice in both Italy and the United States." His first chapter serves as an introduction to the subject and to the author. In Chapter 2, "Revolutionary Constitutionalism," US Revolutionary War, Civil War, he recounts the setting up and interpretation of human rights issues in the US constitution, and compares it to French and German thought. His historical research and presentation, while more than most of us might care to work through or even know, is thorough.

Chapter 3, "The Promise and Betrayal of Italian Revolutionary Constitutionalism: The Southern Italian Emigration," presents the Italian Risorgimento and the subsequent establishment of a national government and is a fine exercise in comparative political science. Richards brings an excellent command of legal and political history to bear on race, an issue that will continue to be a major focus of scholarship into the 21st century.

His Chapter 4, "American Liberal Nationalism and the Italian Emigration," compares African American slaves with Italian immigrants to bring out a number of common experiences, especially in terms of the early formation of identity as

Americans. Richards makes a case for Italian Americans by bringing up cases of race, women and sexual preference rights. He interprets "moral slavery," as the backfiring of a racism created by the denial of basic human rights to people who are dehumanized so that those rights can be denied. This powerful premise is better supported by African American scholars than the Italian Americans, for Richards is better steeped in the African/American intellectual tradition than the Italian/American.

While he rightly notices that such mainstream histories of ethnicity as Ronald Takaki's *A Different Mirror*, ignore Italian Americans, Richards's unfamiliarity with Italian/American sources stands out. Where are the studies that would have not only strengthened his argument, but enabled him to see that he is writing in an established Italian/American anti-racist tradition?

He lets Henry James off too easily, and would have been served by reading William Boelhower's explanations of James's anti-immigrant themes. Richards depends too much on Richard Gambino, whose views on race are one dimensional and not as closely allied with Richards's own as he might think. Here, reference to Patrick Gallo would have provided some balance. Richards's quoting of a misled Gay Talese article to support his claim that there are "only a few" novels "that dealt more fairly with Italian American life" shows his dependence on names and not knowledge. One gets the feeling the author consulted only resources available at the NYU library, and that's the problem for both the author and Italian American studies. The books that would have best served Richards have probably never made it into the libraries where the authors, the caliber of Richards, do their work.

His conclusion, Chapter 5, "Multicultural Identity and Human Rights," offers a "rights-based protest" as a way to counter the effects of moral slavery. Such a protest consists of first "Claiming rights denied in one's own voice" and then "engaging in reasonable discourse that challenges the dominant stereotype in terms of which one's group has been dehumanized." Richards calls for us all to see that: "It is no longer an acceptable basis for any people's Americanization that they subscribe to the terms of American cultural racism."

Richards has brewed a powerful drink that needs distillation for common understanding; his writing works better for those who have experience with the style of writing legal history. To his credit, he regularly repeats his thesis and evidence throughout, as though anticipating one's drifting off and on. A long read, best taken in pieces, better yet studied with a group, *Italian American* should join such works as Eric Yamamoto's *Interracial Justice: Conflict and Reconciliation in Post-Civil Rights America*, in creating an alternative view of US civil rights history and a new way of seeing racial identity in the future.

(January 2000)

David A.J. Richards, *Italian American: The Racializing of an Ethnic Identity* (New York: New York UP, 1999). www.nyupress.og; ISBN 0814775209; $35 (hardcover).

GIOSE RIMANELLI

With *Moliseide and Other Poems*, Giose Rimanelli begins his fifth decade of publishing with a wonderful homage to his origins in the language of his ancestral homeland. Like many authors at the height of their powers in the summit of their careers, Rimanelli turns his eyes back on the roads he's traveled to get to where he is, and there have been some incredibly wild rides along the way.

The Ezra Pound of Italian/American writing, Rimanelli is a man of incredible knowledge — most of it self-taught; he is also, like Walt Whitman, a man of incredible compassion, which comes from his ability to listen. These poems are, in the purist sense, echoes of the world around him, but there is a twist. In the act of responding to stimuli, Rimanelli's poetry draws attention away from itself and toward the object of his inspiration. In this way, the craftsman remains invisible, and these poems can become songs for everyone.

Moliseide has become Rimanelli's *Leaves of Grass*. He has published two previous versions, one with cassette recordings of his lyrics in the music of Benito Faraone, one of his childhood friends. It's as though the longer he lives, the more he needs to adjust the presentation of his past. Rimanelli's wisdom lies in his ability to change the past through verse. And this change ripples back through to the present.

The collection is divided into three parts. Part One is presented in three languages; the original in the dialect of Molise is accompanied by two translations: Italian and English. These poems which form the earliest 1990 version, come at you as pastoral postcards, the struggle between the old world and the new as in "Kawasaki Blues," or pure lyrical myth as in ballads such as "Ballad of the Sorcerer" and "Ballad of the Lizard." More than anything else, the poems in this section give you a sense of what life is like in Molise:

> Molise's World is made of all those things
> that fill our lives with the And the Square
> is always watching who gets married there
> because it wants finest air.
> People arrive and eat, they rest and think:
> "These mornings are a nectar!"
> to see if you make do.

In Part Two, we move away from the Molisani dialect; there are love songs, lighter verse, land travel songs. While these poems might be less didactic, they do offer lessons of what it is like to leave one's ancestral homeland and enter the wide world beyond childhood. One of the lessons taught by association and not words in this section is one found in "Molisan Nights:" "Molisan Nights hanging on the walls; of ancient houses long ago abandoned. Lianas of memories still rooted / in the days of love that went with youth." Nothing is as it was, but that doesn't mean it can't become a song. In Part Three, we return to a trilingual presentation of 23 poems which are reminiscent of Eugenio Montale's "Xenia" poems: more meditations than songs, more chants of wisdom than contemporary tunes.

Appended to the poems is a critical apparatus. As in most of Rimanelli's work — his novels with footnotes, his mythic introductions to academic texts, the author does not separate the creative from the critical. The best of these is Luigi Bonaffini's "Introduction" which gives you not only a sense of what Rimanelli has produced, but the place it has in the evolution of poetry with a capital "P." In the end, the poems are less what the critics say, and more what they do to you, and that is for you to experience. In this way you will come to realize that while Giose Rimanelli may have left the world of teaching, he has not stopped teaching the world to read, to see, and now to sing.

Giose Rimanelli, *Moliseide and Other Poems,* ed. and trans. Luigi Bonaffini (Brooklyn, NY: Legas, 1998). ISBN 1881901149.

&

Since winning the 1994 American Book Award for *Benedetta in Guysterland,* Giose Rimanelli, now a retired professor, has been busy catching up with the many novels, poems and stories he penned as a way of learning the English language nearly 40 years ago. His *Alien Cantica: An American Journey (1964–1993),* published in a bi-lingual edition by Peter Lang in 1995, collected his poems written during this period in a "slangy American for my own practice."

Accademia, his latest publication, is the result of Rimanelli's more than twenty-five years of living in the American academe. The novel is to him what "Lolita" was to Vladimir Nabokov. Rimanelli invites this comparison by setting the novel in Anabasis, Nabokov County, Appalachia USA, a highly symbolic location in which myth-like events occur on streets named after Greek and Roman gods and historical events and places. Like Nabokov, Rimanelli was a well-known author in his native language before immigrating to the United States, took up residence in an American university, and worked at his literary trade in his new acquired language, English. If *Benedetta in Guysterland* was Rimanelli's American primer, then *Accademia* is his graduate thesis, proving that he has not only mastered the English language, but that he's conquered the cultural obstacles that most uneducated immigrants never get the chance to encounter.

So much of the novel is couched in Jungian symbolism that we can't help but see the characters as archetypes. This psychological element enables the novel to reach beyond autobiography and into the lives of everyone whose ever gone to college. Rimanelli structures the novel into two halves; a male point-of-view in chapters 1–9 comes to us through Simon Dona, an Italian immigrant professor, and a female point-of-view in chapters 10–19 through his young, American born second wife, Lisa. The voice of Simon returns for the last chapter.

You don't read this novel to follow a story, but to follow the effect that intellectual development and display has on an Italian immigrant. Simon Dona becomes, for all of Italian America, a trickster who both succeeds and fails at playing his song of life in the key of intellect. Rimanelli uses this trickster character to show us how not to become intellectuals.

Although the novel opens with references to Simon Dona's family (he has two sons from a previous marriage in Italy and one from his younger wife Lisa), family life in this academic environment is all but destroyed. An extended family of friends and colleagues, a weak replacement for the nuclear family, becomes the focus of this Italian narrator's story. As Simon recalls events in the social life of the academe, he rarely mentions his offspring, suggesting that there is little room for the traditional family in this heady, hedonistic atmosphere. The novel becomes a study of the interaction of those scholars whose lives intertwine in the academe making for a richly symbolic story of parodic incest that waxes and wanes on the battleground of male-female sexuality and intellectuality. Each character lives in a self-created labyrinth constructed by social and economic opportunities accepted and denied. In Simon Dona's case, the maze is the American academe, in which he lives in a house made of glass.

Characters in the novel are all obsessed with studying, philosophizing and achieving sexual fantasies, and intellectual superiority at the expense of dealing with, the less desirable, but more stable reality of lasting relationships. Dona is a physical anthropologist who studies the Macaque species, "The most ancient species besides man." But in writing his book, Dona is actually putting forth his research the likes of Madison, a colleague turned lover who studies roaches and names her subjects after people she knows.

The novel is wrought with irony and satire of academic introspection and subsequent self realization. Dona understands the split between public and private life; however as one who lives in a glass house, he knows he can be observed just as the caged animals he studies; the important thing is that Dona can verbalize this: "On the outside we are social saints, and inside our own glass house we are monsters, prisoners of perverted habits, voluntary suicides for the lack of sincerity with ourselves."

Dona reminds us that we all inhabit glass houses and though we may intend for our lives to be open and revealing, we are all victims of the clash between our needs and our desires, a battle between our psyches and our libidos. The results of these interactions are the clouds of doubt and self deceit that clothe our personalities and tint our relationships. As an American academic with international impact, Rimanelli gives us a glimpse into the world of screwed up scholars, an insight that might just save us from becoming like them.

(February 1998)

Giose Rimanelli, *Accademia: A Novel* (Toronto: Guernica Editions, 1997). ISBN 155071015X; $12 (paperback).

E.R. ROMAINE

During a festa people take time out from their daily routines to the celebrate life of someone who has lived an exemplary life and in the process taught us all how to better our own lives. While the stories collected in E.R. Romaine's *Festa*, do not recount the stories of any saints, they do remind us how strange ordinary lives can become when we start paying close attention to them, and how most of us need the patience and perseverance of a saint just to get through some days.

The thirteen stories collected here, mostly set in the Belmont area of New York's East Bronx, take us into and through the lives of some pretty colorful characters. In one of the most hilarious stories, "Counting Wops," we meet Aunt Carmella, "with arms like a stone cutter," who dunks Anna's newly bleached-blonde hair into a sink full of black hair dye to make her Italian again. Turns out Anna, (renamed Ginny by the nuns in school) has a penchant for running away from her Italianess, but her aunts, and her training never let her stray too far. Aunt Mary's game of counting "wops" consists of identifying all the Italian men she finds at the beach, and Ginny can't help but join in. Through this story, and most of the early ones, we get a great sense of the old Italian neighborhood, beyond the boundaries of which, as her father used to day, lies America.

In "Chicken Bet," we meet Joey the Bookie who gets even with Mrs. Fugaso (who once ratted him out to the police) by tricking her into thinking the effects of a church remodeling project are miracles accomplished by her leaving money to the Holy Spirit. Then there's the loan shark of "Agatha Cakes" who falls in love with Lucy, a young widow who can't help but see herself as a potential saint, after losing her husband. Lucy thinks that her melancholia ought to be turned into a thigh-shaped pastry called Lucia's Sigh (in the fashion of the breast-shaped cake named for St. Agatha) that would commemorate her inability to love again. "Tess and the Two Men with the Flowers in their Lapels" features a young woman who parlays witnessing a street shooting into a bright future for her husband.

"Joey the Face Loves Nancy" is a Bronx tale to rival Nancy Savoca's *True*

Love, featuring a mama's boy who turns into a man when he falls in love with the daughter of the local crime boss. "Destino: Lucia's Eagle," combines superstition with intuition to tell a sausage maker and the stories she concocts. Lucia has it all figured out until those around her begin to defy the fate she predicts is theirs. Romaine's work plays with the gangster stuff that riles a lot of the Italian American anti-defamation folk, but she does it with so much fun that it transcends the usual exploitative use to make us, if not laugh, then wonder how anyone can take this stuff so seriously.

A series of stories about young Italian girls' coming of age conclude the collection. In these, such as "Monkey Island," girls rival boys, defying nature even as it begins to situate young ladies in the place where boys use their physical power to get over their emotional weaknesses. Unfortunately, for the girls, even the cute ones, as in "All the Pretty Ones," fall victim to the boys' misdirected violence, and must learn to protect themselves as they try to attract the very ones who could do them harm. All said, the stories are certainly worthwhile reading and could even remind you of own days gone by in Little Italy.

(August 2004)

E.R. Romaine, *Festa: Stories* (Bellowing Ark Press). ISBN 0944920462; $14 (paperback).

Mark Rotella

When Mark Rotella drags his father back to his birthplace of Gimigliano, he begins the process of rediscovering of many stories that he presents in his memoir, *Stolen Figs*. One of the keys to returning to Italy is to walk the land, touch the trees, the walls, and to look into the skies that one's ancestors once knew. To his credit, Rotella never becomes unnecessarily sentimental while doing this. He sees Calabria as a place of hot peppers, good health, good wine, good blood, hard bread, and strong teeth. He makes us aware of just how different life is there:

> Time is different for the Calabresi, who expect that people (for good reason) will run into each other from time to time. This means that the Italians' long sense of history notwithstanding, they are concerned almost exclusively with the present and are not terribly nostalgic.

This is different, he says, from Italian Americans who do long for an old country. Rotella's strength as a writer is that he can make the "old country" new.

He also does a pretty good job of retelling the land's history, from Greek colonization, to today's new immigration. Occasionally, however, he dips into the mawkishly absurd by addressing the reader with sentences like, "Calabria, surrounded by ocean on three sides and mountains on the fourth, was isolated and in need of company. She opened her arms to Hannibal and his Carthaginians...." His extended metaphor of Calabria as a woman, an old, wily putanna, wears thin pretty quickly and reveals the stretch marks of Rotella's talents.

In the process of interviewing relatives he unearths family skeletons and comes to see his life in a new way. When he writes, "My grandfather shot a man over my grandmother," he reveals the gold he's been looking for, but at times it's as though Rotella takes his father's advice to "Never let them know what you're thinking. Never let them know what you're feeling." When he follows that advice he ignores the real wealth of his family's history. He also stumbles on people, like a woman with a sketchbook, whom he describes, then lets go of, as though he was about to say something, but chose not to. We wonder just why he's so hesitant to finish such thoughts. Fortunately he doesn't follow his father's words when writing about his travels.

Calabria is the second-largest producer of figs, but her figs, Rotella tells us, are "taken for granted, and little premium is placed on them." The fig, harvested twice a year, becomes a metaphor for the freshness, the fullness of life in Calabria; they also are like the stories that Rotella has taken away. There's nothing tastier, says his guide Giuseppe, a traveling postcard photographer, as stolen figs, an experience Rotella's father has also recounted to his son. Giuseppe knows the whole region and teaches Mark about Calabrian life while showing him its "scorciatoie" or shortcuts.

We join Rotella on his extensive travels throughout Calabria. Inside castles, to the tops of mountains, and along the sites of ancient history and contemporary feste. A last trip, made with his parents, and his wife, for the Festa della Madonna di Porto, is among the most memorable of his stories. One of the acts of the procession is the coming together of the statues of Jesus, Mary, and Joseph, a scene that reminds Rotella of the way he has reconnected his Old- and New-World families through his travels.

Following Gay Talese's stories of his ancestral Maida, and Paul Paolicelli's tales of his Basilicata, Rotella's *Figs* reminds us that southern Italy is a place of myth, magic, and mundane beauty. Rotella presents a rich Calabria finally accessible to those who only read English.

(May 2004)

Mark Rotella, *Stolen Figs and Other Adventures in Calabria* (New York: North Point P, 2003). ISBN 0865476276; $25 (hardcover).

JANE AND PETER SCHNEIDER

Sicily, the setting for many famous myths such as those we know from Homer's *The Odyssey*, has proven to be equally fertile soil for contemporary mythology and one of its greatest myths that has come to us is that of Mafia. For the most part, in the United States, Mafia has become personality. From the old Moustache Petes like Stefano Magaddino, Joseph Masseria, and Salvatore Maranzano to the next generation of Capones, Lucianos, Bonannos, to the present era of the Gottis, Mafia has become a misguided star system of heroic anti-heroes whose tales have come to replace those of Aneas and Ulysses.

In the US Mafia has also become commodity, and as such there exists a formula for what sells and what doesn't sell. And what sells is simple and exotic lies, what doesn't sell complex truth. Thus, the complexities of mafia in Sicily never really get communicated to the people of the United States.

From its early appearance on the American scene through the popular writings of Luigi Barzini, Sr., through the translations of Sicilian writers like Leonardo Sciascia, to the versions created by Sicilian American writers like Jerre Mangione and Ben Morreale, and Italian American writers like Mario Puzo, Sicily, like a photograph pulled too early from developing chemicals, never had a chance to fully expose itself.

For the dean of Sicilian American writers, the late Jerre Mangione, "destino" was a barrier that kept his relatives from becoming Americans; they contained "strong elements of fatalism" that were

> ingrained in the Sicilian soul by centuries of poverty and oppression.... In their minds, "Destino," the willingness to resign oneself to misfortune, was the key to survival; to refuse to believe that an almighty force predetermined the fate of all people was to court disaster. (*Ethnic* 32)

To avoid disaster, one must not stand out in a crowd. Author Ben Morreale sees this as key to understanding not only Mangione but all Sicilian writers.

> Coming from an island that had been the crossroads of armies bent on world domination for centuries, having insecurities that some have translated into a psychological *paura storica*, or history of fear, the Sicilian has learned not to reveal himself. This reticence might be the core of Sicilian style in literature. ("Jerre Mangione" 41)

Morreale finds a similar style at work in the writers associated with the Sicilian school of Italian literature: Giovanni Verga, Luigi Pirandello, Giuseppe di Lampedusa, Elio Vittorini and the Morreale's contemporary, the late Leonardo

Sciascia. Sciascia is perhaps one of the biggest culprits of the limits placed on Sicilian possibilities. In *Sicily as a Metaphor,* he tells us:

> The history of Sicily is one of defeats: defeats of reason, defeats of reasonable men. . . . From that however comes skepticism, that is not, in effect, the acceptance of defeat, but a margin of security, of elasticity, through which the defeat, already expected, already rationalized, does not become definitive and mortal. Skepticism is healthy though. It is the best antidote to fanaticism. (6)

Morreale, carries on this tradition into American literature. In all his work, Sicily becomes a single dimension of a self that sustains his American rebellion. In his second novel, *A Few Virtuous Men* (1973), he takes us into the mafia experience of Racalmora (the fictional name of Racalmuto). The protagonist is Giovanni Buffa, a priest who recounts his life among "mafiosi." Nicknamed Juffa, after Giufá, the famous village idiot of Sicilian folklore, the priest decides that if he is to serve all God's children he must befriend the "virtuous men" who control most of what goes on in Racalmora. The novel looks at the priest's life before, during, and after he spent nearly a year in America. Before the priest's visit to the US the town was *sistemato,* everything was in its place and its place is determined and kept by the local *mafiosi.* When he leaves Sicily in mid-life he begins to see that system falling apart. On a trip to the US he observes the immigrants leading lives they never would have tried in Sicily In Mario Puzo's *The Godfather,* Sicily becomes for Don Corleone what Krypton was to Superman: a legendary place of origins the experiences of which elevate him to the status of a hero, if not a god. This is exemplified best through the character of Michael Corleone, the one son who is closest to total assimilation into American life. Michael is sent to Sicily to hide out after avenging the attempted assassination of his father. There he meets Dr. Taza, a local professor and historian through which "He came to understand his father's character and his destiny . . . his mother's resignation and acceptance of her role. For in Sicily he saw what they would have been if they had chosen *not* to struggle against their fate" (324).

Simplistic images of the Mafia, from Pitre's perspective of being composed of gallant men of courage, from Sciascia's perspective as being a stable force of traditional power, or Morreale's view of it as people responsible for the "sistemato" state of Sicilian society, and Puzo's narrow fairy tale depictions, are precisely why we so desperately need the work of Jane and Peter Schneider.

For Jane and Peter Schneider, Sicily has become a lifelong study resulting in books like *Festival of the Poor: Fertility Decline and the Ideology of Class in Sicily, 1860–1980* (1996) and *Culture and Political Economy in Western Sicily* (1976). The result of their latest work is *Reversible Destiny: Mafia, Antimafia, and the Struggle for Palermo.*

This couple (she a professor of anthropology at CUNY-Graduate Center, and he a professor of sociology at Fordham) have produced a thoroughly researched and well written interdisciplinary study in accessible language that debunks prevalent myths that conflate Mafia with Sicily. Mafia, we learn, is not a product of ethnicity, but a process of economics and political science.

From what many call the mafia's foreunner, the Beati Paoli, "a mythical eighteenth-century sect," to "covert Masonic lodges," the great maxi-trial of the 1980s and the rise of the antimafia movement, "Reversible Destiny" covers the origins and development of the mafia with great depth and clarity, distinguishing it from banditry, and connecting it to the Sicilian latifundia system and political insurrection. The Schneiders take us into the "intreccii," or intersections of mafia with Italian, US and world politics. They help us to see how cultural foundations of mafia enable it to be a "secret fraternal order whose norms and ritual practices situate its members 'outside' normal society, and, in their minds, 'above it.'"

Earlier writers have tried to explain mafia behavior as part of a traditional Sicilian "passion for death." The Schneiders counter earlier notions of Sicily as a chained to destiny and show us that there has always been a struggle against mafia. A refreshing sense of academic honesty comes when they reconsider their earlier work and revise a number of past observations in light of the new information they've gathered. Through their research and their informants we witness the phases of the 1980s crackdown, the early trials, judicial inquiries, the famous Maxi-trial of 1986 that ended with guilty verdicts for 344 mafiosi the next year, and the subsequent war between state and the mafia during the years 1988–1992 that saw assassinations of public figures like Judge Giovanni Falcone and his successor Paolo Borsellino in 1992.

In chapters like "The Antimafia Movement," "Civil Society Groundwork," "Backlash and Renewal," and "Recuperating the Built Environment" we learn of Catholics and communists and the political terrorism of the "anni di piombo" or the "years of lead" and the rise of the antimafia movement, first among the peasants and later growing to include urbanites. We also get a look at a most interesting development called the "counter anti-mafia movement" that consists of mafia sympathizers and civil liberty watchdogs whose work is symbolically represented through things like the neglect of statues erected to victims of mafia crimes. The final two chapters, "Cultural Re-education" and "Reversible Destiny," show how Palermo as "the world capital of the mafia is struggling to become the world capital of antimafia, its past of moral degradation, and violence, giving way to democratic and civic sensibilities." Ultimately, "Reversible Destiny" counters prevailing notions and images of a Sicily trapped in time of mass immigration. Destino can be manipulated and managed and not simply endured. People no longer have to leave to improve their lives, nor do they have to resign themselves to tradition and the notion of an everlasting cycle of history that keeps repeating itself. Ultimately the Schneiders teach us that citizens are those who get involved in the politics of their lives, and good citizens don't leave their futures up to government.

(*Italian American Review* 2004)

Jane and Peter Schneider, *Reversible Destiny: Mafia, Antimafia, and the Struggle for Palermo* (Berkeley: U of California P, 2003). ISBN 0520221001 (hardcover); 0520236092 (paperback); $24.95 (paperback).

Felix Stefanile

By now the Queens, New York little Italy of Felix Stefanile's past has lived longer in his mind than he ever did within its boundaries. Yet, the further away he has moved, the stronger it has spiritually tugged at his soul. This tension exploded every now and then in poems such as "The Americanization of the Immigrant":

> Like Dante
> I have pondered and pondered
> the speech I was born with,
> lost now, mother gone,
> the whole neighborhood bulldozed
> and no one to say it on the TV,
> that words are dreams.

In his latest book, the poet proves that verse can be just as powerful as television in helping us to recreate the worlds we have lost and to imagine those we have never seen.

Stefanile, recent winner of the John Ciardi Award for life long achievement in Italian/American poetry, and Professor Emeritus of English at Purdue University, has gathered many of his more obviously ethnic eruptions into a collection entitled *The Country of Absence: Poems and an Essay*. These thirty-one poems and an essay become the words that recreate the dreams the poet has had about his life and the life of his ancestors.

The book opens with a masterful essay entitled "The Allegory of the Hyphen." Stefanile sees his own identity in terms of his poetry, an art that serves as the hyphen connecting Italian with American. While immigrant poets such as Joseph Tusiani may use poetry to question the possibilities of having two distinct selves, Stefanile sees his poetry as the bridge that unites the two cultures.

Stefanile's "country of absence," is not Italy, but the place, "where my imagination had never been." One of these places was American poetry, a place the author was brought to by a change of schools and a writing contest that made others aware of his verbal talents. Through the essay, the author reveals what brought the poetry out of the child and the artist out of the man who has been referred to as the "grandfather of new formalism" and "the Godfather of Italian American poetry."

Besides the autobiography, Stefanile includes a section that comments on the roles played by on the role of poets such as Emily Dickinson and Rap artists in crashing through the surface of the acceptable literature formally known as "the canon." In the remainder of the essay the author reads his own work, a treat in the grand tradition of Henry James' "Prefaces." The essay sets up a new way of reading Stefanilie's more obvious Italian/American poems.

Along with two of his translations from the Italian of poems by Umberto Saba and and Cecco Angiolieri, he includes one of his first major publications, accepted in 1950 by Karl Shapiro for *Poetry,* one of the most important literary magazines in this country's history. "The Marionettes" signaled the arrival of a major poet who could make art of the Italian immigrant experience without relying on the sheer weight of the trauma of uprooting for his song: "They're not content to be themselves, / but plot a vegetable sovereignty, / with their sinister, sonorous Italian names / dream some varnished mythology/."

Another masterpiece is "A Fig Tree in America," in which the poet immortalizes his father as the planter of the fig tree: "And here I stand, / amid the brick and business, / over the ultimate exile of his grave, / to marvel at my mortal foreigner, / who struck a flag that still can fly so green./" There's the popular "How I Changed my Name, Felice," the title poem of his last collection, "The Dance at St. Gabriel's," and a whole series based on the author's experiences in World War II which includes "Hubie," a powerfully poetic commentary on friendship and racism.

While these poems have been published before, they create a unique statement in their proximity to each other. *The Country of Absence* lights a side of Stefanile that many of his readers might never have seen, but have always felt; ultimately it is one of the greatest tributes to Italian America by one of its greatest artists.

(April 2000)

Felix Stefanile, *The Country of Absence: Poems and an Essay* (West Lafayette, IN: Bordighera P, 2000). ISBN 1884419283; $9.00 (paperback).

Ross Talarico

Listening to people and turning their lives into literature is one way that Ross Talarico becomes involved in the politics of change. Known throughout the country for his work with local oral history projects, Talarico has had his community work featured on NBC's *Today Show,* National Public Radio's *Weekend Edition,* and in *USA Today.* His books include *Hearts and Times: The Literature of Memory,* produced as a play in Chicago, and *Spreading the Word: Poetry and the Survival of Community in America,* which won a prestigious Shaughnessy Prize from the Modern Language Association.

In *The Journey Home* Talarico turns his poetic eye and his keen sense of community building towards his ethnic ancestors. This collection of eleven oral histories, transcribed and written by Talarico, features Italians from the Rochester, New York area, where Talarico once served as America's only full-time city government sponsored Writer-in-Residence. The oral history project from which Talarico has drawn his work, was created by the Casa Italiana, a center of Italian language, literature and culture for both Nazareth College students and the general public.

Everything about this book speaks to the power of community to create literature and history. The Casa Italiana funded the original project with support secured by New York State Assemblyman Joseph Morelle through a legislative grant from the New York State Department of Education. As the Center's Director Rose Centanni writes in her "Preface," "Talarico presents an Italy in this book that is more a people than a place."

In his "Introduction" Talarico notes that "All the stories describe a time for change in America, not simply of locale, but a change of perspective when life was redefined and 'character,' more than fortune or circumstance, became the prevailing trait of Italian Americans." Talarico's insight into the power of personal story to both create and preserve community history is evidenced by his selections of subjects and observations such like: "It is as if, as Italian Americans, they have displayed what is most distinct in the human species: a passion for life that overcomes the troublesome moments that everyone experiences." The people we meet in *The Journey Home* have as much to tell us about our own lives as they do theirs.

The key to turning one's life history into story is selection. Talarico does a great job of isolating the defining moment of each subject's existence, a moment that he then transforms into art. For Rose Muscarella, it was her mother stooping to scrub the elegant steps of the elegant Hotel Bristol, for Mary Verno, it was the sight of "that first horseless carriage, that Model T Ford . . . with the strange couple dressed in suits sitting so erect, floating effortlessly through the sudden landscape of our dreams." Joe Valentino recalls the revenge he felt when his dog Queenie biting the rear-end of the ornery widow who "represented an adult world that had no sensitivity to children." There are eight other stories ranging from Tony Sciolino's overview of immigration, Mary Ann Sellitto's portrait of her grandfather, and local luminay Johnny Antonelli story of his move from the neighborhood into major league baseball.

In each of the entries, Talarico enacts what I call a sensual intellect. His writing combines body and mind in a way that finds the poetry in the people. The result is a lightning flash of someone's life that, in a moment, illuminates a telling scene that imprints itself one one's psyche and into one's memory forever. Talarico simply finds the words to capture those flashes and send them out to others through words. This is what separates the usual oral history from this unique literary stories.

The collection concludes with Talarico poem, "An Utterance of Joy" through which the author transforms his own grandfather's story into a poem that teaches us all something about the lives of those who brought us here. *The Journey Home* is easy, powerful reading that should be in the hands, home, and head of every Italian American.

(October 2009)

Ross Talarico, *The Journey Home* (West Lafayette, IN: Bordighera P, 2000). ISBN 1884419348.

THOM TAMMARO

We last heard from Thom Tammaro in the *Fra Noi* when his *When the Italians Came to My Home Town* was published back in 1995. His first major book of poetry was well received, and since then he's been editing poetry anthologies, teaching, and working on new poems. Those new poems have found themselves in his latest publication *Holding on for Dear Life.*

This collection of fifty poems divided into four distinct sections that take us Back and forth through the poet's real and imaginary lives. Section One is full of home town memories of a baby boomer born in Pennsylvania. The best poems are filled with stark studies of working class life, so stark is "I And the Village," that it conjures up black and whites photos of the 50s: "Back then, it was all gray skies; / Brown and gray clapboard houses; / Soot on the chrome bumpers / Of black cares, bed sheets...."

He includes some historical subjects like "First Murder in My Home Town," And the "Cuban Missile Crisis" that reminds us of the fears created by air raid drills and being trained what to do if we were captured by communists. "Corpus Christi" is every altar boy's memory who has ever had to walk in the pre-dawn dark to church to serve the first morning mass, pretending to be a priest, and who took communion with unconfessed sins on your soul, just so the priest wouldn't think wrongly of you.

Like many poets of this generation, Tammaro was influenced by Beat writers like Lawrence Ferlinghetti to create poetry in beautiful and clear language. In "The Ferlinghetti Reading" we get a great view of his first Ferlinghetti sighting and the impact it had on his imagination then and now. The act of finding a bottle of "Lupinis" in the gourmet aisle of a grocery store ignites a prose poem that returns the snack to its humble origins. This mock ode of sorts will water the mouths of anyone who's ever purchased a nickel bag of these babies in an old neighborhood store or at a street festival.

Section Two, is perhaps the darkest, and is dedicated to his father who died a slow and eventually painful death from cancer. The poems here recount the experience of being with and away from his father during this time. Tammaro writes in a variety of verse styles, and is especially adept at the prose poem. His "In the Room" recounts the experience of his father renting the house that has the room he knows he will die in. It is one of the most moving poems about death written in recent memory. In Section Three, we move outside the family and into the poet's professional life, and the book concludes with a section of poems primarily about travelling.

Holding on is Tammaro at his best, whether he's meditating on flowers, family, work, laughter, love or death, his poems are class acts of reliving, rejoicing and remembering. He creates a spectacle of the mundane, the everyday matter that we all know and too often ignore in the rush of moving forward. In the sweep of a prose poem and the slap of a tight lyric, Tammaro stops life long enough to craft art out of memory. His meditations on family, work, love, and death help us all to let go of the real and hold on to the spiritual. It's rare to have your own memory so touched by the writing of another.

(April 2005)

Thom Tammaro, *Holding on for Dear Life: Poems* (Granite Falls, MN: Spoon River Poetry Press, 2004). www.spoonriverpoetrypress.com; ISBN 0944024505; $12.95.

GIOIA TIMPANELLI

Few know better than Gioia Timpanelli that to share a story is like sharing one's soul. And few souls are larger than hers. Known as the dean (I prefer *Commare*) of American storytellers, Timpanelli has traveled the world gathering and disseminating wisdom and joy through the medium of storytelling. She has appeared with the likes of Joseph Campbell and Robert Bly, and no matter where she goes, she always brings a little of Sicily into her performances.

With *Sometimes the Soul*, Timpanelli, a master-storyteller, shifts from her familiar stance in front of live audiences to the lonely place behind the desk; she manages this shift from oral to the literary tradition without a hitch. The two novellas that comprise this book are elegant tales that can be read again and again. What makes this possible is Timpanelli's mastery of the written word. Not all oral storytellers can capture all the nuances that make writing more difficult, but Timpanelli has no problem.

In the first novella, *A Knot of Tears*, Signora Costanza has locked herself up in a house for so long that she feels a "knot of tears" that she fears will unravel her if she touches it. On the advice of her servant, a window is opened, and for the first time in a long while she looks out onto the town. At that moment two gentleman catch a glimpse of her and decide that they must meet her. They bet who will be the first to meet her and the quest is on. And while this bet forms the basic plot of the novella, Timpanelli weaves a number of other story lines into the action, including one of a sailor and his storytelling parrot. These other threads intensify the reading and increase its pleasure. You will have to read this a number of times to wring out all the wisdom and Timapanelli's luxurious style will make the rereading a joy.

In *Rusina, Not Quite in Love*, Timpanelli retells "Beauty and the Beast" with a Sicilian slant. A man in debt sends his daughter to serve a rich man's elderly aunt and uncle. Rusina is not hesitant, for leaving home means getting away from her abusive sisters. Rusina finds the service to the old couple a joy and a way to become educated into artistry and womanhood. What she imagines she receives, but what she sees also deceives her. Sebastiano, The master gardener is a warm, helpful sort with a face so hideous it can't be described. Nevertheless, Rusina befriends the gardener and learns much from him, but she can't give in to his requests for her hand in marriage. When she falls in love with a handsome dancer at the ball, she learns to see things in a whole new light.

Both of these novellas are rich with understanding about life, love, nature, writing and storytelling. Timpanelli is especially adept at bringing out the natural strengths of her female characters, something that separates her from other contemporary venues for such stories, such as the Disney machine, that never stop turning out the same old story of weak women depending on strong men. Each story, in its own way, presents the joy of sharing one's story as the antidote to depression. Once this happens, the shell that surrounds us breaks and we are free. Like Costanza, once we look out of our windows, we can begin to see a world that can give us joy.

"Si cunta e si ricunta," is how the traditional tales are begun, meaning "it is told and retold." There should be a similar phrase for reading a Timpanelli story, "Si lettu e si rilettu," "It is read and reread." For Timpanelli takes the old and makes it new, takes the traditional and reworks it into ways of making our lives better by enlarging our souls through story. Timpanelli's first literary fiction has achieved an unqualified success. In both form and content her stories delight and uplift. There is no more we can ask of the writer who has given us *Sometimes the Soul*, except to ask for more.

(May 1999)

Gioia Timpanelli, *Sometimes the Soul: Two Novellas of Sicily* (New York: Vintage Books, 1999). ISBN 0375707220; $23 (hardcover).

BILL TONELLI

Bill Tonelli's *The Italian American Reader* is a collection of 68 selections by American writers of Italian descent. Some of the contributors are well-known champions of their ethnicity, others were dragged along begrudgingly by Tonelli who wanted to reflect a range of approaches to being Italian American. There are novel excerpts such as Don DeLillo's *Underworld* and Mario Puzo's *Fortunate Pilgrim*. Selections from the DeCapite (Michael and Raymond) brothers, Philip Caputo, Josephine Hendin, John Fante, Pietro di Donato, Tony Ardizzone and others. The memoirists include Jerre Mangione, Gay Talese, Barbara Grizzuti Harrison, among others.

Poetry punctuates the prose with selections from John Ciardi, Jay Parini, Felix Stefanile, W.S. DiPiero, Kim Addonizio, Dana Gioia, Rachel Guido de Vries, Joseph Tusiani, Robert Viscusi, Gregory Corso, and others. Short fiction by Anthony Giardina, Rita Ciresi, essays by Maria Laurino, Anthony Valerio Ray "Everybody Loves Raymond" Romano, Camille Paglia, Mary Cappello, Robert Orsi, and Helen Barolini, round out the cast. Tonelli uses themes to organize the collection: home, mom, sex, love and good looks, food, pop, death, work, god, each other, everybody else form the bins into which the writing is placed.

The next time someones says to you, "I never heard of any Italian American writers except maybe Mario Puzo," throw them a copy of Tonelli's collection and tell them to keep the change.

(April 2003)

Bill Tonelli, ed., *The Italian American Reader: A Collection of Outstanding Fiction, Memoirs, Journalism, Essays, and Poetry*, foreword by Nick Tosches (New York, NY: W. Morrow, 2003). ISBN 0060006668; $27.95.

ADRIANA TRIGIANI

When we last left Ave Maria Mulligan of *Big Stone Gap*, she was happily married to local boy Jack MacChensey and settling down to a normal life after an unsettling courtship and a wild Italian honeymoon. In the sequel to her first novel Adriana Trigiani takes us from "The Gap" to *Big Cherry Holler* and further into the lives, losses, and loves of the only Italian in an Appalachian community. Now, eight years and one third grader later, Ave, her husband, and many of their friends are facing near-mid-life crises that occur when the coalmine shuts down, threatening to change the lives of everyone in town.

Ave's different. Not from a long line of miner folk like most everyone else, this "ferriner" can think outside the mine, and that gets her into trouble. Trigiani makes the most of Ave's Italian ancestry, using her difference to both solve and create new problems. In a desperate attempt to do something about her marriage, Ave, with her daughter, visits her father, the mayor of a town in the Italian Alps. As the mountain hikes build her calves and Italian style builds her confidence, she begins to attract attention. But she soon finds out that a similar thing is happening to Jack Mac who has stayed home to work in his new construction business and to figure things out for himself.

From the Alps to the Appalachians, what happens to both keeps the pages flying by in this short but sweet novel about what to do when a once hot love gets cooled off by time, tragedy, and temptation. At times the writing is quite poetic and humorous. Trigiani has a gift of smart dialogue and wise meditation. She never loses her focus on telling a tale in which being Italian is both a curse and a blessing.

Adriana Trigiani, *Big Cherry Holler: A Big Stone Novel* (New York: Random House, 2001). www.atrandom.com; ISBN 0375506179; $24.95 (hardcover).

&

In Adriana Trigiani's *Big Stone Gap*, Ave Maria Mulligan is an Italian American living in a Virginia mountain town who at thirty-something finds herself a stable, independent professional and a spinster. Shortly after her mother Fiammetta dies, Ave finally learns the truth. After getting pregnant by her forbidden love, her mother had run away from home, taking a job as a seamstress. Along her way she met a rich woman named Ave Maria who helped her to America. Fred Mulligan, a local pharmacist and friend of the man who hires Fiammetta, feels sorry for her and marries her despite her pregnancy.

Ave then makes a decision that will change her life. But before she can act on it, life changes her. Instead of settling down, she plans a search for her true father believing it will explain why she can't love the men she finds. Adept at reading books, faces (she's studied an ancient Chinese art), and social situations, Ave can't understand her own dilemma until a jilted suitor derails her plans for escape.

Full of hilarious scenes, such as the campaign visit of Elizabeth Taylor and US Senate candidate Jack Warren, the novel creates a world where being Italian American not only matters, it helps everyone else become better human beings. There's a predictable Hollywood ending — Trigiani did spend ten years of writing and producing shows like *The Cosby Show* — but it doesn't overshadow the down-home goodness of her doorway into a refreshing new world of life in America.

The paperback edition contains a fictional interview of the author by one of the novel's characters and a chapter from the sequel *Big Cherry Holler*.

(August 2001)

Adriana Trigiani, *Big Stone Gap: A Novel* (New York: Random House, 2000). www.randomhouse.com/BRC/; ISBN 0375504036; $12.95 (paperback).

BEA TUSIANI

Subtitled *A Daughter-in-Law's Story of Growing up Italian-American in Brooklyn*, Bea Tusiani's collection of personal stories *Con Amore*, tells the birth to middle-aged story of a woman who could be any woman born to Italian Americans during the post World War II baby boom. In 43 short vignettes, the author revives scene after scene from a pretty normal yet intense life that takes her from the Bushwick section of Brooklyn to Queens, to Long Island, and places around the world.

In some memoirs, the antagonist in the story is an old self, in others, it's a force, or an enemy that helped shaped the writer's persona, but in this book, Tusiani poses her mother-in-law as a possibility. Having married the youngest of Maria Tusiani's sons — the oldest is the famous poet Joseph —, Bea is destined for a long life in the spot light of her mother-in-law. Each chapter opens with a proverb, or a short statement referring to old world traditions or to other beliefs her mother-in-law practices. It is against these short and poignant set-ups that Tusiani's own life comes into focus. "Unlike my mother-in-law who could make soup out of a wasp's nest if she had to, I could be victimized by an army of ants."

Nicknamed, "The Madonna of the Pot," Maria and the author appears on the book's cover photography. They are sitting in a kitchen, smiling for the camera, but you can see there's a tension between them in the stiffness of their hands and smiles. If we try to judge this book by that photo, we might expect frequent battle-like encounters between the two strongest forces in an Italian American married man's life. At first, I was taken aback by how little we actually read about Mamma Tusiani.

For most of the book, the author tells her own story as the daughter of Sicilians on both sides of her family. Her own mother did not live long enough to see Bea get married, and her father, well his second marriage threatens his daughter's. There is more than enough going on in her extended family that we can sometimes forget her mother-in-law is on the cover. After a brief accounting of her mother-in-law's life in the "Introduction," the older woman's story comes to us piecemeal, here and there, as though it was a powerful spice that would overpower the subtleties of Bea's stories if it was used too liberally. Woven throughout the memoir is the life, and death, story of Mamma Tusiani; Bea even includes a letter that Mamma wrote to her sons detailing how she wants to be prepared for her funeral that reflects her modesty and her strong faith.

"My Italian 'suocera' dismissed most anything I did with a backward wave of the hand," but the day Bea when her mother-in-law calls her "my daughter" she "melted into a puddle" and the process is what this book is all about. While most of the vignettes have the substance of family home movies, few of them feel as though they are not your family. Tusiani writes with one eye on reality and the other on her audience's faces. She knows when to stop reminiscing and start pumping up the drama. Anyone can find the drama in the tragic things of life, like the death of a parent, a sibling, a relative or friend, but good writers like Tusiani create the drama in the everyday acts of riding in a car, watching women at work in the kitchen, or men at play on city streets.

(August 2005)

Bea Tusiani, *Con Amore: A Daughter-in-law's Story of Growing Up Italian American in Bushwick* (Boca Raton, FL: Bordighera P, 2004). ISBN 1884419666; $19 (paperback).

Joseph Tusiani

Ethnicity: Selected Poems by Joseph Tusiani is a gathering of poetry on themes of Italian immigration by one of Italian America's great poets. The bulk of the collection is the long-awaited reprinting of *Gente Mia*, first published by the Italian Cultural Center of Stone Park. Editor Paolo A. Giordano has included two of his early essays on Tusiani along with nine other Tusiani poems dealing with Italian American themes.

Whether privately personal, as in "To My Father" and "The Old Chair," or publicly historical such as "The Soliloquy of Philip Mazzei" or "Garibaldi's Candle," Tusiani is a master at capturing dimensions of the immigrant experience. He combines the knowledge of a well-versed scholar with the heart of an emotionally honed human to create formalistic poetry of the most ordinary of miracles and the most extraordinary of historical acts.

Born in San Marco in Lamis, the province of Foggia, Tusiani immigrated to the United States shortly after World War II. Educated at the University of Naples in English Language and Literature, he had written much poetry before emigrating. While his first novel, *Envoy from Heaven*, appeared in 1965, he is perhaps best known for his translations of the poetry of Michelangelo and Tasso. He was the first Italian American to be named Vice President of the Poetry Society of America, a position he held from 1956–1968.

The alienation themes that characterized the episodic writing of the early

Italian/American novelists such as Pietro di Donato are crystallized in Tusiani's work. In his "Song of the Bicentennial," written in celebration of America's 200th birthday, Tusiani, raises the question of the meaning of "Italianita" in America and its relation to the immigrant's identity: "Then, who will solve this riddle of my day? / Two languages, two lands, perhaps two souls . . . /Am I a man or two strange halves of one?" (7). In questioning his own experience as an immigrant, Tusiani also wonders about those who had immigrated earlier, those who had not his abilities to write in either language. More than any other Italian American who has ventured into the arts in America, Tusiani gives voice to those predecessors. In the final stanza of "Bicentennial" he writes: "I am the present for I am the past / of those who for their future came to stay, / humble and innocent and yet outcast. / . . . For this my life their death made ample room."

Through such poems Tusiani takes on the responsibility of speaking for the earlier immigrants. As Giordano points,

> Tusiani shows the reader that the American cultural milieu has absorbed the superficial and stereotypical aspects of Italian immigrant culture while never understanding the true character of this populace. . . . It is up to the poet, who draws his inspiration from the injustice suffered by his people, to assure that their sacrifice will not be forgotten.

Since he has retired from teaching, having taught in American colleges for more than thirty-five years, Tusiani has completed three volumes of an autobiographical narrative epic. The first one is a novelization of his landmark poem, *La parola difficile* [*The Difficult Word*]. The next two were *La parola nuova* [*The New Word*], and *La parola antica* [*The Ancient Word*]. All three were written in Italian and are currently being translated into English.

Giordano has gathered a representative collection of Tusiani's classic poetry that serves as an excellent introduction to newcomers; it is an essential publication for those already familiar with this great poet's work.

(August 2001)

Joseph Tusiani, *Ethnicity: Selected Poems*, ed. Paolo Giordano (West Lafayette, IN; Bordighera P, 2000). ISBN 1884419372; $12 (paperback).

&

More than a century before Shakespeare fell in love, there was Dante in love. And had a Hollywood producer ever been exposed to this poet's life, there no doubt would have been a film or two on the life of this literary giant. Some critics even believe that if there had been no Dante, there would have been no Shakespeare. Whatever the critics say, you can now make up your own mind. You can also save yourself the trouble of learning Italian to find out what he did to woo the ladies in vernacular verse by picking up a copy of *Dante's Lyric Poems*.

This collection contains a selection of Dante's lyric poems, from his earliest compositions at the age of 18 to some his later poems. All are magnificently translated by Joseph Tusiani, an award-winning master poet and translator. Tusiani's previous translations include *The Complete Poems of Michelangelo*, Tasso's *Jerusalem Delivered* and *Creation of the World*, Pulci's *Morgante*, and most recently an edition of Leopardi's *Canti*. Tusiani's English brings an unprecedented faithfulness to Dante's Italian rhythms and rhyme.

The "Introduction" and notes are provided by Dante Scholar Giuseppe Carlo Di Scipio, Professor of Italian and Chair of the Department of Romance Languages at Hunter College. Di Scipio's research and insights into the poetry and the context of each poem help us to understand the impact Dante's "stil novo" or new style, had on the evolution of the Italian language and love poetry. As Di Scipio points out, the "comprehensive view, as presented in this volume ... provides a concrete understanding of Dante's poetic growth and constant experimentation with forms, techniques and themes."

Included in this revised and expanded edition is the entire *La Vita Nuova*, through which we gain access to the "conscience and history" of Dante's poetry. Though not a goal for Tusiani, it would have been nice to have an English translation of this important work included in this fine publication. Dante's *Lyric Poems* is a must for scholars, and more importantly, is accessible to the general reading audience.

(September 1999)

Joseph Tusiani, trans. *Dante's Lyric Poems,* intro. and notes by Giuseppe C. Di Scipio (Brooklyn, NY: Legas, 1992). ISBN 0921252196.

ANTHONY VALERIO

As we know so well through the work of Giambattista Vico, if history is to live it must be imagined. This is why what survives from prehistoric times comes to us in images and not philosophy, in sounds and not sound bites. This is a lesson well learned by novelist and story writer Anthony Valerio who applies the same remarkable storytelling skills that gave us *The Mediterranean Runs Through Brooklyn, Valentino and the Great Italians,* and *Lefty and the Button Men,* to the life of

Anita Garibaldi — revolutionary and wife of the famous Giuseppe Garibaldi.

In Valerio's hands, the little we know of Anita through earlier accounts, becomes enlarged and takes on a life of its own. Beyond the boring facts of history we gain the spirit that made those facts important enough for us to remember over a century after her death. *Anita Garibaldi: A Biography* is a mosaic portrait composed from dozens of sources and different voices, united through story as bonafide history. While what little we have in writing about Anita Garibaldi has been known for some time, Valerio provides new insights to this historical information, not by coming up with new information, or by revising earlier accounts, but by applying the novelist's tricks to the biographer's trade. This synthesis brings us new perspectives on a life that is normally overshadowed by her husband.

Born Ana Maria de Jesus Ribeiro da Silva in Brazil, Anita lost her father when she was 12 to a work accident; six years later she first caught sight of Giuseppe Garibaldi and joined him in the fight to free her country. The recreation of her earlier years, about which very little is actually known, helps us to understand how Ana could leave her home and her life to fight alongside her lover in Brazil, Uruguay and Italy.

We know that Garibaldi first spied his future wife through a telescope, but Valerio's imagining of the encounter makes us feel it from both sides of the instrument.

> Her admiration was clear, transparent. In her smile he'd been seeing the vitality and tenderness some knowledge of him aroused in her.... Her appearance possessed "una bellezza irregolare," an unusual, stark beauty, a beauty outside the ordinariness of the lady-like norm. So powerful was the impression she made on him that he ordered the dinghy put down.

When Garibaldi begins rowing her way, we are there cheering him on.

Just as Valerio varies sentence length and sounds to create various paces throughout the work, he also varies the length of the chapters so that they become more like scenes in a dramatic film and less like sections of a predictable documentary. Most of the writing is so good you'll almost forget it has an academic base until you consult the endnotes, bibliography, or index, all accurate and useful.

A "Foreword" by Philip Cannistraro, Distinguished Professor of Italian American Studies at CUNY Graduate Center and Queens College, nicely situates Anita's story in the history of the democratic struggles that lead to the development of modern nation states. 20 pages of illustrations provide fixed images that serve as a static relief to the moving images in the prose.

This biography, along with Dorothy Bryant's novelization of her life in *Anita, Anita*, is a good place to start if you know nothing about this amazing woman who died at 28 years of age, living more in that period than most people having three times the years. For those who know everything, Valerio's ability to imagine her passion and purpose will help you know it even better.

(July 2002)

Anthony Valerio, *Anita Garibaldi: A Biography*, foreword by Philip V. Cannistraro (Westport, CT: Praeger, 2001). www.greenwood.com; ISBN 0275969371 (hardcover); 027596938X (paperback); $18.95.

&

Anthony Valerio, author of *Valentino and the Great Italians*, *The Mediterranean Runs through Brooklyn*, and *Bart: A Life of A. Bartlett Giamatti*, has always been one of the leading voices of literary Italian America. In his earlier books, Valerio wove imaginative chiaro/scuro flights into Italian/American history and his own life to create original takes on the meaning of Italian/American sensibilities in a post-immigration culture.

In his latest book, *Conversation with Johnny*, he pushes even further ahead by tackling two stereotypes that have plagued Italian Americans: the gangster and the lover. In this sometimes parodic, sometimes sardonic, but always entertaining look at crime and culture, Valerio attempts a literary hit on those stereotypes. While he might not eliminate them, he certainly paralyzes both of them long enough for us to see that "the cult of 'The Godfather' is over."

The seed of this novel is a short story Valerio published back in 1990, in the first issue of *Voices in Italian Americana*. "The Last Godfather," which appears as a chapter in *Conversations*, sounded a death knell for the gangster as representative for Italian America and resurrected the Italian/American writer as a hero in its place. *Conversations* wraps that story in a context that leaps the ghetto boundaries of Italian/American storytelling.

Nicholas, whose family has nicknamed Mootzie, "after mozzarella itself," is a writer as obsessed with the women he has loved as he is with the stories he must tell. When his latest affair with a married redhead writer he calls "Lefty" begins to wilt, he decides it's time to get some advice from an old neighborhood buddy who has risen to the position of Don.

Nicholas wants to become an ordinary man and so seeks advice on how to stop being a lover. Having sacrificed family for women and writing, Nicholas comes to Johnny, whose over-developed family includes the entire Bensonhurst neighborhood. During the conversations, in which Nicholas confesses the intimate details of his sexual escapades, Nicholas and Johnny pose challenges to each other: Johnny can give him money, can make him Maitre d at a famous restaurant, but can he give Mootzie what he really needs, like advice on creating a family or a retirement home for Italian/American writers? Nicholas gives a reading in Johnny's home of his story, "The Last Godfather," which presents Johnny with an honorable way out of his life of crime.

Against Johnny the pure criminal and Nicholas the cultural pioneer, Valerio introduces Bob Nardack, the "Kid Professor," whose name hides his Italian origins and whose behavior in public mocks his true love. Nardack serves as a foil to both Nicholas the writer/lover and the gangster. The kid professor, is a public gangster storyteller and private lover who puts down his true love in public to elevate his own intellectual work; after all, how can a man who professes love be taken seriously as an intellectual?

A strange tension develops between the kid professor and Nicholas when the attention the kid gives to Italian Americans in crime shadows the developments of Italian/American culture. Nicholas asks Johnny to take the kid aside and steer him straight, away from an identification with crime and toward the development of culture; he wants Johnny to deliver the message that "For the time being, we have to tolerate our crime and our culture, but your job is to promote the culture, not the crime." As the kid professor needs Nicholas to claim a culture, Nicholas needs the kid professor's academic skills to engrave his contribution on the larger society's cultural memory, but he can't allow the kid to push his work in one breath and tell stories about his own petty criminal exploits in the next.

The novel's segments, like a good stand-up routine, are well timed and while each can stand on its own, they all combine to create a novel that comes together only at the end when the characters transform into another story. The key to this novel is the sound and fury of the language used by Valerio to raise simple storytelling to the art of literature.

Ultimately the novel is about the balance that must be created between history and imagination so that a culture's history can be used to create art. And this is what Valerio achieves in this slightly romantic parable about the relationship between love and friendship. "Conversation with Johnny" is a gourmet novel concocted by a master literary chef, a literary potion that could just be the antidote to break the spell cast on Italian American by Mario Puzo's *The Godfather*.

(October 1997)

Anthony Valerio, *Conversation with Johnny: A Novel* (Toronto: Guernica Editions, 1997). ISBN 1550710524; $12 (paperback).

2009 Editor's Note: It now can be purchased as *Lefty and the Button Men* through Xlibris Corporation, www.xlibris.com.

STEVEN VARNI

Through twelve connected stories, Steven Varni's novel, *The Inland Sea*, explores the making and breaking of a nuclear family that could be yours or your neighbor's. Varni strikes a nice balance between style and story to create an extraordinary novel out of the ordinary experiences of a young man's coming of age and coming to terms with his childhood.

Divided into Part One, Innocence, and Part Two, Experience, *The Inland Sea* invites comparison to William Blake's *Songs of Innocence and of Experience*. Blake, a major English Romantic poet, used poems and illustrations to depict contrasting stages of human life youth and adulthood. Like Blake, Varni creates art that impacts the psyche.

The stories of Innocence begin when the protagonist and sometimes narrator, Vincent Torno, is not yet able to read, though he can mimic what his mother reads to him. As we follow Vincent's development we learn that his mother has a mental illness requiring occasional hospitalization. Vincent cannot separate himself from her sickness until he grows older. He has a father who "forced each issue ... [while] his mother tore each one to pieces." This combination creates a series of conflicts that shape the way Victor learns to read their world. There is a sense of distance between Vincent and the reader that is enhanced by having all but one of the stories in this section written in third person. Varni shifts modes to create an entirely different mood in Part Two.

Of the six stories in Experience, four are in first person and bring us closer to the personality that has now become our narrator. If Innocence was about learning to read life, then Experience is about learning to write life, to express one's thoughts and ideas in language that enables Vincent to gain control over his life and sometimes the lives of others. Part Two covers Vincent's growth away from his family and toward his life work of writing. Since his older brother goes into the family business the pressure is off Vincent so that he can go off to college where he begins to develop a stronger sense of self.

Varni captures well the time in a boy's life when knowing meanings go from being unnecessary to vital for mental and physical survival. As Vincent Torno returns to the past to extract some understanding of where he is at, he reminds us that this is something we all do, but something that when done by good writers, helps us know our own lives a little bit better.

The Inland Sea is a wise novel built with patience and the author's wonderful ability to catch the detail that puts us inside the characters, as in this scene when Vincent is watching his brother and friends work in the shed:

> Only rarely could Vincent actually see their work; a box or a head or someone's back inevitably blocked his view. But he listened to the sober metallic sounds of the tools, to his brother's and his friends' comments, quite voices diminishing with increased effort. He watched the contortions of their shirtless torsos, the beads of sweat tracing the lines on their shoulder blades and taught necks, where they bend to work beneath a caged droplight.

Varni's narrator, whether first or third person, creates a mood not unlike the calm in the eye of the storm. All hell can be breaking loose in the Torno family business or home and we watch it all as though we were invisible and knew it.

Varni has given us a fine look into the lives of the children of immigrants and the family they have created. Ultimately *The Inland Sea* reminds us that it doesn't matter what gets lost or retained from a culture through assimilation, it's the effect that experiences have on our psyches that really counts.

(November 2000)

Steven Varni, *The Inland Sea* (New York: W. Morrow, 2000). ISBN 0688169066; $22 (hardcover).

RICHARD VETERE

It is not often that a good book gets made into a good film, but this is exactly what has happened with Richard Vetere's *The Third Miracle*. First published to critical acclaim in 1997, this writer's first novel has just appeared in paperback on bookstore shelves, roughly the same time the film version was released on video.

A statue of Mary in a Queens church begins crying tears of blood whenever it rains in October. The miracle is attributed to Helen Stephenson, a holy woman from the parish who abandoned her daughter, believing she was called to minister to the poor. When news of the event reaches Cardinal Cahill, he appoints his best investigator, Father Moore. A leading Church intellectual, Moore is going through a trying time in his life as a priest. Having just disproved a case that "destroyed" the faith of another community, he is hesitant to take on the task, but does so a favor to his friend the Cardinal.

As years pass, the miracle becomes part of a strong case to canonize Helen. After a number are claimed in her name, the Vatican sends over a team to see if the necessary three miracles can be confirmed. Over the course of this religious thriller, we come to learn how human is the spiritual. Vetere takes us behind the scenes of a Church wielding its temporal power through heroes who fight the forces of evil that surface whenever there's a surge in holiness.

It's easy to see why this novel made a good transition to the screen. Vetere's a natural writer of dialogue. He has a fine ear for voices and an ability to get different voices down on the page without dragging a quick paced narrative. His characters are well developed and balanced, not the usual stereotypes. A veteran playwright of successful Off-Broadway productions such as *Gangster Apparel*, *The*

Marriage Fool, and *First Love*, he recently starred in the production of his new play *Safe*. A film adaptation of his play, *How to Go Out on a Date in Queens*, is currently in production.

(July 2001)

Richard Vetere, *The Third Miracle: A Novel* (New York: Scribner Paperback Fiction, 1998). www.SimonSays.com; ISBN 0684847426.

Robert Viscusi

Author's note: What follows is part of a review that covered two poets. The second part appears in this volume under the Paola Corso entry.

Robert Viscusi and Paola Corso are two very different poets, at verydifferent places in their careers, who have recently published their first full-length collections of poetry.

For years now Viscusi, best known for his American Book Award winningnovel, *Astoria* and his humorous and controversial, *Oration Upon the Most Recent Death of Christopher Columbus,* has been has been penning and performing poetry around New York and in Italy. Some of this poetry has been collected in *A New Geography of Time.*

More focused on thought than sound, more dictum and rhythm than meterand rhyme scheme, his is a poetry characterized by phrase turnings and not verse rhyming. You'll remember the ideas long after the sound has stopped echoing. But you may have a problem memorizing them, for Viscusi does not follow the rules of typical oral traditions.

Viscusi is more of a thinking person's poet; he champions the absurd thought that makes sense only when you let go of your way of looking at the world. For Viscusi doesn't see things the way most of us do. He can, and that's what makes his prose accessible to students and scholars alike, but when it comes to poetry, he's not trying to teach his readers anything. Rather, his goal is to make them see things differently.

There is some of his classic Italian Americana here, but for the most part this collection moves us out of Little Italy and into the new world. Whether it's a meditation on website or a view of St. Anthony's Basilica in Padova, these forty some poems force you to you to look beyond belief and create new ways of understanding how to live with imperfections and how to imagine the real.

(June 2005)

Robert Viscusi, *A New Geography of Time* (Toronto: Guernica Editions, 2004). $10 paperback). ISBN 1550711830.

Justin Vitiello

For many years, Justin Vitiello, poet, translator, and professor at Temple University, has labored to build cultural connections between Italy and the United States. He has translated the likes of Michelangelo, Gaspara Stampa, Dino Buzzati, Danilo Dolci and Ignazio Buttita from Italian and dialects into English. His books include *Vanzetti's Fish Cart, Sicily Within*, and a major study *Poetics and Literature of the Sicilian Diaspora: Studies in Oral History and Story Telling*. All this creative, scholarly and critical writing work has helped him to claim the culture of his ancestors and infuse his American life with a good dose of Italianita.

His latest book, *Labyrinths and Volcanoes: Windings Through Sicily*, a compilation of the prose and poetry he's produced on Sicily, is more proof that this scholar is also an adventurous artist. Vitiello's incredible knowledge of Sicilian culture is cleverly juxtaposed with words from the various inhabitants he has met over the twenty-two years of travelling and there. Some of the material has been published before, but it all comes together for a different effect in this volume.

Vitiello's observations are punctuated with insights such as his commentary on the treatment of strangers:

> But the ultimate protection is the dialects the natives have developed so as not to be totally understood or conquered. Resisting nature and alien civilization, Sicilians mitigate these two ageless forms of supreme hostility by offering strangers the sweetest fruits that stone can produce.

At times traditional, at times experimental, Vitiello's style echoes Italian writers such as Elio Vittorini and Luigi Pirandello. While his language can sometimes be stiff, it is always accessible. One thing's for sure, he's radical in the true sense of the word. Vitiello gets back to the roots of his origins and gathers oral histories of artists, artisans and community organizers. We meet those who fear and those who defy the mafia. Sprinkled throughout are some fine folk stories.

As he tells one of his Sicilian friends,

> It it's possible to teach anyone anything, Sicily's taught me this: that existing harmony and integrity with the life you've been plunked down to live, you might choose to make it worth cultivating and spreading around. Perhaps that's dangerous, but if you're scared pluck out your heart!

In the end, *Labyrinths and Volcanoes* is a documentary in the form of an appetizer of one's man's life journeys to Sicily.

(October 1999)

Justin Vitiello, *Labyrinths and Volcanoes: Windings Through Sicily* (Brooklyn, NY: Legas, 1999). ISBN 1881901165.

CHUCK WACHTEL

Writing in the shadows of 1930 proletarian novelists and among post-modern attempts to avoid realism, the contemporary American writer who has emerged from the working class has not fared well in American literary publishing and studies. But if Chuck Wachtel's novels are any indication, the future of American literature might just belong to this long ignored, rich resource of storytelling.

Wachtel's first novel, *Joe the Engineer*, published in 1983 and winner of a prestigious Pen/Hemingway Citation, tells the story of Joe Lazaro, a Vietnam War veteran who has returned home ready to enter the traditional American working class life. When he realizes that there must be more to his life than his job as a water meter reader and his marriage to a neighborhood girl, he begins to doubt the whole foundation of his life.

Through Joe, Wachtel crafts a philosophy of working class life in street language.

> He did what was expected of him. Got married, went to work, came home, sat with his elbows on the kitchen table.... Nobody likes their job. You're not supposed to. His father hated his. He did it because it's expected of you. Which was his mistake.... You don't do what's expected of you. You do what you want.

The novel's tension builds as Joe works his way through this dilemma. Wachtel captures the seventies without the sentimentalism and sensationalism that are characteristic of other novels of this period. The five months we spend in the claustrophobic neighborhood of Joe Lazaro is both a disturbing and dynamic reminder that there is a Joe in all of our lives. In Wachtel's hands, literary realism is resurrected. Recently republished in Penguin's Contemporary American Fiction series, *Joe the Engineer* will no doubt become a classic of American neo-realist literature.

Wachtel's new novel, *The Gates*, is a much more complex work than his first. The protagonist, Primo Thomas, is born to an African/American doctor and his Italian/American wife — a characterization that's unique. While Wachtel does not spend much time on giving us the details of Primo's mixed ancestry, he reminds us that while there are many ways in which these two cultures are different, there are many more in which they're similar. A prime example comes when Primo and his friends attend a Saint Anthony festa in Little Italy.

An Italian/American family is staring at Primo in obvious hatred. Primo walks up to the family and says, "When my mother made 'moolinyam,' she'd never used too much cheese. She used to say real Italians know that God made eggplant so you could taste it, not disguise the flavor. . . ." And then turning to the daughter, he continues, "My mother also used to say that the dark, shiny skin of an eggplant was beautiful. It was a mystery to her how anyone could make a bad word out of something so beautiful. She like to kiss my arms when she said it. Your mother ever kiss your arms?"

While Primo's black skin might keep others from recognizing his Italianess, his memory of his mother, sustained through his Aunt Olivia, keeps him connected to a past that continues to nurture him long after his parents have died.

Primo, at age 36, returns to New York City after a two years of teaching at a rural New England college. An academic more at home on the streets than an ivy-walled campus, he is a teacher of English as a second language who's not afraid to get involved in the lives of his students. And while it may hurt (emotionally and physically) to do good, Primo understands that in the long run, it could hurt even more to do nothing.

We follow Primo as he readjusts to city life and comes to terms not only with his past, but with old and new loves. A turning point in his life comes when he travels to Nicaragua with a delegation of American teachers who tour the area learning how the revolution has changed the people. Each experience becomes a gate which Primo must confront, pass through and move on with his life. As Primo faces changes in his life, we learn that the boundaries which separate self from other, US from Latin America, rich from poor, immigrant from citizen are arbitrarily constructed, and difficult to overcome. Education and love can sometimes create gates through which we can move through these barriers and make sense of life in the twentieth century. Primo does this by connecting to his students, by learning Spanish, and by risking his life to help justice enter into places where it has been denied.

As in *Joe the Engineer,* Wachtel has created a thoroughly real character through which we learn not only about a time period in American history, the 1980s, but also a lot about ourselves. He paces his narrative so that it never superficial, nor does it stop moving forward.

Wachtel, who is half Italian on his mother's side, and half Jewish on his father, is also the author of *The Coriolis Effect,* a collection of poems and short prose. He teaches in the Creative Writing Program at Purdue University, and in the M. F. A. Program for writers at Warren Wilson College.

(April 1995)

Chuck Wachtel, *The Gates* (New York, NY: Viking, 1994). ISBN 0670838861; $23.95 (hardcover).

Chuck Wachtel, *Joe the Engineer* (New York: Morrow, 1983). ISBN 0688015484; $10.95 (paperback).

JANET ZANDY

In 1922, John Valentino wrote in the March issue of *Survey* magazine that "Immigrant children may yearn for freedom to live untrammeled American lives; but they can do so only by abandoning, physically as well as intellectually their own households."

While Valentino's advice was meant to help immigrant children in the assimilation process, following it, more often than not, would create a great psychological distance between a family's generations. The move from working-class to middle-, and at times even upper-class was not made without problems that we are just beginning to understand.

In *Liberating Memory: Our Work and Our Working-Class Consciousness*, Janet Zandy presents a wide array of testimony to the consequences of being born into working-class culture. Her introductory essay, and the autobiographical and creative writings by twenty-five contributors, help us to understand the struggle to maintain both connections to the class one is born into and the class one is assimilating into.

Born Janet Ballotta, Zandy grew up in Hoboken and Union City, New Jersey. Her father, the son of Italian immigrants was her "intellectual companion," and his death at the age of 49, from cancer attributed to his job in a chemical plant, created a void in her life that she began to fill with formal education. Her mother, the daughter of a German/Austrian Jewish and Italian immigrants, instilled in her a sense of responsibility to family and community. Zandy attended college on a scholarship awarded to her by the company that employed her father. Of her education she writes, "I loved school almost as much as I loved my parents. But, the more schooling I got, the more separate I felt from them." *Liberating Memory* explores this separation and examines its effect on the lives of those born into working-class families.

Part One, "Memory, Not Nostalgia," opens with an essay and short story by Carol Tarlen who, in spite of her graduate school education, has remained an activist in the working class culture into which she was born. Joseph Nassar, a college professor recalls the day his cousin's body came home from Korea, and uses the experience to launch into an account of how his own military service affected his life. Sue Doro, a working-class poet, and Lennard Davis, a professor and literary critic, complete this section with powerful essays that demonstrate how the past can help only if we move beyond nostalgia and into the understanding of how that past has shaped not just our lives, but even the way we remember.

In Part Two, "A Language of One's Own," Masani Alexis DeVeaux creates a vibrant account of her experiences by infusing her prose with poetry that connects the voices of her past to the hopes of her future. DeVeaux provides a model of how we can use our own language to grow. Jim Daniels, a celebrated poet, recounts how writing became his detour around the grim future of a factory worker. Joan Maria Vasconcellos, a Portuguese/American, appears in this section through an essay and the script of a one-woman show she produced which examines the relationship among feminism, ethnicity and laughter.

Of particular interest to Italian Americans is M. Bella Mirabella's contributions in Part Three, "Places and Displacements." In "Connections," Mirabella, of New Rochelle, New York, recalls her visit to the old country and how she made it new, and her "The Education of an Italian American Girl Child," chronicles her odyssey to college and the community college compromise which kept her from aspiring to greater possibilities.

In Part Four," Cultural Work," poet Wilma Elizabeth McDaniel recounts the experience of "Okies" leaving the devastated Oklahoma Dust Bowl in the 1930s for the hope of "green" California. Pat Wynne's "Days of a Red Diaper Daughter," and her song lyrics, demonstrate how art and politics can combine to make for a life that uses, as it celebrates, working-class values.

Part Five, "The 'We' Inside the 'I'," features essays that examine the complexities of establishing self-identity within the context of family and community. Florence Howe's "Am I Her Daughter? Am I at Home?" characterizes the way working-class culture and identity can sustain hopes for a future in which we all will feel at home on the job, in the classrooms, and in the cultural arenas of America.

Liberating Memory is an extension (and expansion) of Zandy's earlier collection of working-class literature. In *Calling Home,* an anthology of writing by working-class women, Zandy gathered established writers such as Sandra Cisneros, Meridel Le Sueur, Tillie Olsen, Marge Piercy and Nellie Wong, along with unknown writers such as 86 year old Rose Venturelli, to create a dynamic collection of voices that speak to the values of working-class culture.

Zandy's work, as she writes in *Liberating Memory,* provides us with "the missing identifying principle" which can help us "see each other's history" and "construct a viable paradigm that addresses multiple oppressions." This is the most important work we can do in our attempts to keep peace in this country so often plagued by the differences inherent in diversity.

(January 2002)

Janet Zandy, ed. and introd., *Liberating Memory: Our Work and Our Working-Class Consciousness* (New Brunswick, NJ: Rutgers UP, 1995). ISBN 0813521211 (hardcover); 081352122X (paperback); $45 (hardcover); $16.95 (paperback).

Janet Zandy, ed. and introd., *Calling Home: Working-Class Women's Writings* (New Brunswick, NJ: Rutgers UP, 1990). ISBN 0813515270 (hardcover); 0813515289 (paperback); $38 (hardcover); 13.95 (paperback).

Review Essays

"Could This Be the End of... Gangsters in Fiction and Fact"

With the appearance of the film *Donnie Brasco* just a few months after yet another Mario Puzo mafia novel that's a planned t. v. miniseries, we once again face the question, what's stronger the facts or the fiction about Italian/American gangsters? *Donnie Brasco,* while an interesting story based on truth, continues to milk the myth, popularized by Puzo, that organized crime is monopolized by Italian Americans. If Puzo admitted that everything in "The Godfather" was made up, then why do Italian Americans wince when Hollywood sends out another formulaic gangster film? Why should fiction be so upsetting?

The answer lies in the fact that for nearly a quarter of a century, mafia gangsters have been Italian/American culture in the eyes of America's filmgoers. That the mafia myth has proven stronger than the truth is reason enough to wish every new gangster film away. And while *Donnie Brasco* might be a new look at an old scene, without Al Pacino, no one would pay attention to this tired, old tale. What the film does well is blur the lines between good government cop and bad street soldier. But this is no new insight. Pacino's acting, and the film's staccato-documentary style may have kept *Donnie Brasco* from becoming a mediocre made-for-t.v. film, but they won't be enough to renew the gangster genre.

Away from the big screen, there are signs that the Italian American-as-gangster stereotype is losing its ability to make big money. After a much shorter than expected stay on the bestseller list, Puzo's latest novel is evidence that the mafia myth might just be weakening its hold. The characters in *The Last Don* come to us as silly ghosts of his earlier thugs. Domenico Clericuzio, the aging head of a New York crime family looking to take over legitimate businesses, Alfred Gronevelt, who runs the Xanadu Casino Hotel in the wild world of Las Vegas gamblers, and Eli Marrion, the head of LoddStone Studios in Hollywood, all fashion themselves to be gods, and, as in most mythology, it's the mortal children of the gods who can destroy what their parents created.

To ward off the inevitable decay, the Don tries repopulating his "Bronx Enclave," with nothing but new Sicilians, whose very birth in the old country somehow keeps them ever obedient to his rule. But even this can't keep his family loyal. Times change, and systems built in the past can't always survive, though try telling that to the Don, who, at the outset is planning for his succeeding generations to be legit by trading in an empire of crime for restaurant chains, Wall Street firms, legalized gambling and building construction businesses. However, before the transition can be made, the family needs a few sacrifices.

Lacking the concentration, and originality of Puzo's earlier vision, *The Last*

Don ultimately becomes a story about a novelist's lack of dedication. In a recent interview with Larry King, Puzo — fresh from by-pass surgery and pumped up on Prozac — admitted that once again he wrote for the money. Whatever gold *The Last Don* mines will only be the result of having a large audience made ready by a mass marketing campaign that is more creative than the author deserves. Whatever the reason, let's hope that this is the last word on gangsters and gamblers from the man who gave us the first Don.

What makes the gangster a titillating subject for the Hollywood dream machines is the subject of one of four recent publications which attempt to help us understand how the image of the gangster has captured the lion's share of the Italian America's public image. This demythologizing is just what we need to replace the distorted image of America's Italians.

In *Inventing the Public Enemy: The Gangster in American Culture, 1918–1934*, David Ruth, an assistant professor of history at Pennsylvania State University, explores the evolution of the gangster through a study of the media images that began appearing in 1918. His main argument is that as the American urban centers grew, as the US economy was becoming more corporatized, and as the government became more bureaucratized, the American was losing the traditional sense of individuality. Amidst this social upheaval, writes Ruth, "the gangster was a central cultural figure because he helped Americans master this changing social world."

Ruth begins his argument with a brief look at the image of the criminal in American post World War I culture and finds that it usually "confirmed the individual's loss of agency in an impersonal world." More often than not crime was presented through a deranged individual who performed his deeds single-handedly in dark and dreary urban ghettos. Against this trend, Ruth finds that in the 1920s the scenes of crime in films such as *Scarface*, *Little Caesar*, and *Public Enemy*, moved from ethnic ghettos to downtown commercial centers, the criminal became more like those in the rising business class, and less like the dark, ethnic foreigner of earlier depictions. As technology improved business, so it improved crime. The pistol and knife were replaced by the machine gun.

From the comparison of crime to business, Ruth moves into the examination of how the growth of a new consumer society in the late 1920s created a fascination with the gangster. Easier access to stylish consumption, through fancy dress and cars, argues Ruth, blurred the earlier lines that separated social class. And as street criminals began associating with the upper echelons of society, it became harder to tell the gangster from the corporate elite.

Just as the gangster came to represent America's attempts to struggle with the advent of image-driven consumption, Ruth sees the gangster as moving ideal masculinity away from its traditional basis in "male honor" to one based in violent and aggressive behavior that reflected a man's ability to control his world. Nowhere was this more obvious, writes Ruth, than in the representation of the gangsters' treatment of women. A defender of "conservative gender values" on the one hand, the gangster also depicted an "openly expressive sexuality [that] had become a nearly ubiquitous element of modern urban life." This changing sexuality, which gave women power over men, could also lead to a woman's demise.

Ruth concludes his study with a fascinating examination of the impersonation of the gangster in Al Capone. Ruth sees Capone as an "attractive and repulsive" figure that "illuminated the lives of urban Americans." Capone's story, as a microcosm of how the individual could "escape from obscurity to wealth, power, and fame," also epitomized the gangster's adoption of corporate strategies through the need to "organize or perish." Ultimately, as Ruth writes, "Survival of the fittest, whether due to natural selection or machine guns, alternately justified celebrating the victors and damning the system."

Ruth stops his study at 1934, with Capone in Alcatraz, Prohibition repealed and the advent of stricter Hollywood censorship. And while the study needs to go on, Ruth's success is that the provides a solid foundation for future work, which for Italian Americans, would provide a long awaited explanation for why one ethnic group has managed to maintain the dubious distinction as the home culture of the gangster in America. While Ruth never goes into the rationale behind the plethora of criminal figures that have represented Italian Americans since the 1930s, he does a valuable service to us all by reminding us that the gangster reflected the entire society, and not just the Italian segment.

Not so passive about noting extreme prejudice against Italian Americans is Ronald A. Farrell's and Carol Case's *The Black Book and the Mob: The Untold Story of the Control of Nevada's Casinos*. In this fine study of the sociology of business and crime, the authors explain and historically document the establishment and maintenance of the Las Vegas *Black Book*, a blacklist that bans people from casinos who might be perceived as a threat to the public image of gambling. Besides being a sound, and welcome historical study, *The Black Book and the Mob* is a strong argument that "selection of individuals for the Black Book, ... reflects stereotypes of evil, cultural conflicts and the differential ability of groups to institutionalize their interests."

The evidence is *The Black Book* itself, which since its 1960 inception has listed 38 people, the overwhelming majority of whom are of Italian/American heritage representing a tiny minority of minor figures in the industry's history. *The Black Book*, developed by the dominant White Anglo Saxon powers to maintain control over the gambling industry in Nevada, was created at a time when the image of the mafia seemed to threaten all of America.

Farrell and Case point out that prior to the early 1950 Kefauver hearings, which placed gangsters on television in an attempt to determine the source of organized crime in America, gambling in Nevada was overseen by city and county officials. But with the threat of government intervention, ignited by the 1947 murder of Bugsy Siegel and fanned by the McClellan investigations into organized crime in 1957, the state leaders decided that self-control was needed. Their solution was the 1959 Gaming Control Act which created a five-member Nevada Gaming Commission that had the power to license and regulate gambling establishments and the ability to investigate improprieties and enforce industry regulations.

The timing of the public organized crime hearings and investigations, which concluded that a mafia of Italians and Italian Americans did exist and "formed the basis for an 'alien conspiracy theory' of organized crime," led to the majority of the first blacklisted being of Italian ancestry. "While no more criminal than many of their more businesslike counterparts in the industry," the authors write, "those whose names have been placed in the book tend to be caricatures of the mafia stereotype."

The Black Book follows the growth of Nevada's gambling industry from its roots in strong individual entrepreneurs to the corporate conglomerates of today. Examining the stories of most of the Black Book entries, Farrell and Case use actual hearing transcripts to bring excitement to what could have been a dry presentation. The insight offered by Farrell and Case goes a long way to helping us understand how Italians have been systematically denied access to legitimate businesses in Nevada.

Perhaps the most interesting question raised by Farrell and Case is why Italians were singled out when Jews, who actually had a stronger industry presence and more actual power, and who were just as "alien" to the dominant society as Italians, were virtually ignored. The authors' explanation lies in the perpetuation of yet another stereotype of Jews as "good investors and businessmen, a stereotype that may over the years have included the regulators to look upon them more favorably. This image, along with the pejorative one that Italians are dumb as well as criminal and violent, may also explain why it is that Italians use Jews to make their rackets profitable." That Mormons "doctrinally identify with Jews," is one more piece of evidence offered by the authors to explain why Italians were so singled out, and why Jews not only avoided "entry into the Black Book, but also [were able] to have obtained major interests in the industry."

What Farrell and Case's work does to debunk the myth of a mafia ridden Las Vegas, Richard A. Capozzola's *Finalmente! The Truth About Organized Crime* does to explain America's "mafia mania." Capozzola, a retired New York State educator and administrator, who also served as police commissioner for Westchester County of New York from 1974–1978, presents a basic, and often controversial argument that the defamation and denigration of Italian Americans through the news media and Hollywood should be "equated to ethnic genocide."

Capozzola finds the origins of the mafia mania in the Kefauver Senate Crime Committee hears of 1950–1951. Based on the information provided by John Scarne, "the worlds foremost authority on gambling," and author of *The Mafia Conspiracy,* Capozzola makes a strong case for the idea that the mafia is a government fabrication designed to keep authorities' eyes on Italians, all the while overlooking the real sources of crime in America. Capozzola's point is that anti-Italian sentiment born out of the mafia myth, has kept the best of Italian/American culture out of sight and the worst of it in everyone's face.

His self-illustrated history covers a twenty year period and stops at the murder of Joseph Colombo, but not short of suggesting that the shooting of Colombo was orchestrated by a government agency interested in eliminating the Italian American Civil Rights League. Capozzola's evidence comes from his own feelings and from a conversation Scarne had with gangster Frank Costello who said "no mob guy did the job." But more than leave the reader with something to think about, Capozzola suggests things to do and provides a quiz that should challenge any American to identify Italian Americans who have made valuable contributions to American culture. Capozzola wants us all to see the real Italian Americans, and this is what Alan Balboni does in his new study.

The actual picture of Italian America, reflected in Balboni's regional portrait of Italians in, *Beyond the Mafia: Italian Americans and the Development of Las Vegas,* demonstrates the great disservice done to the vast majority of Italian Americans by books like *The Last Don* and films like *Donnie Brasco.* This wide view of the Las Vegas historical landscape makes figures like Tony Spilotro (glorified in Martin Scorsese's *Casino*) look as tiny, and as insignificant as ants in the desert.

Balboni's expansive survey of the history of Italian presence in Las Vegas is based on his interviews of over one-hundred and fifty Italian Americans who live in Las Vegas. These stories of the successes and failures are great ammunition in the fight against the prevailing mafia myth. Unfortunately, these are the stories that never make the news, and so remain in the shadows of those that do. From pioneer laborers to early business builders, Las Vegas Italians, are quite unlike those who much of America has come to know through mass media. Balboni traces the Italian presence in Nevada to miners working on the famous Comstock Lode. He tells us that Nevada offered greater opportunities for quick money making and just as quick assimilation than most other areas in the United States. Balboni's support for this "fluid assimilation" argument comes from the facts that there were never any ethnic neighborhoods, that it wasn't until the post-World War II era that Italian American organizations would come into being, and that there was never a need to organize "the Italian vote" before an Italian American could be elected.

Balboni's history documents important Italian American contributions to the rapid growth of Las Vegas and its most recent prominence as one of the fastest growing cities in the United States. He concludes with a survey of Italian American Organizations and a brief summary that demonstrates that in spite of such discriminatory tools such as *The Black Book,* the lives of most Italian Americans have not been significantly affected by the mafia mystique. Balboni balances his book research with oral histories, and while it reads a bit dry at times, it does lack the scholarly jargon that makes such studies difficult for most readers. For Italian America, Balboni has provided yet another chapter in the history of Italians in America that should go a long way to proving that there is beauty beyond the mafia.

In spite of these recent books, the regrettable truth is that the fiction of the gangster is stronger than the facts, and the facts of Italian/American history will never be as attractive as the fictional myths. We know that the gangster figure meets a fundamental need by allowing Americans to reclaim a sense of power in a society gone out of control. But as these recent publications prove, the mafia has been a convenient and relatively safe dragon for American heroes to chase. In the meantime more terrible monsters terrorize the American way. And as long as the media has the mafia, they don't have to admit that we are failing in the real fight to make America safe. Up until this point, Italian America has been defined by the myth of mafia, but in the face of contrary evidence, what we do in response to the myth will define us and determine the future of our community and identity as Italian Americans.

(April 1997)

Mario Puzo, *The Last Don* (New York: Random House, 1996). ISBN 067940 1431; $25.95 (hardcover).

David Ruth, *Inventing the Public Enemy: The Gangster in American Culture, 1918–1934* (Chicago: U of Chicago P, 1996); ISBN 0226730077 (hardcover); 02267 32185 (paperback); $42.50 (hardcover); $15.95 (paperback).

Ronald A. Farrell and Carole Case, *The Black Book and the Mob: The Untold Story of the Control of Nevada's Casinos* (Madison, WI: U of Wisconsin P, 1995). ISBN 0299147509 (hardcover); 0299147541 (paperback); $17.95 (paperback).

Alan Balboni, *Beyond the Mafia: Italian Americans and the Development of Las Vegas*, foreword by Jerome E. Edwards (Reno: U of Nevada P, 2006). ISBN 0874176816 (paperback); $27.95 (hardcover).

Richard A. Capozzola, *Finalmente! The Truth About Organized Crime* (Five Centuries Books). Phone 407–862–6880; $3.95 (magazine format).

"THE ITALIAN AMERICAN AUDIENCE: CAVE PEOPLE CULTURE"

Recently I've seen a couple of films and two new plays, all of which used Italian American characters to get their stories told. It seems there's a renewed demand for Italian American characters and that audiences can't get enough of them. I have this habit of watching the audience whenever I'm in a theater or attending any public event. And lately, at every event, I have noticed many Italian Americans in the crowd.

In all cases the Italian Americans in the audience seemed to thoroughly enjoy the stereotypical stage and screen depictions of other Italian Americans. They, for the most part, found the jokes hilarious, and were anything but offended by the portrayals of Italian Americans as sluts, thugs and monosyllabic maniacs. In fact, they seemed to thrive on the images, to grow stronger and more proud with each succeeding slur.

During the intermission of one of the plays I heard an Italian American comment, "That's just how they act in Melrose Park." Now, despite some superficial similarities, the Italian Americans in this performance were not at all like those in Melrose Park, nor any place else in Italian America. The sad things is that this reaction was quite typical of those I've observed during the past few months.

One excuse for reactions like this could be that only a bad sport could take such portrayals seriously. After all, isn't anything fair game when the goal is to get a laugh? But why were they laughing when I wasn't? Was I just being a bad sport? Or was I the only one sick and tired of the same old stories being used as formulas for making a buck. Did the woman whose laughter shook her so hard that her gold chains jangled annoyingly throughout the play see something I didn't? What makes the man who saw people from my hometown in the characters on stage so proud that he announced his observation in public?

Now most ethnic purists might explain this enjoyment by suggesting these audiences were culturally ignorant and blind to the abuse of Italian American culture that's going on. And the audience, in defense, might refer to such purists as a snobs. But this type of interaction only bruises egos by igniting useless arguments. I have no doubt that there is intelligence behind both responses. But there is another approach to this situation which might help us come to terms with both points of view.

We need new ways of seeing and new ways of examining the images that come to us inside our homes through television, and on the stages and screens of the theaters we attend. These new ways must shake us out of passive states of catatonic reception and into more active ways of perceiving the deceptive images and the destructive ideas they mask.

Culture is a mirror of our society. And two things can happen when we look into today's mirrors. Either we don't see ourselves, and begin to wonder if indeed we do exist, or we become so used to the distortions that not only do we learn to live with them, but we, in our attempts to survive, learn to like them. And sometimes we learn the lesson so well that we even emulate these reflections.

We need to be able to see the critical irony inside Martin Scorcese's portrayals of Italian American gangsters or the romantic idealism in Coppola's godfathers; we need to see the shallowness of the humor created by a John Patrick Shanley (*Moonstruck* and *Italian/American Reconciliation*) or a Tom Dulack (*Breaking Legs*). In other words, we need to be able to tell the difference between the outsider's abuse of the Italian American character in order to get a cheap laugh, and the insider's use of similar characters to criticize life in America and in Italian America.

Plato once wrote of an experience in which people are chained in-place inside a cave. They are limited to viewing only the shadows of images passing before a fire; these shadows become their reality. One day a man breaks away, leaves the cave, and enters the sunlight; his eyes are hurting; he's shocked and afraid. Eventually he grows accustomed to this new reality. He returns to the cave with news of what's outside, hoping that he can liberate his people by telling them about the new reality he has experienced in the world outside the cave.

Perhaps Italian Americans, like the people in the cave, are so accustomed to the distorted images of their culture that society projects that in an effort to survive in their environment they have come to accept them. Perhaps that explains why there was so much Italian/American support of television programs such as *The Fanelli Boys*, films such as *Moonstruck*, and plays like *Italian-American Reconciliation* and *Breaking Legs*.

Now I don't expect every Italian/American to react the same way to a cultural experience, but I wonder why so many of us do. Can we, like Plato's cave people, afford to ignore the those who have left the cave and who have returned to tell us that there are other realities? Can we learn to challenge the distorted reflections in our cultural mirrors by intelligently criticizing them, or more positively, by supporting the positive images that are cast by our own artists? Or is it just easier to remain chained to the false belief that it's all just entertainment innocently designed only to make us laugh while the other guy makes a buck?

(April 1998)

"Italian Americans Over the Edge"

There's a fine line between making a "bella figura" or "brutta figura," and once that line is crossed, Italian Americans tend to keep quiet in fear of bringing shame or even envy on themselves or their families. This tradition of silence is broken by three recent publications: *Short Time*, a novella by Fred Misurella; *Nice Boy*, a novel by George Veltri; and *Jimmy & Rita*, a collection of poetry by Kim Addonizio. These authors use a variety of characters and techniques to force us to take harsh looks at contemporary life. Their defiance of the silence that surrounds moments of "brutta figura" demonstrates that there is as much to learn from the bad times as from the good.

In *Short Time*, Misurella, a veteran story writer and critic who teaches literature and writing at East Stroudsburg University, takes us for a short visit into the life and mind of Nick, a Vietnam Vet who is asked by his daughter if he ever killed any one "over there." The answer takes the shape of a long, short story in which Nick recalls his killing of a villager who could have been the enemy. In the span of just over fifty pages, Misurella takes us back to the days when body counts were an everyday item on television news, when young men had to make life changing, often life-threatening, decisions based on faith in their government and family. Nick didn't have pressure from his family to volunteer to fight in Viet Nam, "But the feeling was in there, inside me, whether from books, movies, or televiwion, I'll never know. I just felt that I had to go, as if I owed something."

Nick sees becoming a soldier as a way of becoming a man, of "cutting the apron strings." "Short Time" refers to the tail end of a soldier's tour of duty, and with two weeks left, Nick, looking forward to returning home, gets called back early to attend his mother's funeral. At the Saigon airport he thinks: "I had survived, others hadn't. But there would come a war, hot or cold, that would get me too."

In Misurella's understated style, the ordinary becomes magnified so that his war stories recall the battle we fight everyday for sanity. When his daughter, who smokes cigarettes, yet jogs, criticizes his generation as "touchy-feely," "innocent — and phony," we're given a good look at the new generation gap that replaces the earlier one between him and his parents. And like Nick, who wonders if he'll ever find, "Peace...without the ground blowing up beneath my feet," readers will ponder the possibilities of finding peace in our short time on earth.

Peace is something that Gregory Zassiccia is looking for in George Veltri's first novel *Nice Boy*. And for a while he thinks he's found it through drugs. Veltri, in a catchy style of writing that mimics the lapse in synapses of a drugged out speaker, takes us on a wild trip, from a working-class kid's innocent entree to drugs: "I took a lot of them screwy head chemicals, mixed up with speed drugs, and got a reputation like, wow-wee-wow, devil may care, high-wire crazy boy. But still a good boy. Nice boy. Didn't do no harm. Least it seemed that way"; through his descent into addiction: "So how come nobody notices that something's not right with old Gregory boy. He's acting strange, ain't he? Well some people do notice, real obvious to them, but they're reluctant to speak up. Don't want to accuse. Not their business"; and ends up in recovery at which point: "Family got all this new meaning to me now" and "something long buried" begins to surface."

Nice Boy is as hilarious as it is horrific. Veltri finds the humor in a tragic story, and never slips into the dismissal of drug use as an interesting experiment. Gregory's story of addiction becomes a cold, slap in the face to those of us who believe these things happen to those who deserve it. The author keeps this junkie human through family interludes such as Gregory's visits to his nonna's house and his great description of the creation of his family's "Italian American basement."

Veltri holds back no punches in this powerful account of a nice boy gone bad. Gregory's tale of survival becomes a testimony to the power of a family to save its own, especially when its own want to be saved.

Kim Addonizio's second collection of poetry, *Jimmy & Rita* is a love story filled with all the grit and glitter of contemporary urban life. The collection is a fast-read, reminiscent of the story of the infamous punk rock couple Sid Viscious and Nancy. Rita is a good girl gone bad. From working in massage parlors, to turning tricks on the streets, Rita's sense of survival begins where her body ends. Her guide into self destruction is her girlfriend Diane through whom Rita meets Jimmy, a street tough who takes her on a journey away from her past and into an unknown future.

Addonizio's gift is the ability to give us a haunting story through poetry without any whining, even when there's much to complain about. A poetic novella of sorts, *Jimmy and Rita* flashes by like a short film. Through a series of free verse and prose poems, Addonizio shifts between Jimmy's and Rita's point of view to create a wild sense of each watching and listening to the other. We can sit back and watch their lives intertwine and unravel, but we can't do a thing about the terror they put themselves through.

Jimmy and Rita are characters who could have stepped out of Veltri's *Nice Boy*, but they lack Gregory's innate sense of right and wrong. Doing what they can to survive day-to-day, they live without hope or a philosophy through which a world without drugs can make sense. Addonizio presents the worst of street life and its tales of self and other abuse in language that is simple, graphic and loud. Her tough and edgy writing will no doubt shake up even the most daring of readers. The price of witnessing this tragedy is the knowledge we gain about our society, our culture, and a better understanding of how ignorance and our silence and apathy contributes to the nightmares of those we know and love.

(May 1998)

Fred Misurella, *Short Time* (West Lafayette, IN: Bordighera, 1996). ISBN 1884419070; $7 (paperback).

George Veltri, *Nice Boy: A Novel* (San Francisco: City Lights Books, 1995). ISBN 0872863026; $9.95 (paperback).

Kim Addonizio, *Jimmy & Rita: Poems* (Rochester, NY: BOA Editions, 1997). ISBN 1880238411; $12.50 (paperback).

"Radically Italian American"

In these days, when cultural differences are exploited more than similarities are explored, when the idea of working-class unity is clouded by the competition for leisure time and credit card possibilities, it's hard for us to even imagine that there was a time when what happened to the working class mattered to intellectuals. But these days, as more and more radical intellectuals are reclaiming their working-class backgrounds, it is important to remember the cultural work done by those immigrant intellectuals who dedicated their lives to the working class cause.

In the early 1900s Luigi Fraina, who later changed his name to Lewis Corey, concentrated his efforts on social, economic and political analysis, and was one of the earliest writers to publish Marxist literary criticism in the United States. His life work represents the preoccupation of radical immigrant intellectuals with the obstacles they encountered in adapting to life in the US.

The story of Fraina's life is an important one for American social history, and one that might have been forever a footnote, if Paul Buhle hadn't found the significance in Fraina's struggle to advance the thinking of Socialist Labor Party leader Daniel DeLeon. Buhle's early interest in the US Left began with a Bachelor's thesis on DeLeon at the University of Illinois directed by Rudolph Vecoli. Buhle shifted attention to Fraina for his Master's thesis, directed by A. William Hoglund, at the University of Connecticut. *A Dreamer's Paradise Lost* is an expansion of that thesis and the first book-length study of this remarkable figure in US history.

Buhle, the director of the Oral History of the American Left Program at New York University and currently Visiting Scholar in the American Studies Program at the University of California, Santa Cruz, is a leading historian and scholar of American radical culture. His recent and forthcoming books include *Images of American Radicalism, The Immigrant Left, From the Knights of Labor to the New World Order,* and a second edition of *The Encyclopedia of the American Left*. In *A Dreamer's Paradise Lost,* his study of the life and times of Luigi Fraina, Buhle combines history, biography and cultural criticism to review an important period in American culture when intellectuals concerned themselves with what was going on in the streets.

In the book's first chapter, "The Immigrant and the American Radical Movement," Buhle introduces us to "an immigrant boy-intellectual and budding socialist," whose father, "a radical republican in Italy," had immigrated to the US in 1897, "for the freer political atmosphere of New York City." The young boy's experience in the city's slums of selling newspapers turned him into a hungry reader of fiction, poetry, and social science. At the age of seventeen he published his first essay, "Shelley, the Atheist Poet," in *The Truth Seeker*. The essay, sets the tone for his adventure on the road to freedom from the constraints of traditional institutions such as the Church. What Buhle does so well in his opening is provide us with the socio-historical context by which to understand how this one man's life can matter to us all. Fraina's path took him through such movements as the Socialist Party, the International Workers of the World movement and the Socialist Labor Party, as lead by Daniel DeLeon. As a writer, a spokesperson and an activist, Fraina's thinking impacted all of these movements at critical times in their development. Even if you have no interest in the story of Fraina, the immigrant radical, Buhle's synthesis of radical history is well worth the read.

In many ways, Fraina's own growth as a radical parallels the rise and fallof radicalism in America, and this is the story that Buhle wants to tell. In chapter 2, "Bohemian Rebel and Revolutionary Agitator," Buhle recounts the 1910s, a decade which, as he writes, "offered the possibility of simultaneous radical change in economics, politics, morals and art" unlike any other until the 1960s." Buhle examines what he calls Fraina's project of "socialist modernism," which Buhle sees as seeking "to interpret the distance and interplay between working-class life and cultural modernism." Fraina articulated his thinking through essays, reviews and even fiction published in the *Daily People*, the *New Review*, and *Modern Dance*. Buhle orients us to Fraina's prolific publications and critically analyzes the key articles of Fraina's early career which led to the publication of his first book, *Revolutionary Socialism*, in 1918.

In chapter 3, "On the Verge of Communism," Buhle uses Fraina's life to show how a budding communist society in Russia led the American Left to rush into "imitations of Russian formulae" with the effect that "The less likely the short-term revolutionary transformation of the United States seemed, the more Russian slogans and affiliation gained in luster." Buhle's description and his analysis of the various immigrant ethnic groups' responses to the possible alternatives offered by communism is first-rate and key to understanding current interest in the relationship between ethnicity and socio-political history. Buhle's presentation prefaces his analysis of Fraina's introduction and editing of Lenin and Trotsky's *The Proletarian Revolution in Russia*, the first major documentation of the Russian Revolution, which Buhle believes ranks with John Reed's journalistic, *Ten Days that Shook the World*.

Fraina's struggle to reconcile the tension between the requirements of an international and national communism is quite representative of the times, and in chapter 4, "Tangled Journeys: The Road Out and the Road Back, 1919–29," Buhle follows Fraina's progress which led him to change his name to Lewis Corey. Buhle's strength in this chapter lies in his ability to avoid romantic notions in his portrayal of Fraina's problems with the Communist Party, which accused him of spying in Moscow, extorting Party funds and fleeing to Mexico. Fraina becomes a cultural chameleon through various name changes, but continues his intellectual expression through the pen name Lewis Corey. In chapter 5, "Political Intellectual at Large," Buhle analyzes Corey's contributions to the history of monopoly capitalism through articles in the Encyclopedia of the Social Sciences and his book length studies, *The Decline of American Capitalism*, *The House of Morgan*, and *The Crisis of the Middle Class*, and reasserts Corey's importance as a radical economist and historian whose writings were prophetic about the Great Depression.

In the final chapter, "The Perils of Disillusion," Buhle explains that Corey's shift to American liberalism as a militant anti-Communist, at least in sentiment, "brought him no more satisfaction than his final years as a Marxist and radical had." In the later years of his life, Corey went from a professorship at Antioch College, to historian for the AFL Butcher Workmen's Union, for which he wrote Meat and Man, work which led him away from academia and into a job as educational director for the Amalgamated Butcher Workmen in Chicago. In 1950 the US Justice Department sought to deport Corey as an illegal alien because his parents had entered the US without papers. He died awaiting deportation and two days later he received a Certificate of Lawful entry.

In many ways, Buhle's study of Fraina/Corey, is a document of an ignored legacy that contemporary radicals of the American left could use in rethinking their role in light of the fall of Soviet Communism. But this legacy could have been clarified had the last chapter reinforced the relevance of Fraina's struggle for freedom and justice to the battles being fought on today's cultural fronts. Through a short essay reconnecting this legacy to the present, Buhle might have provided us with a better synthesis of the mass of information he presents. But then again, this could become the task of someone who reads this important book and carries on the work that Buhle has begun.

A Dreamer's Paradise Lost is the recovery of radical history at its best and the right antidote to the ethno-historical amnesia that has helped to keep working class realities out of the nation's larger historical consciousness. Buhle has once again accomplished an important task in cultural history that will benefit historians, scholars, students and activists across the political spectrum.

(*Voices in Italian Americana* 1997)

Paul M. Buhle, *A Dreamer's Paradise Lost: Louis C. Fraina/Lewis Corey (1892–1953) and the Decline of Radicalism in the United States* (Atlantic Highlands, NJ: Humanities Press, 1995). ISBN 0391038508; 0391038494 (paperback).

"Working Class Culture"

A recent conference on working-class studies at Youngstown State University gathered over 200 scholars, writers and artists around the theme "Working-Class Studies and the Future of Work." This was the second conference at Youngstown State, which has created a Center for Working-Class Studies, devoted to examining working-class culture, and evidence that the desire and the need for studying working class issues is growing at a rapid rate.

Two new publications reflect this growing interest in working-class culture and present ways we might begin to organize approaches to the study of this too-long neglected region of American life: one is a guide to working-class films and the other is an anthology of fiction, poetry and memoirs produced by writers of the working-class.

Tom Zaniello's compilation of films, *Working Stiffs, Union Maids, Reds and Riffraff,* is a must-have publication for anyone curious or serious about studying working-class culture. This incredibly useful, accessible and interesting compendium of over 150 films is the result of years of painstaking research and analysis by Zaniello, a professor of English at Northern Kentucky University and a visiting professor at the George Meany Center for Labor Studies.

After a brief "Introduction" in which he explains the process by which he created the listing, discusses trends and themes he found both in his own original research and his reading of the few previous studies, and orients the reader to the guide, Zaniello launches into an alphabetical listing of the titles. Each listing includes a guiding phrase or sentence that summarizes the film's focus from Zaniello's perspective. These captions can be poetic, parodic, descriptive, or just plain corny, but no matter, they add a bit of garnish to the staple reference fare he serves up. Under the captions is the year the film was made, the MPAA rating (when available), the cast, an energetic description, a critical commentary and production details. Zaniello goes the extra mile for scholars by providing suggested films of related interest, annotated references for further reading, and an availability index complete with addresses where the film can be bought, borrowed or rented. His inclusion of a thematic index — a big help to those wanting to create college courses around related issues — and an address list of sources, round out a work that should become the new standard for reference publications.

Zaniello's book transcends its reference value through its clear writing and entertaining voice. As he tells us in the introduction, this result of 20 years of work is still a work-in-progress, and you can help him expand and refine the work by writing to him directly.

Over forty poets and story writers from the US working class contributed to *Getting By: Stories of Working Lives,* an anthology edited by David Shevin and Larry Smith, with introductory essays by each of the editors and a preface by poet Sue Doro. These introductory writings join those by Janet Zandy in *Calling Home* and *Liberating Memory,* and the essays by Tom Wayman, to form the core of the developing theories surrounding working-class writing. Smith's essay, creates theory out of autobiography as he recounts his experiences signing book at a mall. As he writes, "the working class is the one class seeking to deny itself — to disappear." But Smith, Shevin, Doro, and the writers included in this important anthology, won't let that happen.

An anthology is difficult to characterize in a review, and the number as well as the variety of writers Shevin and Smith have found resist any generalizations, and rightly so. But each of the entries reminds us is that work can be honorable, boring, necessary, life-saving and life taking. Working-class experiences lend themselves to a rough texture, both in the living and the recounting of work; at first glance, some of these entries seems more surface than depth oriented, but this probably comes from the conditioning we have received in literature courses which typically ignore working-class writing.

Entries range from the mainstream smooth poetry of Philip Levine to the rough and ready style of Randy J. Abel. Italian/American writers are represented by the able work of P. J. Corso and the challenging poetry of Joe Napora. But the one thing we learn by reading all of the entries is that work has a way of making an individual's experiences matter to the entire community. The beauty of creating an anthology around work is that it is a theme that can help us all to transcend differences created by categories such as race, gender, lifestyle, and ethnicity.

The anthology is organized into five sections: "Carpenter Aunts: Family and Neighborhood"; "Working Class Education — That Working State of Mind"; "The Sweeper: Ingenuity and Persistence"; "Where You Go When You Don't Work: Struggles and Getting By"; and "Cleaning Stalls in Winter: Work Ethic and Dignity." While this might be too neat of a way to bring a sense of order to the selections, it might help someone trying to use it in a course.

It is difficult hard to single out individuals in an anthology, especially when there are no weak links in the literary chain. Suffice it to say that what does characterize the writing gathered in this anthology is its lack of pretension and its lack of experimentation which probably comes from the need and struggle to show us how work affects all of us. *Getting By* does that well enough to make it required reading, not just for those who attend conferences on working-class studies, but for anyone interested in expanding their notions of good American literature.

(*Voices in Italian Americana* 1997)

Tom Zaniello, *Working Stiffs, Union Maids, Reds and Riffraff: An Organized Guide to Films about Labor* (Ithaca: ILR Press, 1996). ISBN 0875463525 (hardcover); 0875463533 (paperback).

David Shevin and Larry Smith, eds., *Getting By: Stories of Working Lives* (Huron OH: Bottom Dog Press, 1996). ISBN 0933087411.

"Writing as a Reader: The Deserted Village of Jay Parini"

Jay Parini's new novel, *The Apprentice Lover*, comes to us soon after a biography of Robert Frost, a book of poetry, another of essays, and an historical novel based on the life of Walter Benjamin — rather prolific for a guy who teaches and participates in panels and workshops throughout the year around the country. And that doesn't include the number of books he's edited during the same period. Parini's concern with how much writers produce surfaces in an essay exploring the pros and cons of being prolific. He tells us that while over-productivity might hurt, it also can heal. The greater danger he warns is "The critics won't keep up with them. Their books will be reviewed in isolation from their previous works, and their careers will resist categorization" ("On Being Prolific" 56–57).

Categories work primarily for shelving and selling books, and while you can find Parini in many sections of your local library and bookstore, the only category that fits him as an author is that of the contemporary old fashioned man of American letters. Like any number of his predecessors, Parini creates in his new novel a protagonist who finds American culture not sufficiently inspirational for a literary wannabe. Henry James's flight east to England and Italy might not have been the model for Alex Massolini, the protagonist of *The Apprentice Lover*, but it certainly is an important precedent for considering much of Parini's writing, especially this new novel. This comparison takes on greater significance when we realize that Parini served his own literary apprenticeship in Europe.

The success of old fashioned master writers is deeply connected to their work as master readers. Writers like Parini and James are not afraid to read, and know that in order to write, one must read, and in order to improve one's reading, one must write. Any author who tells you they don't read, is either lying or not worth reading. It's as simple as that. Parini's reading creates his writing and his writing creates his reading. His expression finds its way through novels, biographies, critical studies, short fiction and poetry, fiction, nothing but commercial crap is out-of-bounds for him. Like Henry James, Parini is a public intellectual of the highest calling. He contributes regularly to literary and political discussions alike. He leads and participates in workshops designed to pass along his skills to new generations. And he's not afraid to spend time reviewing books. I say all this by way of introducing my discussion of his new novel because in many respects, this novel, contains much of what Parini has been working on his entire career.

The protagonist of *The Apprentice Lover*, Alex Massolini, is an avid reader, but it seems most everything he's been reading lately "is about love or war, the two subjects that sat like deadweights on my chest" (3). He is a beginning writer, he's written a few poems, but is not sure of how he can go from being a serious reader to a serious writers. When his brother dies, he loses his sense of career direction and drops out of his Ivy League school just before graduation. This upsets his family and starts Alex to thinking about what he's going to do with his life. A student of the classics and a budding young writer, Alex sends some of his poetry to Rupert Grant, a famous Scottish writer who lives on Capri. Grant offers Alex a chance to work as his secretary, and thus begins Alex's soul searching journey to the land of his ancestors.

Set in the US and Italy during the Viet Nam war, *The Apprentice Lover* tells the story of Alex's trip to "a fresh landscape and" his attempt to cash "the blank check of time unmeasured by parental or institutional expectations." He is looking for, "a canvas where I could paint myself into the picture, adding or subtracting traits at will, a place where I had no former history which I had to be absolved" (12). Thinking he can "cut loose from the overfilled barge of [his] youth" (3), Alex abandons his family only to stumble into a deeper sense of the past. "It seemed ungrateful of me to reverse the journey my grandparents had made with such difficulty. . . . They had abandoned their families — poor, illiterate, well-meaning people — and made their way across a vast, threatening sea" (11). Alex might not face the physical dangers of his ancestors, but the psychological risks are no less. The poetry of Parini's writing here is not just in the sound of much of the novel's prose but also in the precision by which his words create the imagery. "My parents Vito and Magarita, who had loomed so large through my past two decades, dwindled as the strip of rubbery water between myself and them lengthened, stretched to a point of unbearable tension, then snapped" (10).

The Apprentice Lover is a story about the relationship of history and story, of classic and contemporary and how they continue to influence each other. History is stasis, it doesn't change as quickly as we do; stories can change everytime they are told and can also alter our sense of history. In this sense, storytelling becomes an anti-static force. This novel moves along by juxtaposing varying notions of story and history, a pattern not new to Parini's work. In his historical novel of the last years of Walter Benjamin's life he wrestled with the very same ideas.

Benjamin believed that the equivalent of a Copernican revolution in thinking must occur. Fiction would replace history, or become history. The past, "what has been," had previously been accepted as the starting point; history stumbled toward the dimly lit present through the corridors of time. Now the process must be be reversed; "the true method," said Benjamin, "was to imagine the characters of the past in our space, not us in theirs. We do not transpose ourselves into them: They step into our life." One does not proceed by seeking empathy with the past: Einfuhlung. This was historicism of the old mentality. Instead, he argued for what he called Vergebenwartigung: "making things present" (*Benjamin's Crossing* 73).

In another historical novel on the last year of Leo Tolstoy's life, Parini has Tolstoy say: "Fiction is for people who have not yet begun their search for God" (*The Last Station* 13). This juxtaposition of fiction and theology, of fact and story, that create a dynamic tension throughout most of Parini's work, comes to the surface in this new novel.

Divided into a prologue, six parts and an epilogue, *The Apprentice Lover* covers a little less than a year in Alex's life, but it's a time that changes the entire trajectory of his being. In the "Prologue" we learn that Alex's brother Nick is killed in the Viet Nam war. Nick appears throughout the novel in interestingly formed letters from Viet Nam that Alex periodically recalls or rereads. "brothers, as the old Neapolitan saying goes, are versions of each other" (127). The letters reveal an intensity, a sense of personal history, of immediacy, of reality that Alex has yet to encounter. When Nick writes, he says things he probably could not have said to his brother's face, for the both come from a family in which "it was considered a failure, a mistake, for a man to show emotion, to lose his temper and lash out. Men controlled themselves. They managed to stifle emotions before they could root and grow into visible feelings" (8). In one letter, Nick tells him: "everybody (except Dad) thinks I'm a piece of shit and only you got brains. Only you are 'college material.' Only you are 'college material'. I'm just there, a kind of accident, an unfortunate case. Hardly even Italian" (238). But it is Nick's experience that makes him a powerful writer, and it is through these letters that Alex learns how to be a writer by learning how to reveal those emotions on the page. In many respects, it's is more interactions with his brother's ghost that with any living mentor that teach him how to write. Like one of his earliest novels, *The Patch Boys*, *The Apprentice Lover* is about a young man's attempt to find a place for himself in the worlds of and outside his Italian American family. His father, Vito, is a veteran of World War II who left his fighting spirit back with the ghosts on Salerno beach. He submits to his wife's wishes and lashes out at Alex when he doesn't do the same. Margarita is an overweight control freak given to creating public spectacles over her inability to pull all the strings all the time. His namesake grandfather, Alessandro, urges him forward to Italy with the warning that the United States is the future, Italy is not much more than an interesting place from his past. And then there's his only sibling Nicky, whose death challenges Alex to find a way to get to the other side of death. At the funeral, Alex, in a fit of family loyalty and responsibility tells his parents he will do what was expected of his brother hand he survived the war. He will come into the family construction business. But Alex's college education has left him totally unfit for such a future and his family knows it. So he takes off for Italy.

The title of Part One, "Sic transit," begins the first of many classical allusions. Translated as "So it goes. This first phrase of the famous saying: "Thus goes the glory of the world" launches Alex on his journey to the auspicious Villa Clio, home of the Scottish poet, his wife and their entourage. Named after the muse of history, often portrayed sitting with a scroll and books, the Villa becomes a place made of words and haunted by history. Clio is also said to have teased Aphrodite's love of Adonis, and this unstated allusion adds a dimension that imbues static history with a vibrant sensuality.

Living at the Villa Clio is Rupert's wife, Vera, 20 years younger than her husband and an author of cookbooks who promises Alex that she will "tell [him] the truth, if and when it matters" (39). She lives up to her name only when she can hurt the few who are weaker than she. There's Grant's English assistant, Holly Hampton, beautiful and seriously aloof, at least to Alex. Grant also employs an Italian researcher, Marisa Lauro. Both girls service the man more than his letters, and become objects of desire for Alex. Other minor characters include, Patrice, a gay acquaintance from France whom Alex meets on the ferry over from Naples. Alexi, as Patrice calls him, saves Patrice from drowning during a swim in the famous Blue Grotto, and the two gain a spiritual connection that surpasses their different sexual orientations. There's Luigi Aurelio, a local priest who is a literary translator and a convenient confessor for Alex from time to time as he works his way back to a Catholic sense of the spiritual.

Besides a few local servants who tend to the mundane needs of life at the Villa, there are of course the many house and dinner guests including some of the world's top writers W. H. Auden, Graham Greene, and Gore Vidal. Each of these writers come to us in charming vignettes, but none are drawn with the detail of one Dominick Bonano. A Puzo-like writer of "multigenerational sagas about

Mafia families" with titles like *The Last Limo on Staten Island* that become potboiler bestsellers, Bonano is a grand, obnoxious American who thinks enough of Alex to introduce him to his daughter. Whether intentionally or not, this author's name reveals much about Parini's attitude toward the type of fiction that "nobody takes seriously" (45). The usual spelling of the name, as in the late gangster Joe Bonanno, uses 2 "n"s. Ano, Italian for anus, and Bon, good. Bonano will not do as a model for Alex who has come with the hopes of finding a mentor.

> In retrospect, I suppose this yearning for mentors had something to do with my own father's remoteness, although this sort of speculation didn't interest me at the time. All I know was that Rupert Grant immediately inspired in me the feelings of longing. He represented a world I desperately wanted to possess myself. (46)

This is not the first time Parini has written about mentors. In fact, what he has to say in the novel about mentors had been rehearsed in an essay collected in *Some Necessary Angels: Essays on Writing and Politics*. From the Scottish poet Alastair Reid, in many ways the major source from which Parini drew to create Rupert Grant, he leaned to edit, and to see cooking as an analogue to writing. From Robert Penn Warren, he learned to "Cultivate leisure. That's the best thing a writer can do for himself. Good work never comes from effort. It comes easily. If it doesn't, it isn't ready" ("Mentors" 11). And from Gore Vidal, he learned responsibility to society. When Rupert tells Alex that the only way a particular story might work is if the characters are sitting atop a bomb, Parini is taking this from advice that Vidal had once actually given to him. Alex finds the writer in himself by first learning to see it in others, and what he sees is not always easy to emulate.

In Part Two, entitled "Gradus ad parnassum," we see the young man taking his steps toward becoming an artist. The "Steps to Parnassus" refers not only to the sacred mountain of the museses, but also that classic work on Latin verse containing rules and examples for good writing. As he begins his internship in the writing business he find out that "Lo pazzo d'isola [the island madness], as the locals called it, permeated everything, but it was worse at the Villa Clio" (83). Capri has always figured strongly in Parini's work. His friend Gore Vidal has a villa there; Parini and his wife, Devon, have spent time there, and that is where Walter Benjamin met his wife Dora and his lover Asja Lacis. In Crossing Benjamin, Parini uses Asja's perspective to comment on the island:

> What I liked about Capri was its feeling of survival; many conquerors had come and gone, but the island itself remained — a glittering rock of freedom in the bright green sea. It was timeless and equal to anything history could give it. (*Benjamin's Crossing* 161)

But as history ages, it has a tendency to lapse into myth. And through the myth of Capri, the island becomes a theater where the "sexual outlaws, revolutionaries, artists, wealthy pleasure seekers" (213) come to see and be seen. Alex later begins to tire of the beauty and says, "Capri, a corrupt and jaded island full of snobs and dissipated intellectuals. This was definitely 'not' the Italy my grandparents recalled and sentimalized"(207).

Rupert renames Alex to Lorenzo, as though baptizing him into literary life. But the new life Alex realizes is not what he has expected. When Rupert tells him "Writers are all murderers in disguise," Alex is shocked.

> My idea of a writer was far different from this. To me, a writer was a healer, a builder, a creator. Not a destroyer. When I suggested as much to Grant, he shook his head sadly and clucked his tongue. "If you're really a writer, Lorenzo," he said, "you'll slay your next of kin first, and proceed from there. It's a bloody business. A bloody goddamn business." (92)

Yeah, it's not always great to know the man inside the writer, and sometimes it's just better to stick to the writing and leave the writer alone. But you can't do that when you're the apprentice, so Alex must learn how to process his master's personality.

Unlike his brother Nick, who let outside forces dictate what experience he would gain, Alex has been able to, if not totally control, then at least point to the direction in which his experience would come. Alex comes to believe that he must constantly search for experience that will ultimately give some meaning to his life. In the meantime he encounters those whose lives begin to represent different was of seeing and being in the world. Through Rupert's relationship with Holly and Marisa, we can see two very different portrayals of decadence. Alex, acting as the good apprentice is quite attracted to his mentor's women and even considers the possibility of sleeping with Rupert's wife, something offered to him by Rupert as well as Vera. Alex soon finds himself imitating his mentor in the worst way in order to find a place for himself in this strange, new world.

In the novel's shortest section, Part Three, entitled "Amo, amas, amat," after the singular conjugation of the Latin verb "to love," things begin to heat up. As Alex pines for Holly, Marisa comes to his room one night and helps persuade him to "love the one you're with." Alex, whose sexual experience prior to this trip has been nothing but a few forays into the shallow end of the pool, is after more than the sex, but it seems that all of his friendship with females (Bonano's daughter Toni, and later with Holly) turns sexual. But as Alex expands his sexual experience he finds the social world of Capri constricting.

Parts Four "Ars longa" and Five "Vita Brevis" break up the famous quote of Hippocrates, "Art lasts, life is brief," and in these sections Alex's prose gets sharper under Grant's guidance, but his moral vision is getting blurry. Alex returns to fighting childhood mother/son, father/son battles with Rupert and Vera as surrogate parents. When his father calls to say mother's sick, Alex contemplates returning, but in the end decides that he's not going to fall under his mother's spell this time. And soon the drama heightens as life is short refers to a suicide that could be read a suffocation of the spirit of youth by Rupert's egocentric behavior. The possessive and demanding love displayed in many of these characters is reminiscent of the obsessive love that Parini portrayed in his very first novel, *Love Run*. And it's connections like these that suggest the possibility that every work of art contains all of the artists previous works.

War and the place of the intellectual are ideas Parini has played with in previous writings, most dramatically in historical novels like *Benjamin's Crossing*. Character Lisa Fittko writes: "In time of war, people become obsessed with their own past, with the story of their lives; they begin to live everything all over again, sifting for evidence of a kind that cannot be found" (*Benjamin's Crossing* 113). This is what Alex's brother Nick does in his letters and it forces Alex to do the same. Parini, as a public intellectual, creates a place for such a figure in novels such as *Benjamin's Crossing*. Again, this comes to us through Lisa Fittko:

> For me, Benjamin was the European Mind writ large. Indeed, as I later realized, Old Benjamin was everything the Nazi monsters wanted most to obliterate: that aura of tolerance and perspective that comes from having seen many things from many angles. Even that rueful laugh of his was part of the aura. Here before us was the last laughing man, I thought. The last man to laugh the laugh of ages. From now on, history would be tears, and the work of intellectuals would be the work of grieving. (187)

Parini's writing reminds us that it is the world that makes us writers, and that nothing can be better than living the writer's life. As he writes about Tolstoy in his novel, *The Last Station*, "He has always been happiest within his work, dreaming his grand, sweet dreams" (3). In the novel, Tolstoy's daughter mentions that her father believed: "'It is the duty of an author to present himself to the public. To say, *this will do, and this will not do*'" (53). There is a number of similarities between Tolstoy's amanuensis, Valentin Fedorovich, and Alex. Valentin writes in his diary:

> I am not among the great ones, but I understand what must be done — or not done — to become like them. I have to give up desire and loathing. I have to delight in what happens, whatever is given. I should not struggle or exert my own petty will. (*The Last Station* 107)

This is the place of the apprentice, the one who stands near, but never in the place of, the master. In a similar vein, Alex's writing, while perceptive, reveals the young man's tendency to elevate and explain his master's behavior:

> Grant's world was so purely aesthetic, a maze constructed to hide some mythical beast that frightened him. He had created a dazzling thing, employing his talents to the fullest, and yet those around him scarcely understood what he'd done, or what their part in his fantasy might be. (257)

The apprentice must learn to subjugate his self to the needs of the master, but then there must come a time when the apprentice attends to his own needs, at the cost of separating himself from the master.

In a trip he takes with Holly to the mainland, Alex comes upon a scene that Parini uses to give his protagonist an unearned epiphany. When Alex goes to the beach at Salerno he feels a connection to his father's experience of landing there during the Allied invasion of World War II.

> My knees weakened, and I knelt in the sand as the day brightened, with a red sun tinting the water. I believed I had seen something there, in Salerno. Heard and smelled it, even tasted it. And it would never leave me. It would become part of who I was, making it far more possible for me to connect to my father when I went home. (256)

Somehow he believes he has connected to his father simply by imagining the scene. This is one of the few possibilities never fully realized by Parini in this work.

As he begins to connect to his father's past he begins to disconnect himself from Grant. This separation begins earnestly In Part Six, "Gloria mundi." after Alex is able to verbalize his own earlier delusions:

> I refused to criticize it [Villa Clio], taking for granted its small guilts and large assumptions. I bought greedily into Grant's view of things, and did my best to make him believe I shared his opinions. Yet now I found our conversations painful. (277)

In the end he realizes that knowing the artist's humanity is what keeps him from becoming a god and keeps Alex from living the rest of his life as a faithful devotee. This realization alone enables Alex to assert his own identity as an artist, as by the novel's Epilogue, Alex has become a master writer whose work as a poet and novelist has brought him some degree of fame and comfort. He publishes a piece on Rupert that later gains him an invitation back to the Villa Clio from Vera. When Alex returns he finds the island overcome by commercial success and Rupert overcome by senility. In their final encounter Alex realizes he will never know if he ever did get through Rupert the way Rupert had gotten through to him.

In the end, *The Apprentice Lover* is not really the coming-of-age novel, as other critics have suggested. It is a coming to one's senses novel, a piercing through the illusions the ego builds as obstacles to achieving one's goals. Every apprentice writer fears the power of the great ones whose works have taunt them to give it a try. When Alex realizes that he cannot write like Shakespeare, he fears he is destined to write crap, that if he does not live like Rupert, he will never be able to dedicate himself totally to the art. But the more Alex learns about Rupert, the more confused he becomes. He wonders if one needs to become an asshole to be great. And he learns the great lesson that if it wasn't for assholes, we'd all be full of shit. If it wasn't for artists, we'd all be a little less human.

Every work of art is a home the artist lives in for a while and then abandons for others to inhabit. The problem is, if we go searching for the artist in one of his deserted homes, we will never find him, for he's gone off to live somewhere else. So while there is much of Jay Parini to be found in *The Apprentice*, and much of his previous work that echoes throughout the rooms of this work, we'd be hard pressed to make a case that Parini is somewhere hiding in this novel, as most likely he's off somewhere down the road reading himself a way to write himself a new home for us to read, inevitably creating, through a lifetime of writing, a deserted village for us to wander through and wonder about.

(*The South Atlantic Quarterly* 103.1 [Winter 2004]: 159–68)

Works Cited

Jay Parini, *The Apprentice Lover* (New York: HarperCollins, 2002).
___. *Benjamin's Crossing* (New York: Anchor, 1998).
___. *The Last Station* (New York: Henry Holt, 1990).
___. *Love Run* (Boston: Little, Brown and Company, 1980).
___. "Mentors," *Some Necessary Angels: Essays on Writing and Politics* (New York: Columbia UP, 1997). 3–17.
___. *The Patch Boys.* (New York: Holt, 1986).

INDEX: BOOKS REVIEWED

Accademia: A Novel, Giose Rimanelli	151
[The] Apprentice Lover, Jay Parini	197
Are Italians White? How Race is Made in America, Jennifer Guglielmo and Salvatore Salerno, eds.	109
At the Copa, Maria Labozzetta	119
Between Salt Water and Holy Water: A History of Southern Italy, Tommaso Astarita	18
Beyond the Mafia: Italian Americans and the Development of Las Vegas, Alan Balboni	183
Big Cherry Holler: A Big Stone Novel, Adriana Trigiani	165
[The] Big Hunger: Stories 1932–1959, John Fante	89
Big Stone Gap: A Novel, Adriana Trigiani	166
[The] Black Book and the Mob: The Untold Story of the Control of Nevada's Casinos, Ronald A. Farrell and Carole Case	183
Black Madonnas, Louisa Ermelino	83
Blackshirts in Little Italy: Italian Americans and Fascism, 1921–1929, Philip Cannistraro	39
Blood of My Blood: The Dilemma of the Italian-Americans, Richard Gambino	97
Blue Italian, Rita Ciresi	49
Bookend: Anatomies of a Virtual Self, Joe Amato	13
Calling Home: Working-Class Women's Writings, Janet Zandy, ed. and introd.	179
[A] Canticle for Bread and Stones, Emilio DeGrazia	69
[Al] Capone: A Biography, Luciano Iorizzo	114
"Che Bella Figura!": The Power of Performance in an Italian Ladies' Club in Chicago, Gloria Nardini	136
Chiaroscuro: Essays of Identity, Helen Barolini	22
[John] Ciardi: A Biography, Edward Cifelli	48
Claiming a Tradition: Italian American Women Writers, Mary Jo Bona	32
Clay Creatures, Mark Ciabattari	47
[The] Closer We Are to Dying, Joe Fiorito	93
Con Amore: A Daughter-in-law's Story of Growing Up Italian American in Bushwick, Bea Tusiani	167
Conversation with Johnny: A Novel, Anthony Valerio	172
[The] Country of Absence: Poems and an Essay, Felix Stefanile	159
[The] Country of Marriage, Anthony Giardina	98
Cutter's Island: Caesar in Captivity, Vincent Panella	138
Dances with Luigi: a Grandson's Determined Quest to Comprehend Italy and the Italians, Paul Paolicelli	141
Dante's Lyric Poems, Joseph Tusiani, trans.	169
dark mother: african origins and godmothers, Lucia Chiavola Birnbaum	30

[The] Day Laid on the Altar, Adria Bernardi	28
Death by Renaissance, Paola Corso	60
[A] Dreamer's Paradise Lost: Louis C Fraina/Lewis Corey (1892–1953) and the Decline of Radicalism in the United States, Paul M. Buhle	192
East Liberty, Joseph Bathanti	27
Ethnicity: Selected Poems, Joseph Tusiani	168
Fabrizio's Passion, Antonio D'Alfonso	64
[The] Family: A Novel, Maria Puzo	147
[John] Fante: A Literary Portrait, by Richard Collins	89
[The John] Fante Reader, Stephen Cooper, ed.	56
Feast of the Dead, Anthony Fragola	94
Festa: Stories, E.R. Romaine	153
Finalmente! The Truth About Organized Crime, Richard A. Capozzola	183
[A] Fortune in Gold, Michael Palma	137
Full of Life: A Biography of John Fane, by Stephen Cooper	89
Gambler's Daughter, Rachel Guido DeVries,	66
[Anita] Garibaldi: A Biography, Anthony Valerio	170
[The] Gates, Chuck Wachtel	178
Getting By: Stories of Working Lives, David Shevin and Larry Smith, eds.	195
Giovanna's 86 Circles, Paola Corso	58
Here in the World, Victoria Lancelotta	122
Holding on for Dear Life: Poems, Thom Tammaro	162
Hollywood Italians: Dagos, Palookas, Romeos, Wise Guys and Sopranos, Peter Bondanella	35
In Bed with the Exotic Enemy: Stories and Novella, Daniela Gioseffi	106
In Italics: In Defense of Ethnicity, Antonio D'Alfonso	62
In Our Own Voices: Multidisciplinary Perspectives on Italian and Italian American Women, Elizabeth Messina, ed.	131
In the Garden of Papa Santuzzu, Tony Ardizzone	17
In the Gathering Woods, Adria Bernardi	29
[The] Inland Sea, Steven Varni	173
Inventing the Public Enemy: The Gangster in American Culture, 1918–1934, David Ruth	183
Italian American: The Racializing of an Ethnic Identity, David A.J. Richards	148
[The] Italian American Experience: An Encyclopedia, Salvatore La Gumina, et al, eds.	115
[The] Italian American Reader: A Collection of Outstanding Fiction, Memoirs, Journalism, Essays, and Poetry, Bill Tonelli, ed.	165
Italian American Writers on New Jersey: An Anthology of Poetry and Prose, Jennifer Gillan, Maria Mazziotti Gillan, and Edvige Giunta, eds.	99
Italian Stories, Joseph Papaleo	143
Italian Women in Black Dresses, Maria Mazziotti Gillan	101
Jimmy & Rita: Poems, Kim Addonizio	190

Joe the Engineer, Chuck Wachtel	178
[The] *Journey Home*, Ross Talarico	160
Labyrinths and Volcanoes: Windings Through Sicily, Justin Vitiello	177
[The] *Last Don*, Mario Puzo	183
Liberating Memory: Our Work and Our Working-Class Consciousness, Janet Zandy, ed. and introd.	180
Lincoln's Foreign Legion: The 39th New York Infantry, The Garibaldi Guard, Michael Bacarella	20
[The] *Logic of a Rose: Chicago Stories*, Billy Lombardo	127
[The] *Loss of the Miraculous*, Ben Morreale	134
[The] *Lost World of Italian-American Radicalism: Politics, Labor, and Culture*, Philip Cannistraro and Gerald Meyer, eds.	40
Lucchesi and the Whale, Frank Lentricchia	124
Madonnas That Maim: Popular Catholicism in Italy Since the Fifteenth Century, Michael P. Carroll	45
Making the Wiseguys Weep: The Jimmy Roselli Story, David Evanier	88
[A] *Matter of Honor: One Cop's Lifelong Pursuit of John Gotti and the Mob*, Remo Franceschini	95
[The] *Milk of Almonds: Italian American Women Writers on Food and Culture*, Louise DeSalvo and Edvige Giunta, eds.	79
Miss Giardino, Dorothy Calbetti Bryant	36
Moliseide and Other Poems, Giose Rimanelli	150
More Italian Hours, and Other Stories, Helen Barolini	25
[The] *Music of the Inferno: A Novel*, Frank Lentricchia	125
[A] *New Geography of Time*, Robert Viscusi	176
Nice Boy: A Novel, George Veltri	190
Night Bloom: A Memoir, Mary Cappello	42
Nothing Grows in One Place Forever: Poems of a Sicilian American, Leo Luke Marcello	129
Old Italian Neighborhood Values, Stephen DeFelice	67
On Going Home Again, June Avignone	19
Paper Fish, Tina De Rosa	74
Paperwork, David Citino	54
Pink Slip, Rita Ciresi	51
Recollections of My Life as a Woman, Diane di Prima	80
Reversible Destiny: Mafia, Antimafia, and the Struggle for Palermo, Jane and Peter Schneider	156
[The] *Right Thing to Do*, Josephine Gattuso Hendin	112
Roman Candle: The Life of Bobby Darin, David Evanier	87
Rosa, The Life of an Italian Immigrant, Marie Hall Ets	86
[Carlo] *Rosselli: Socialist Heretic and Antifascist Exile*, Stanislao Pugliese	145
[The] *Saints in the Lives of Italian Americans: An Interdisciplinary Investigation*, Salvatore La Gumina, et al., eds.	116

Say That to My Face: Fiction, David Prete	144
[La] scoperta dell'America: Un'autobiografia, Carmine Biagio Ianacce	113
Short Time, Fred Misurella	190
Sicily, the Hallowed Land: A Memoir, Ben Morreale	133
[The] Sisters Mallone: Una storia di famiglia, Louisa Ermelino	84
Sometimes I Dream in Italian, Rita Ciresi	52
Sometimes the Soul: Two Novellas of Sicily, Gioia Timpanelli	163
Stay with Me, Lella, Marisa Labozzetta	120
Stolen Figs and Other Adventures in Calabria, Mark Rotella	1543
[Una] Storia Segreta: The Secret History of Italian American Evacuation and Internement during World War II, Lawrence DiStasi, ed. and introd.	821
Studies in Italian American Folklore, Luisa Del Giudice, ed.	71
[The] Sun and Other Things, Peter Carravetta	43
Taking It Home: Stories from the Neighborhood, Tony Ardizzone	15
[The] Test, Dorothy Bryant	38
Things My Mother Told Me, Maria Mazziotti Gillan	105
[The] Third Miracle: A Novel, Richard Vetere	175
To Sleep with the Angels: The Story of a Fire, David Cowan and John Keunster	61
Travelers' Tales Guides: Italy, Anne Calcagno, ed.	39
[The] Trouble with Mental Wellness, Joseph Colicchio	55
Umbertina: A Novel, Helen Barolini	24
Under the Southern Sun: Stories of the Real Italy and the Americans It Created, Paul Paolicelli	139
Underworld, Don DeLillo	73
Unsettling America: An Anthology of Contemporary Multicultural Poetry, Marria Mazziotti Gillan and Jennifer Gillan, eds.	103
Vertigo: A Memoir, Louise DeSalvo	77
Voices of Italian America: A History of Early Italian American Literature with a Critical Anthology, Martino Marazzi	128
[The] Voices We Carry: Recent Italian/American Women's Fiction, Mary Jo Bona, ed.	33
Were You Always an Italian: Ancestors and Other Icons of Italian America, Maria Laurino	122
Where I Come From: Selected and New Poems, Maria Mazziotti Gillan	103
White on Arrival: Italians, Race, Color and Power in Chicago, 1890–1945, Thomas Guglielmo	110
Winter in Montreal, Pietro Corsi	57
Wop! A Documentary History of Anti-Italian Discrimination, Salvatore La Gumina	117
Working Stiffs, Union Maids, Reds and Riffraff: An Organized Guide to Films about Labor, Tom Zaniello	195
Writing with an Accent: Contemporary Italian American Women Writers, Edvige Giunta	108

SAGGISTICA

Taking its name from the Italian–which means essays, essay writing, or non fiction–*Saggisitca* is a referred book series dedicated to the study of all topics, individuals, and cultural productions that fall under what we might consider that larger umbrella of all things Italian and Italian/American.

Vito Zagarrio
The "Unhappy Ending": Re-viewing The Cinema of Frank Capra

Paolo A. Giordano, editor
The Hyphenate Writer and The Legacy of Exile

Dennis Barone
America / Trattabili